Popular Culture in the Middle Ages

Popular Culture in the Middle Ages

Josie P. Campbell

Bowling Green State University Popular Press
Bowling Green, Ohio 43403

Library of Congress Catalog Card No.: 86-71408

Copyright © 1986 by Bowling Green State University Popular Press

ISBN: 0-87972-339-4 Clothbound
      0-87972-340-8 Paperback

Contents

Preface

The present collection of essays represents an effort to provide publication for a variety of contributions on Popular Culture in the Middle Ages. All of the essays except three, D. Thomas Hanks, Jr.'s " 'Quike Bookis'—Corpus Christi Drama and English Children in the Middle Ages," John M. Theilmann's "Medieval Pilgrims and the Origins of Tourism," and my "English Cycle Drama: 'Thou art a pilgreme,' " appeared in the *Journal of Popular Culture,* 14 (Summer 1980); this second printing is an attempt to bring the essays together in a single volume more readily accessible to students and readers of medieval literature and of popular culture.

I am grateful for the assistance of the contributors to this volume and to Pat Browne, the editor of The Popular Press. I wish to acknowledge my indebtedness to Robert Worth Frank, Jr., who first introduced me to the delights and wonders of medieval literature when I was a student at the Pennsylvania State University. My special thanks go to Donald A. Campbell, my severest critic and my dearest friend.

I also wish to acknowledge my special gratitude to the Faculty Development Fund at the University of Rhode Island, URI Alumni Association, for its generous support of this publication.

Josie P. Campbell
University of Rhode Island
Kingston

Introduction

When I accepted the task of editing a collection of essays on medieval popular culture, I considered the possibility of seeking papers united around a common theme, but soon abandoned the idea as impractical and possibly too restrictive. The culture of the Middle Ages was as complex, if not as various, as our own, and the difficulty of examining medieval popular artifacts is often compounded by lack of data. Thus, the following essays cover a wide range of topics, from church sculpture as "advertisement" to tricks and illusions as "home economics." Still the papers do fall into a not entirely arbitrary order, with Charles Altman's and Bruce Rosenberg's papers providing a neat, although perhaps not quite closed, frame for the total collection.

If Bruno Roy in his paper "The Household Encyclopedia as Magic Kit: Medieval Popular Interest in Pranks and Illusions" shows us the zest for life, the sense of humor and fun, apparent in the Middle Ages, Norman Smith in his "Portent Lore and Medieval Popular Culture" provides the opposite as he reveals some of the culture's darkest fears and anxieties. These fears and anxieties frequently were projected on women, especially those women who may have been alienated from community life or who appeared estranged; Elizabeth Tucker points out in her paper, "Antecedents of Contemporary Witchcraft in the Middle Ages," that such women were often thought to be witches, sometimes fulfilling dual roles, either the healer bearing magic herbs or the destroyer carrying poisonous death. Similar attitudes, however modified or amplified, toward the duality of women are also shown to exist in various literary forms and popular spiritual treatises which deal with presumably "normal," not aberrant, women.

Popular attitudes of a culture are always difficult to define, however, within the context of the total culture. This is especially true when we deal with attitudes toward a given group of people because they cannot be reduced to a single and static given pattern, although as Shirley Marchalonis suggests in "Above Rubies: Popular Views of Medieval Women," it is often tempting to take the easy way out and to be reductive in dealing with various attitudes toward women in literature, which remains more "fixed" than life. Today, with an emphasis on much-needed feminist studies of the popular images of women in various cultures, it may be necessary to remember that such images change from time to time and that these changes can only be understood by looking at their coherence within a *complete cultural context. Such understanding is sometimes more desired than realized, particularly in medieval studies, where important pieces of information and integral links between gender-defined roles and economic exigencies are either missing or unknown to the literary critic or art historian.*

Caroline Eckhardt in her essay "Woman as Mediator in the Middle English Romances" reminds us also that fiction is not life, even when there may be similarities between the two. The Paston Letters, for all their wealth of information, give us but one example of the experiences of women in the Middle Ages; we should like to have more to see if other strong-willed and determined women could marry as they chose. Might they not risk family ostracism and perhaps economic sanctions? The question arises as to how valid and limited our generalizations may be from a specific family in medieval England to what surely must have been diverse familial arrangements.

Yet, for all such supposed diversity, there is a long history of a rather inflexible perception of women in medieval literature and spiritual treatises, as Maureen Fries demonstrates in "Feminae Populi: Popular Images of Women in Medieval Literature"; women are either the ideal (the Virgin Mary) or the negative opposite (Eve). The only mixed type seems to be the Magdalene, who begins her career in the negative fashon of Eve but dramatically changes to a more positive image similar to that of Mary. The difficulties of viewing literature within the context of the experienced life as presented in writings like the Paston Letters are being addressed; in recent years, significant work in medieval urban culture, economics and social history has added greatly to our insight into the meaning of the portrayals of women in art and literature as they relate to the culture of the time.

The two essays on popular culture in Scotland by Evelyn S. Newlyn ("Robert Henryson and the Popular Fable Tradition in the Middle Ages") and by W. F. H. Nicolaisin ("Tension and Extension: Thoughts on Scottish Surnames and Medieval Popular Culture") range from Henryson's use of practical, yet symbolic, use of Scots names, which gives us useful information about work patterns, kinship structures and population movement. Edmund Taft's essay, "Surprised by Love: The Dramatic Structure and Popular Appeal of the Wakefield Second Shepherds' Pageant," is concerned with the popular appeal of that drama to a diverse audience, an area frequently overlooked. D. Thomas Hanks, Jr.'s " 'Quike Bookis'—Corpus Christi Drama and English Children in the Middle Ages," examines the drama as both entertainment and education for medieval children. While they may have enjoyed watching the stage-children, villains, and games, they learned a complex concept of history as well as religious stories. Hanks argues that these children may also have learned a revolutionary view of the upper classes. Michael Stugrin is equally concerned about the effective quality of a variety of popular literary and spiritual texts upon their audience and what these texts tell us in terms of medieval popular taste ("Innocence and Suffering in the Middle Ages: An Essay about Popular Taste and Popular Literature").

These essays taken as a whole display generally a literary basis; John M. Theilmann's examination of the historical beginnings of tourism, "Medieval Pilgrims and the Origins of Tourism," may seem at first glance an exception, but even here are numerous cross-references to the literature of the time. My own essay, "English Cycle Drama: 'Thou art pilgreme___' " has obvious connections to the institutions of pilgrimage explored by Theilmann. Indeed, each of the authors represented in this text shows to a remarkable degree the ability to move rather comfortably from one discipline to another, for example, from literature to art history or from linguistics to sociology or history. My intention from the beginning was to include scholars from various disciplines, and it is coincidental that the contributors' backgrounds are primarily in the areas of literary study and languages. Nonetheless, the strong, if implicit, evidence from the essays reveals a commitment to multi-disciplinary approaches to the study of popular culture.

For the most part the essays on medieval popular culture have an air about them of healthy skepticism and inquiry; Charles Altman's paper, "The Medieval Marquee: Church Portal Sculpture as Publicity," is a model of popular culture theory that also demonstrates its usefulness by classifying and defining (or explaining) certain medieval artifacts, in this case popular church statuary, while Bruce Rosenberg ("Was There a Popular Culture in the Middle Ages?") recognizing the significance of Altman's work, raises the unpopular but necessary question of how much we learn about popular culture from such classification.

His point is well taken. For example, in my own area of study, medieval drama, we know that the Corpus Christi plays were immensely popular, lasting well over a hundred years, but what does this tell us about how the drama interacts and plays off against other segments of the culture, the visual arts, other forms of poetry, or the ceremonious, not merely ecclesiastical, but political and social? We have only limited information about the interaction between the plays and their audience: certain lines of dialogue in the drama at times indicate rowdy response or lack of audience attention, for example. Even though the Chester drama explicitly defines what the interaction between the plays and audience should be—"the augmentation and Increase of the holy and Catholic faith of our Saviour Iesu Christ and to Exort the minds of Common people to good devotion and to holsome doctrine there-of"—how much interaction is effected or even if it is effected is not always clear.

In Corpus Christi drama, the Church takes the role of the entrepreneur, but the process of the Church's popularizing dogma and biblical narrative is complicated by the means of production, the middle-class burghers, the guilds-men, who paid for, staged and acted out the plays, before a largely middle-class audience, but one with enough diversity to necessitate inclusion of material that would appeal to "more and lesse, / gentillys and yemanry." Just as with the church sculpture that Charles Altman describes, the Church had to "sell" its product, while maintaining the beliefs and values it stood for. We are left with a number of questions about the drama concerning the exchange between Church and burgher, to say nothing of the exchange with the audience. For example, we can tell what kinds of social criticism were allowed by reading the plays themselves, but what kinds were disallowed, and what does this finally tell us about the interaction between entrepreneur (the Church) and the means of production (the guilds-men) and the consumers (the audience)? Even more *significantly, what does this particular segment of medieval popular culture, the drama, tell us of the culture as a whole?*

Similar questions arise when one studies the visual arts of the Middle Ages. Certainly from the 13th century on, sculpture and strained glass reveal a heavy emphasis on physical and emotional suffering; the figure of Christ becomes strikingly human in its placement and form. Numerous examples of the pieta in painting and sculpture of this time depict profound sadness akin to the sorrow expressed in Giotto's "The Lamentation" (1305-06), in which the stooped forms of the mourners are bent in anguish over the simple massive weight of Christ. Even the grotesque sinners in scenes of the Last Judgment no longer evoke merely horror but compassion. The shift to an intensely emotional response to suffering and destruction can be explained partly, as Michael Stugrin points out in his essay, by looking closely at various historical, economic and social events: religious tensions, repeated crop failures, the Black Death of 1348, the Hundred Years' Wars. We can only begin to understand the popularity of certain forms and their content when we see them in interaction with other segments of the culture.

All essays published here demonstrate the need for more truly multi-disciplinary efforts in popular culture studies, whether of the Middle Ages or of the present time, as envisioned by Victor Turner (quoted in Rosenberg's article) in which there is a "creative collaboration" among the literary critic, the art historian, the anthropologist, the sociologist, and so on. Whether this kind of collaboration is possible, given the economic situation and the academic structure along clearly defined disciplinary lines is another question. Until the time when scholars from various disciplines pool their research efforts, popular culture studies will in large measure continue to be conducted by scholars who individually cut across disciplinary lines. This is not necessarily bad, particularly for the scholar, for he or she is forced to broaden his or her intellectual boundaries, and it is an old story to the medievalist who traditionally is educated to work in more than one discipline.

This collection of essays, then, not only deals with the question of a popular culture in the Middle Ages, but provides new material on the topic. In addition the essays suggest a variety of methods of approaching popular culture, especially a culture in which there was no mass means of production or distribution as we know it. At the same time, they implicitly look to the future when there might profitably be a more collaborative effort among scholars from different disciplines toward solving certain problems of popular culture study. Finally, and most significantly, we discover in this study of medieval popular culture, in many ways so different from our own, not only where we have been but also traces of what we are.

Josie Campbell is professor of English at the University of Rhode Island; she has published on medieval drama and on popular Canadian and American fiction.

The Medieval Marquee

The complexity of movie marquees is well-known to those who frequent films with the avidity of the penitent seeking heaven. The symbolic content of a marquee that has the name of the late John Wayne in The Searchers *is subtly but forcefully apparent; we know what values are contained in the lean and lone figure of Wayne, and behind him the values in Hollywood as transmitted through John Ford, the director. So it is with the "medieval marquee," the Church portal sculpture, as Charles Altman makes clear, with the Church proclaiming its values, as it shores up the common people's belief in salvation and ensures the status quo of a class structure. The Church in the Middle Ages, according to Altman, is the entrepreneur, just as the film industry today mediates public taste with its seductive appeal; in both instances, it is the "well-planned marquee" which lures its customers inside.*

Charles Altman is an associate professor of French and Italian at the University of Iowa and has written on medieval literature and on French and American film.

The Medieval Marquee:
Church Portal Sculpture as Publicity

Charles F. Altman

How may we speak of popular culture in a world where transportation is inadequate, mass communications non-existent, and printing not yet invented? We meet elite culture at every turn, in the carefully turned Latin phrases of learned clerics, in the polished language of the courtly lyric and romance, in the exquisite workmanship of the goldsmith or enamelist. Folk culture is everywhere present—in the oral performance and rough syntax of the vernacular epic, in the scabrous short tale, in the pre-Lenten carnival festival. Given current definitions, however, we must conclude that popular culture as such is not a phenomenon which we may associate with the medieval period. Only by extending and reformulating the accepted definition may we arrive at an approach to popular culture less historically limited than current ones, an approach which gives primacy to functional relationships rather than technology.

Let us begin by unpacking the current notion which ties popular culture to the mass media. This simple claim in fact covers two separate principles:

1). The artifacts of popular culture achieve wide distribution among all classes of society. They are easy of access, inexpensive to consume, and made of relatively cheap materials.

2). Popular culture is by definition a mediated culture. Between the popular artist and his public stands an institution which publishes the popular text for its own ends—profit production and self-preservation. This mediatory publishing institution strongly influences the form of the popular text, making the popular artist only partially responsible for the form in which the work is disseminated. He may choose what to write, but the publisher (network, manufacturer) decides what will actually be produced.

The first of these principles has long been recognized. The second has not been adequately acknowledged, yet it lies at the heart of popular culture's special position within society. We may appreciate this more fully by comparing popular art to its elite and folk counterparts. In general, folk art is unmediated art. Not only *for* the people, it is also *of* and *by* the people. The folk artist belongs to the same class as his audience and has regular personal contact with the members of that audience. Performers are live, thus permitting on-the-spot interaction between artist and audience; typically each performance is different because the performer reacts differently to each audience. Furthermore, the distinction between performer and audience is not permanent and irreversible; at any moment a member of the audience may take up the guitar and become a performer. According to the romantic notions which color every aspect of our sense of elite art, the elite artist is a demiurge, a seer, a *vates* who creates because he must. Art in the post-romantic world enjoys the status of religion. The elite artist thus creates his art work totally oblivious to the media which will distribute it, on the understanding that they will faithfully transmit it to the public. Any editor or producer who alters the finished product of a T.S. Eliot or an Orson Welles is immediately labeled a charlatan. For the conventions of elite art declare the art work to be the inviolate creation of a sacred individual: the inspired artist. Tampering with such a holy institution is tantamount to sacrilege.

In contrast, the popular artifact is always tainted, soiled by the spectre of monetary gain, less than immaculate conception, and the heretical hand of the artistically inept publisher, producer, or press agent. Where the elite or highbrow artist—at least in theory—writes in a vacuum and is eventually published by an organization convinced of the artistic value of his work, the popular artist is for all practical purposes the employee of a publishing institution with its own values and vested interests. Consequently, the popular text typically speaks with two voices:

1). Written for the people, the popular text panders to the people's supposed preferences, reaffirming their values, encouraging their dreams, playing to their fantasies. Indeed, the very presence of this populist voice tends to make the public unaware of another voice which it masks.

2). Distributed by an institution, the popular text serves that institution's vested interests, in particular the institution's drive for survival. The popular text thus always functions as an advertisement for the institution which produced it. This self-advertisement may take the blatant form of praise for the text's very medium (e.g. the importance of reading competence for Horatio Alger's heroes, the laudatory treatment of Hollywood in the musical). More often, however, it is the producing institution's values which are celebrated by the popular text (e.g. the Hollywood film's incessant rewarding of romantic love, boy scout virtue, and free enterprise).

How then do these general precepts about the nature of popular culture affect the study of the field in the pre-modern period? In general we may formulate the following guidelines:

1). Popular culture may be said to exist when a given text achieves wide dissemination through the efforts of a publishing institution (taken in a broad sense) with a vested interest in survival.

2). Therefore, use of mass media is not a necessary condition for the existence of popular culture.

3). Conversely, broad dissemination of a particular artifact does not constitute a sufficient condition for the existence of popular culture.

4). Analysis of the popular text must take into account both aspects of the text's rhetoric—the voice which advertises the publishing institution's values and services as well as the voice which appeals to the public's pre-existing tastes and self-interest.

These four principles will be kept in mind as we pursue a specific example of medieval popular culture.

II. From Altar to Portal Art: Taking the Sacred Image to the People

During the course of the 11th century in Western Europe there occurred an innovation in church decoration which was to have a profound effect on the arts in general throughout the middle ages. Prior to the romanesque period the church building regularly took on the appearance and structure of a fortress, its walls serving to separate a sacred space within from the secular space without. The outside of the edifice bore little if any witness to the activities taking place within. In contrast to the coarse exterior of wood, stone or brick, the inside was commonly aflame with the bright colors of mosaic, fresco, embroidered cloth or precious metals. Though from time to time the nave may have been decorated with hieratic or narrative compositons, church art of the first millennium was in general concentrated in the altar area. Often this art work was distributed into three separate levels: the crypt, where relics were displayed (frescoes, decorated sarcophagi, reliquaries fashioned out of precious metals, rare stones or carved ivory), the main altar, where the scripture was read and the mass celebrated (finely wrought paten and chalice, sumptuous candelabra or chandelier, embroidered altar cloths, illuminated manuscripts), and the vault above (where God's dominion over the universe is figured in mosaic or fresco). Of all the arts displayed in the altar area, most remained only marginally visible to the faithful; those which presented figures large enough to be recognized—such as the apse *Majestas*—served not so much to teach or persuade but only to illustrate the Christian message to those already familiar with it. The church art of the first millennium is thus a radically private art, limited to the believer and to the most sacred parts of his place of worship. Like the mass which the priest celebrates even when no one is present to participate, early church art exists primarily for the glory of God and not for the rhetorical effect which it might have on man.

Altar art never disappears entirely from the Christian repertory, but during the romanesque period it is rapidly replaced as the primary mode of religious art by another type of art with a radically different location and function. Given its status as sacred fortress, the early church (baptistry, mausoleum, etc.) pays little attention to entrances and exits, unless it is to limit them and assure their impenetrability to the unfaithful.

Beginning in the 11th century, however, the churches of Western Europe begin to pay increased attention to the *Westwerk*, the western end of the church which is henceforth often endowed with twin towers and multiple portals. Now in previous churches, a door was most often just a door, an entrance or an exit with practical rather than symbolic value. With the romanesque church, however, this practical approach to the portal is radically modified. By surrounding the door itself with a sculptural program ranging from a band of ornamentation to tens of square yards of narrative sculpture, the 12th-century church turns the portal area into a symbolic dissertation on the place of the door in sacred geography. In the early church, the door—except for that fleeting instant when an individual is passing through it—constitutes part of the wall separating secular and sacred space. In the romanesque church, however, the portal must simultaneously figure both in the separation between the holy and the worldly and their potential continuity.

Not only does representational art, previously reserved for the church interior, spill over onto the jambs, tympanum, archivolt and facade of the romanesque church, but in so doing it changes character radically. If altar art is static art designed to celebrate God's glory, portal art combines that celebratory sense with a narrative impulse revealing the process by which one may pass from secular space to sacred space (a process obviously prefigured by the act of passing through the church portal itself).[3] Scenes of the Last Judgment, parables with a clear moral lesson (e.g. the Wise and Foolish Virgins), episodes from the lives of well-known saints all provide the faithful with an example to be followed as well as a counter-example to be avoided.

Furthermore, portal art is no longer private, limited access art, as was altar art. The tympanum dominates not the altar but the town square— secular space supreme. Visible at any time of the day or night, portal art becomes a part of the townspeople's daily lives, whereas altar art was a Sunday experience. Portal art is thus by its very nature *evangelical* art, and as such addressed to a far wider and more varied public than altar art could ever have been. Instead of simply expressing a truth, it seeks to communicate that truth, to convince someone of it. Portal art interfaces, as it were, the eternal repose of the church within and the hustle-and-bustle of the world without. In general the rise of representational and narrative sculpture in romanesque art may be related to this desire to evangelize, to make truths live for the masses.

At the risk of oversimplification we might summarize the preceding comments in the following way:

Early Altar Art	Romanesque Portal Art
ritual reaffirmation	evangelism
static	narrative
private	public
precious or perishable materials	stone
designed to be contemplated primarily during religious ceremony	available at any time, freed from any specific relationship with the Holy Office
part of a unified religious experience	part of an uncontrolled secular scene

In short, romanesque portal art has many of the characteristics which we associate with the popular arts. Produced in general by lay masons working in close connection with the church, romanesque portal art displays the apocalyptic subjects and narrative representational techniques which have the best chance of appealing to the people at large.[4] Relying on the familiar image rather than the written language, west facade programs typically reach a far larger percentage of the population than any previous religious art form. It remains to be seen, however, how the popular imagery of romanesque portal art manages simultaneously to fulfill the needs of its varied public as well as the requirements of the text's publisher—the Church.

III. Beggar and Rich Man at the Church Door: The Function of the Dives and Lazarus Parable in the Portal Program

Of all the subjects carved in medieval portal programs, the most common are undoubtedly apocalyptic scenes, often accompanied by episodes from the life of Christ. Indeed, so many romanesque churches display such scenes that it would be impossible in an article of this length even to begin an analysis of their form and function. Instead, I will concentrate on the fascinating and often represented parable of the rich man (*Dives*) and the poor beggar Lazarus (Luke 16: 19ff).[5] Beginning in the 11th century, this parable was represented throughout Europe in every medium and location imaginable: as a nave fresco,[6] in stone capitals located in every part of the church,[7] in manuscript illustrations,[8] even in bronze and glass.[9] By far the most common location for the Dives and Lazarus parable, however, is the area directly adjacent to or above the church entrance: the tympanum,[10] in a series of porch capitals,[11] or in a sequence of reliefs.[12] Why, we may well ask, is this particular story so often chosen as part of a portal program? What function does it play in terms of the overall program? As popular narrative—in every sense of that expression—does the Dives and Lazarus story have particular appeal to the uneducated masses? Does it carry any self-advertisement for the church (the work's "publisher," though not its immediate author)?

As analyzed by medieval artists, the Dives and Lazarus story is typically divided into four segments:

1). The rich man at his table feasting, accompanied by a small number of revelers (at least one of whom is a woman), and often attended by a servant.

2). Lazarus lying at the rich man's door; he is covered with sores which are licked by a trio of dogs.

3). Lazarus is shown comfortably nestled in Abraham's bosom.

4). The rich man is licked by the fires of Hell; the common gesture of reaching out toward Lazarus is explained by the text as a request for a drink of water to relieve his parched throat.[13]

The first two segments are invariably combined in a single composition; the third and fourth segments—depending on the space available—are either combined or treated in similar but separate scenes. However these four basic segments are arranged, the parable's basic structure becomes apparent.[14] Just as Lazarus is offered not even the crumbs from the rich man's table, so the rich man is refused divine sustenance in the afterlife. The tale's operative dualities are clearly defined by the four-part division of the text: rich/poor, salvation/damnation, worldly life/eternal life.

On the surface this parable seems obviously addressed to the urban poor. Take heart, it says to them, for your condition is a sacred one. Those who wield power and enjoy the pleasures of this world are doomed to a life of eternal torture unless they share their worldly treasures. Viewed in this way Poverty takes on something of the sacred character which the mendicant orders would confer on it from the 13th century on. In fact, according to Emile Male, the Dives and Lazarus story is particularly appropriate to the area surrounding the church entrance, because it was there that the medieval poor congregated to beg alms.[15] Transfigured by the tale of poor Lazarus, the beggar might expect a more generous gift from the rich parishioner.

To this socio-historical explanation of the popularity of this parable as part of a portal program we may add a formal justification. The church portal, as we have seen, represents both the dividing line and the passageway between secular and sacred space. On one side the dealing of the marketplace, where men are judged by their pocketbook; on the other side the church—early symbol of the heavenly city—where only spiritual riches may be counted. This same duality is clearly reflected in the story of Dives and Lazarus, where the first and second segments take place in this world, while the third and fourth are projected into a realm beyond time. In other words, Dives and Lazarus in the first diptych are to the world outside the church as Dives and Lazarus in the second diptych are to the hallowed space within. This parable thus serves as a guide to the symbolic meaning of the portal itself. To enter in is to adopt certain values and leave others behind.

To the poor beggar seated at the church door, the meaning of the parable is hardly ambiguous. Radulphus Ardens sums it up well in a 12th-century sermon: "By this example the poor and the sick learn not to complain about their misfortunes, nor to condemn the rich, but to praise God and to blame their suffering on their own sins."[16] The promise of a reward in the next world serves to divert any criticism which the lower classes might be tempted to level at the moneyed classes. The Dives and Lazarus story thus serves the rich and poor alike: to the impoverished masses it is a tale which dignifies poverty and promises paradise; to the rich burgher or nobleman it is a defense against potential revolt. To the church, however, this parable might seem nothing short of an implicit condemnation: just as Lazarus lies penniless at the rich man's door, so the city's beggars sit unrewarded at the church portal. By carving the story of Lazarus at the church door, the church paradoxically places itself in the position of the rich man, the affluent institution which refuses to share its wealth with those who have none. Why then place this story in a position which underscores the church's formal correspondence to the uncharitable Dives?

To answer this question we must momentarily desert portal sculpture and consider instead a tradition too often forgotten in the interpretation of church art: the homily. Every year, on the second Sunday after Pentecost (first Sunday after Trinity), in churches all across Europe, the Gospel passage for the day was taken from Luke 16: 19ff; that is, the parable of Dives and Lazarus. Following the reading of the Holy Scripture, the priest would expose the meaning of the passage to the faithful. This homily was not, however, entirely of the priest's invention. In general, nearly every aspect of it would be borrowed from a long line of Church fathers stretching from Jerome and Augustine through Gregory and Bede to more recent glosses believed to be the work of Walafrid Strabo and Hugh of Saint-Victor. From the 4th century through the 12th, not much changes in the standard interpretation of this familiar parable. The rich man is given no name because at the final hour God will not know him; Lazarus is named because his name is written in the Book of Life.[17] The rich man represents the proud Jews, Lazarus the humble Gentiles hungry for knowledge. But the Jews refuse to share their Law with the Gentiles, so Lazarus is condemned to lie at the door where the dogs lick his sores. Now the sores of the flesh clearly figure, on the moral plane, the sins of the Gentiles, which can be opened only by confession, thus paving the way for the confessor's saving counsel (represented by the dogs curative licking).

Two aspects of this interpretation require particular attention; not surprisingly it is in regard to the dogs, the unexpected heroes of this reading, that more information is needed. Now the original intent of the parable can hardly have been to underscore the rich man's avarice by opposing it to the animals' charitable attention, for the dog as pet, as household companion and faithful friend, is a Western innovation. In the Middle East two millennia ago the dog was a scavenger, a coprophagous pest, hardly a fit hero for a tale of poverty rewarded. In the first century, then, the presence of the dogs must have evoked horror, graphically expressing the depths of Lazarus' misery and the extent of the rich man's lack of concern. The medieval church's interpretation of the parable thus differs radically from the original; whereas the oriental version reveals no agent of change, no method whereby Lazarus is transfigured from lowly beggar to heavenly vision, the medieval version treats the dogs as intercessors, as institutional intermediaries between this world and the next. But who exactly are these intercessors, these charitable figures who by opposition to the rich man's avarice seem somehow like a prefiguring of paradise? Here the commentators reveal a most interesting progression. Whereas Jerome in the 4th century identifies the dogs with teachers (*doctores*), nearly all commentators after Gregory the Great stress the role of the preacher-confessor.[18] In the 12th century the allegorical interpretation regularly likens the dogs to preachers (*praedicatores*).[19] The Victorine *Allegoriae in Novum Testamentum* (generally attributed to Hugh of Saint-Victor) sums up this approach quite succinctly: "the dogs lick the wounds of the pauper, because preachers by preaching take away sins—as if they were touching wounds they lead the sinner to salvation—thus the wounds of the flesh are cured when they are licked."[20]

Now this standard version of the parable must have been preached literally hundreds of thousands of times during the middle ages. No faithful parishioner could have remained unaware of this accepted interpretation.[21] Viewed in this light, the parable of Dives and Lazarus takes on a new function within the portal program. Far from simply extolling Poverty or criticizing Avarice, the parable now becomes an advertisement for the activities which take place within the church, an invitation to partake of the preaching which alone can guarantee the masses a passport to paradise. The Church's typological identity with the Heavenly City is thus reinforced and the portal's function as passageway from the secular to the sacred underscored. The hero of the portal program is thus the preacher; far from being implicated as an uncharitable institution by the parable carved at its door, the church is recognized as the dispensary of heavenly rewards.[22]

For the common people, the parable of Dives and Lazarus represents a call for charity from the rich and promise of ultimate reward. For the church this parable represents the perfect publicity, a well disguised but nevertheless effective indentification of salvation with the church and its preachers. Like a well planned theater marquee, which appeals to the customer's taste only in order better to attract him inside, the romanesque portal program remains constantly self-conscious of its position and function. Deploying representational carving and narrative sequences to a degree never before displayed, the romanesque portal complex provides the Western world with its first truly popular genre, replete with the institutional rhetoric which will characterize popular culture right down to the present era of mass media.

Notes

[1] In an interesting paper which greatly helped to refine my own ideas, Stephen G. Nichols, Jr. has suggested that typanum art represents a projection of apse art onto the church's facade. In one sense this is clearly true, for romanesque tympanum iconography borrows heavily from Byzantine apse iconography. The narrative dimension of the romanesque portal area represents novelty, however. Nearly every west facade program combines scenes recalling Christ's first coming, usually narrative in nature, with a static vision of Christ's second coming. It is the

combination of these two impulses which characterizes romanesque portal art. (Nichols' paper was delivered to the Medieval French Literature section of the 1977 meeting of the Modern Language Association in New York City.)

[2]On the preference of the medieval lower classes for apocalyptic material, see Norman Cohn, *The Pursuit of the Millenium: Revolutionary Millenarians and Mystical Anarchists of the Middle Ages* (New York: Oxford Univ. Press, 1970; revised and enlarged), pp. 53ff.

[3]"There was a rich man, who was clothed in purple and fine linen who feasted sumptuously every day. And at his gate lay a poor man named Lazarus, full of sores, who desired to be fed with what fell from the rich man's table; moreover the dogs came and licked his sores. The poor man died and was carried by the angels to Abraham's bosom. The rich man also died and was buried; and in Hades, being in torment, he lifted up his eyes, and saw Abraham far off and Lazarus in his bosom. And he called out, 'Father Abraham, have mercy upon me, and send Lazarus to dip the end of his finger in water and cool my tongue; for I am in anguish in this flame.' But Abraham said, 'Son, remember that you in your lifetime received your good things, and Lazarus in like manner evil things; but now he is comforted here, and you are in anguish. And besides all this, between us and you a great chasm has been fixed, in order that those who would pass from here to you may not be able, and none may cross from there to us.' And he said, 'Then I beg you, father, to send him to my father's house, for I have five brothers, so that he may warn them, lest they also come into this place of torment.' But Abraham said, 'They have Moses and the prophets; let them hear them.' And he said, 'No, father Abraham; but if some one goes to them from the dead, they will repent.' He said to him, 'If they do not hear Moses and the prophets, neither will they be convinced if some one should rise from the dead'." (Revised Standard Version)

[4]Frescoes—Italy: Sant-Angelo in Formis, Brindisi (Santa Maria del Casale); Spain: San Clemente de Tahus (partial); Germany: Burgfeldun; England: Hardham (Saint Botolph); France: Vicq-sur-Saint Chartrier (Eglise Saint-Martin), Ponce (Eglise Saint-Julien), Saint-Junien (collegiale).

[5]Capitals—nave: Vezelay (Basilique Sainte-Marie-Madeleine); aisle: Besse-en-Chandesse (Eglise Saint-Andre); exterior blind arcades: Vigeois (ancienne priorale Saint-Pierre); cloister: Moissac (ancienne abbatiale Saint-Pierre), Monreale (cathedral).

[6]Manuscript illustration—*codex aureus Epternacensis*, Nuremberg, Germanisches National museum, hs. $2^0$156142, fol. 79 recto; a copy of the above, Escorial Codex Vitrinas 17, fol. 117 verso; Herrad of Landsberg, *Hortus Deliciarum* (destroyed in the Strasbourg fire of 1870; for a copy see A. Straub and G. Keller, Herrade de Landsberg, *Hortus deliciarum*, Strasbourg: Monuments historiques d'Alsace, 1879-99; illus. 32bis); New York, Pierpont Morgan Library MS 521, recto (a leaf which may have prefaced the Eadwine Psalter); Godefridus, Abbot of Admont, *Homilies*, Library of the Abbey of Admont (Styria); *La Somme le roy, Millar MS (published in Eric George Millar, La Somme le roy*, Oxford: Roxburghe Club, 1957; fol. 188 verso).

[7]Bronze—the column at Hildensheim; stained glass—Bourges (Cathedrale Saint-Etienne, choir).

[8]1Sympanum—Avila (San Vincente), York (now in Museum of Yorkshire Philosophical Society), and possibly Ruffic (north blind doorway of Saint-Andre).

[9] Porch capitals—Toulouse (Saint-Sernin, the south door known as the Porte des Comtes), Lescure d'Albigeois (ancienne priorale Saint-Michel), Autun (Cathedrale Saint-Lazare, north door), Nevers (Saint-Sauveur, part now in Musee Lapidaire).

[10]Reliefs—Moissac (ancienne abbatiale Saint-Pierre), Lagrauliere (Eglise Saint-Marcel), Argenton-Chateau (Eglise Saint-Gilles), Lincoln (Cathedral), Rouen (Cathedrale Notre-Dame, south portal known as the Portail de la Calende).

[11]The popular 12th-century preacher Radulphus Ardens (Raoul Ardent) outlines six parts: "There are then six parts of the parable in question; first the worth of the rich man is set forth, second the worth of the pauper, third the reward of the pauper, fourth the punishment of the rich man, fifth the rich man prays for himself, sixth for his kin, but his prayers are not answered." Migne, *Patrologia Latina* (hereafter PL), vol. 155, col. 1962. The last two sections as outlined by Radulphus Ardens are never to my knowledge represented in medieval iconography.

[12]This claim holds only for the romanesque period. Gothic treatments of the Dives and Lazarus parable tend to split the narrative into a continuous progression of minuscule segments, thus sacrificing the parable's exemplary dualism to realistic representation and cause-and-effect sequentiality. It is interesting in this respect to note Emile Male's misconceptions about the 13th-century popularity of this parable. In *The Gothic Image: Religious Art in France of the Thirteenth Century* (trans. Dora Nussey; New York: Harper, 1958, 1958; orig. 1913) Male lists the Dives and Lazarus parable as one of the four most common in 13th-century French art. In fact, of the thirty-

three locations listed above, some twenty-eight are either 11th or 12th century, while only four are from the 13th century.

[13]Male, *op. cit.*, p. 200; see also Raymond Rey, *La Sculpture romane langue-docienne* (Paris: Didier, 1936), pp. 77ff.

[14]Radulphus Ardens, PL vol. 155, col. 1963.

[15]The fact that Lazarus is the only named character in any of Christ's parables gives rise to a great deal of interesting commentary on the specific genre of the Dives and Lazarus story. The 9th-century *Glossa Ordinaria* (falsely attributed to Walafrid Strabo) says that the story seems more like a narrative than a parable ("magis videtur narratio quam parabola," PL vol. 114, col. 316); Radulphus claims it is not only a parable but also a story ("non solum parabola sed etiam historia est," PL vol. 155, col. 1962); Werner of Saint-Blasus in the Black Forest points out that naming a character is more appropriate to narration than parable ("Nota cum parabolae non ponant nomina, et Dominus per humilitatis approbationem pauperis hugus nomen dicat, non parabola, sed rei gestae narratio haec est," PL vol. 157, col. 1004-05; Zacharias Chrysopolitanus gives word for word the same passage, ultimately borrowed from Ambrose and Petrus Chrysologus (PL vol. 186, col. 337).

[16]Jerome, PL vol. 30, col. 594; Gregory the Great, PL vol. 76, col. 1301 (*Homiliae XL in Evangelia*, but see also *Moralia in Job*, book 25, ch. 13); Bede, *Expositio in Lucae Evangelium*, PL vol. 92, col. 533 (also his homily on the parable, PL vol. 94, col. 267); Smaragdus, PL vol. 102, col. 348.

[17]Werner, PL vol. 157, col. 1007; Godefridus, PL 174, col. 387; Zacharias Chrysopolitanus, PL vol. 186, col. 337.

[18]Hugh of Saint-Victor, PL vol. 175, col. 822.

[19]The sermons which I have quoted are all conserved in Latin, but students of the medieval homily have repeatedly insisted that these Latin originals served as the basic text for vernacular sermons. See L. Bourgain, *La Chaire franciase au XII e siecle* (Paris: Societe generale de Librarie catholique, 1879), p. 186; more recently Michel Zink has dealt with the same problem in *La Predication en langue romane avant 1300* (Paris: Champion, 1976), pp. 85ff.

[20]In the later middle ages the connection between the Dives and Lazarus parable and preaching is further reinforced by an identification of Lazarus and/or his dogs with the mendicant preaching orders, especially the Dominicans. Known by a common pun as the bloodhounds of God (*domini canes*), the members of this order mixed poverty and preaching in a manner clearly reminiscent of the Dives and Lazarus parable. It is thus not surprising to find Lazarus interpreted as a Dominican in the Bible Moralisee of the later middle ages or represented as a talented preacher in the Middle English *Dives and Pauper* (ed. Priscilla Heath Barnum; London: Oxford Univ. Press, 1976; Early English Text Society, No. 275.

Portent Lore

Norman R. Smith begins his essay by pointing out that there is no such thing as "popular" monster lore (teratology) in the Middle Ages, but goes on to say that a knowledge of the teratological thought of, say, Isidore of Seville, may give us a very good insight into the popular thought of the day. Ideas concerning "monstrous births," considered portentous until recent times, tell us a great deal about the concepts men had of themselves in relation to their world, their god, and their historical place, factors which illuminate the imaginatively constructed ideas and their popularity during the Renaissance. Monster lore, of course, remains popular in our own day, hence our passionate interest in the Loch Ness Monster and our devotion to the myriad types of Frankenstein that have appeared recently, a fact that perhaps links us and our time in a rather startling way to the Middle Ages.

Norman R. Smith received his Ph. D. from the University of Illinois and works for I.B.M., Trenton, N.J.

Portent Lore and Medieval Popular Culture

Norman R. Smith

In studying the monstrous portent in medieval popular culture, several clarifications need to be made from the start. First of all, a portent can be anything from an overdeveloped lobe on the liver of a sacrificial animal to a comet or a disastrous earthquake, and for reasons of convenience, I have concentrated on one particular type of portent, the monstrous birth. Secondly, so far as I can tell, there is no such thing as a "popular" monster lore in the Middle Ages. In the medieval period, monster lore, or *teratology*, was the property of the learned classes—those who could read cosmographies and encyclopedias, the works of Isidore of Seville and Vincent of Beauvais. But an analysis of the teratological thought of the medieval savants might well tell us what went on in the popular mind. Indeed, when printing makes books cheaper and learning more accessible in the Renaissance, teratology does in fact become popular culture.[1]

Until comparatively recent times, the births of deformed creatures—human or animal—were considered portentous: such births represented either divine comments on contemporary conditions or divine revelations of the future. Such ideas date back at least to Babylonian-Assyrian cuneiform tablets of 2000 B.C. The Babylonians developed an extensive science of monster interpretation based on emblematic symbolism: "If a woman gives birth to twins united at the sides, the land ruled by one will be controlled by two,"[2] and so on.

Though the idea has been entertained, it seems doubtful that Babylonian portent lore had much effect on the development of teratology in the West. Of greater importance are ideas that evolved in Greece and Rome. From Greece came the idea that entire races of monstrous human beings lived in remote regions of the earth. Herodotus, for example, notes that in Libya there is a race of dog-headed men as well as headless men whose eyes and mouths were in their chests (*Histories* IV. 191). Ktesias of Knidos, a Greek physician contemporary with Hippocrates, wrote a geography called the *Indika*[3] in which India is populated by hosts of bizarre human beings: the dog-headed *cynocephali* (pp. 21-5); the one-footed *monosceli* (or sciapods) who hold their single giant foot umbrella-fashion above their heads when the sun is hot (p. 61); a race of men (later called the *panotii*) whose ears are so large that they can be wrapped around the body like cloaks (p. 60), and so on. Ktesias' monsters are taken up in *The Life of Alexander of Macedon*, a late-classical romance that became incredibly popular in the Middle Ages,[4] and in the popular seventh book of Pliny's *Natural History*. Pliny, of course, was also widely read, and his discussion is picked up by such writers as St. Augustine (*Civ. Dei* VXI. viii) and Isidore of Seville (*Et.* XI. iii. See Fig. 1).

A friendly dog-head in far-off India is not a very threatening being, and one finds marvel rather than fear in many Greek discussions of the monstrous. This is totally unlike the feeling one detects in most Roman monster and portent lore. The earliest collection of Roman law, the *Twelve Tables,* codifies a mandatory death sentence for monsters.[5] Livy enlarges upon this theme. For Livy, Rome has fallen on dark days of impiety and disregard of the gods; he chooses to record the frightening monsters and portents of Roman history in order to show divine involvement in human affairs (*Livy* XLVIII. xiii. 1-3). Of a hundred or so portentous events in Livy's history, at least fifteen are frightening monsters, such things as "a pig born with a human face" (XXVII.iv.14-5) and a boy with the head of an elephant (XXVII.xi. 4-6)—portents that often had to be atoned for with sacrifices by the pontiffs.

Other Roman writers are concerned with monsters. Livy inspired the shadowy late-classical figure Julius Obsequens to write an entire work on the subject of Roman portents. Julius's *Prodigiorum Liber*[6] was ultimately printed at the Aldine Press in 1508 and it became very popular in the monster-obsessed Renaissance. Closer to Livy's own time, Tacitus endowed the monster with an intense sense of catastrophic portentousness. His *Histories* is a dark and bloody chronicle of the coups and usurpations of first-century Rome, and among the divine portents of these disasters are animals that "give birth to strange young" (I.lxxvi). Only Cicero, in his *De Divinatione*, refuses to believe that monsters and portents are messages from the gods or that they are valid indications of future occurrences. Cicero, it should be noted, is not an original thinker; he follows very closely the teratology of Aristotle, who in his *Generation of Animals* argued that monsters are caused by physiological dysfunctions. "A monstrosity... belongs to the class of 'things contrary to nature',," wrote Aristotle, "although it is contrary not to nature in her entirety but only nature *in the generality of cases.* So far as concerns the nature which is *always* and by *necessity*, nothing occurs contrary to that" (*G.A.* IV.iv.770b.10-15).

Aristotle, of course, had a very idiosyncratic view of God and nature—

Fig. 1. The monsters of India: a sciapod, cyclops, Janus-head, one of the *blemmyae*, and a cynocephalus. From Sebastian Munster's *Cosmographiae Universalis* (Basel, 1550), p.1151.

his god is withdrawn from the hustle and bustle of the cosmos; he spends his time contemplating his own perfection, and does not bother to violate the laws of nature by way of causing monsters or miracles. Implicit, however, in the Babylonian and Roman views I have discussed is the notion that divinity is indeed involved in the affairs of this world, and that god or gods do indeed cause monsters, portents and miracles in order to warn men of coming disasters. This idea is carried forward into the Christian Middle Ages.

The Bible itself contains few monsters—there are the hideous creatures of Daniel and of the Apocalypse, as well as Behemoth and Leviathan in Job. As Robert M. Grant has noted, there is much of a portentous and miraculous nature in the canonical scriptures and there is a great deal more in the Old Testament apocryphal and pseudepigraphical material.[7] But there is nothing beyond a warning to the decadent Israelites that "women in their uncleanness will bear monsters" in II Esdras V.8 to indicate that the prophets thought at all about the monstrous birth.

Nonetheless, the idea of portentous monstrous births is so congenial to Christian thought that it is not long before classically-trained Church Fathers are discussing them in patrology. For example, we find Tertullian arguing in his *Apologeticus* that Christian "divination" is as potent as the pagan brand; the Bible foretells everything, including God's overturning of the order of nature and sending signs by means of monsters and portents, *quod et monstris et portentis naturalium forma turbatur* (*Apologeticus* XX.iii)—the very language here is reminiscent of such Roman teratological writers as Livy and Cicero. When Eusebius comes to write some of the first Christian history, he finds it logical to include such distinctly Roman events as cows giving birth to monstrous lambs during the seige of Jerusalem (*Eccl. Hist.* III.viii. 1-11). This is highly significant, since Eusebius, along with Paulus Orosius, had such a profound influence on the historiography of the Middle Ages.[8]

It is Saint Augustine who, in the fifth century, established a definitive Christian doctrine of the monstrous which was to remain influential for over a thousand years. Augustine was a highly credulous thinker; it has been noted, for example, that he was unsure whether Apuleius' transformations in the *Golden Ass* were fiction or nonfiction (Grant, p. 216), and he seems to have little trouble in accepting the bizarre creatures of Pliny's seventh book (*Civ. Dei* XVI.8). More importantly, Augustine vigorously attacks Aristotle's teratological rationalism—indeed, he attacks the whole of Aristotelian thought with regard to the ability of God to interfere with the normal order of things. "The freakish births of animals," Augustine writes, are "portentous events" (*Civ. Dei* X.16). They occur because "God, Who made the visible heaven and earth, does not disdain to work visible miracles on heaven and earth, whereby He may quicken the soul, hitherto given up to visible things, to worship Him, the invisible" (*Civ. Dei.* X. 12—. Augustine's God is not constrained, like Aristotle's, to obey the laws of nature: "He is assuredly called almighty for no other reason except that He can do whatever He wishes. He was able to create many things that would surely be thought impossible unless they were made manifest. . .(XXI.7).

Augustine stops short of suggesting that the future can be divined by the interpretation of monstrous births. In fact, he holds that predicting the future involves trafficking with demons (*Civ. Dei* V.7). But his warning seems to have had little effect on subsequent thinkers. Surely, if God bothers to overturn nature in order to cause these creatures, then monsters must be indications of future events—thus reasons, for example, Isidore of Seville: *quaedam autem portentorum creationes in significationibus futuris constitutae videntur. Vult enim Deus interdum ventura significare per alliqua nascentium noxia*—(*Et.* XI.iii). Isidore is followed nearly word-for-word by Rabanus Maurus (Cf. *De Universo*, Migne, *PL* CXI. Col. 197), and there is nothing in any of the treatments of monsters over the next seven or eight hundred years to indicate that there was any disagreement on this point.

For most of the Middle Ages, however, it was not the portentous monster, but rather the monstrous races of India that held men's interests. The races are discussed in the 8th-century cosmography of Pseudo-Aethicus of Istria and in the 11th-century *Gesta Hammaburgensis* of Adam of Bremen. In the 13th century they are discussed in the *Image du Monde* of Gautier of Metz, in the *Tresor* of Brunetto Latini, and in the chronicles of Rudolph of Ems and Gervase of Tilbury.[9] By the 13th century the Indian monsters had worked their way into bestiaries, those typically medieval documents in which the Book of Nature is read by interpreting the characteristics of animals.[10] A bestiary in the Bodleian Library is a good example: it describes the "cynocephali which have dogs' heads and which signify detractors and discord" and the "panothii which have ears capacious to bad news."[11]

The emblematic interpretation of monsters that we see in these examples becomes increasingly typical of teratology as we move toward the Renaissance. The massive writings of Vincent of Beauvais contain several good examples. Vincent is interested in all kinds of monsters, from the Gorgons and Chimera of mythology[12] to the Indian monsters. But Vincent is just as interested in portentous births of the sort which so fascinated and terrified the Romans—and later the Renaissance. The following tale, which was popular in the Renaissance and was repeated by Pierre Boaistuau[13] and Jacopo Filippo Foresti da Bergamo[14] (variations of the tale were offered by Petrarch[15] and Raphael Holinshed[16]) is told by Vincent of the period just before the invasion of Britain in 1066:

In those days in the confines of Normandy and Britanny, a portent was seen in one, or rather in two women. There were two heads and four arms, and everything was twin to the navel, but beneath everything was totally unified. One laughed, ate, and talked; the other wept, fasted, and was silent. They chewed simultaneously, but one directed the motion. One died and the other survived, in frightful straits, for three years, carrying the dead one about...finally dying from the odor of the cadaver. Some have supposed and written that these women signified the English and the Normans, who although once divided, were united under one lord (See Fig. 2; *Spec. Hist.* XXV.xxxviii.)

Vincent mentions another fascinating creature, which, though the encyclopedist himself offers no emblematic interpretation for it, comes to be emblematically interpreted as we move into the Renaissance. It is a satyr-

Fig. 2. The two-headed monster of Vincent of Beauvais. The 16th century illustrator has neglected to show all four of the creature's arms. From Pierre Boiastuau, *Histoires prodigieuses* (Paris, 1560; rpt. Paris, 1961), p. 69.

like cynocephalus (Vincent says it liked wine and women and had a *genitale membrum magnum*) which is captured and brought before a certain King Louis (*Spec. Nat.* XXXI. cxxvi). According to Jakob Mennel, a humanist in the court of Maximilian in the late 15th century, the creature signified "those times in which mindless men shifted about as if they were barking dogs" (See Fig. 3).[17]

Monster lore truly becomes "popular culture" only with the Renaissance, a fact which presents no problem as far as the present discussion is concerned. We think of the Renaissance as a period of progress in technology and scholarship, an era of development of the critical spirit, at least in certain fields such as anatomy, archeology, historiography, text analysis and so on. But Renaissance teratology, with few exceptions, does not show evidence of progress in any of these areas; indeed, it represents an extension of ideas present in the Middle Ages. The essence of Renaissance monster lore may be what Marshall McLuhan called "the hypertrophy of the unconscious,"[18] a phenomenon he associated with periods of revolution in media technology: the advent of print in the 16th century created a great need for sensational materials to be broadcast, and this need caused ideas that formerly had been only lurking in the dark recesses of men's minds to come floating to the surface. These ideas often seem as though they would have been more appropriate in earlier, more superstitious eras.

That such ideas are properly to be called part of the popular culture of the Renaissance is seen from the sheer output of teratological material. Julius Obsequens' collection of Roman prodigies, the *Prodigiorum Liber*, first printed by Aldus Manutius in Venice in 1508, is reprinted dozens of times in the 16th century,[19] and fresh works on the subject of teratology are written by Italians,[20] Germans,[21] and Frenchmen.[22] The forerunner of the modern newspaper, the broadside, is largely devoted to reporting and interpreting the contemporary monstrous births[23]—truly a significant fact from the viewpoint of popular culture, since broadsides, often luridly illustrated and sensationally written, were bought on street corners and at fairs by the barely literate masses. The great reformers Luther and Melanchthon used the broadside medium to popularize their propagandistic and anti-Catholic versions of two of the most famous monsters of the Renaissance, the Monk-calf of Freiburg and the Pope-ass of Rome (see Figs. 4 & 5).[24] Furthermore, one of the great bestsellers of the 16th century was the *Histoires prodigieuses* of Pierre Boaistuau (Paris, 1560), a sort of Renaissance Ripley's Believe-It-Or-Not containing marvelous tales on everything from the man who washed his hands in molten lead to the miraculous properties of gemstones. Seventeen of the *Histoires'* forty tales are about monsters, a fact which may explain why the book was republished anywhere from ten to twenty-two times and translated into Dutch, Spanish and English.[25]

I have suggested that though this 16th-century monster lore is broadcast by means of a Renaissance revolution in media technology, it is still medieval in character. This is a vast subject, but perhaps one illustration will suffice. One of the revolutions that comprise the Renaissance is a radical change in the way history is viewed. Throughout the Middle Ages, history was written on the pattern of *The Seven Books of*

Fig. 3. A cynocephalus is presented to King Louis. From Jakob Mennel's 1503 manuscript, *De Signis, Portentis, atque Prodigiis* (Vienna, N.B. Cod. 4417), fol. 9.[7]

Das Munchkalb zu freyberg

Fig. 4. Luther's Monk-calf of Freiburg. Martin Luther, *Werke* (Weimar, 1900), XI, 373.

Der Bapstesel zu Rom

Fig. 5. The Pope-ass of Rome. Illustration from Melanchthon's antipapal pamphlet, in Martin Luther's *Werke* (Weimar, 1900), XI, 371.

History Against the Pagans of Paulus Orosius and the *Chronicon* of Eusebius. Each of these works is heavily influenced by the Christian idea that the things of this world are unimportant compared to the realities of the heavenly world. Such a notion has a distorting effect on written history: the historian is less interested in the dynamics and the human interplay of an epoch than in the isolated events that seem to betoken the activities of the deity. Thus, a comet or the birth of a monster, occurrences thought to be messages from God, become more important than the motives of a tyrant, the migrations of peoples, or the movements of great armies. Medieval history becomes a shopping-list-like chronicle of disjointed and mostly unimportant events.

Historiography began to change with Petrarch and advanced by a quantum leap with Machiavelli early in the 16th century. For Machiavelli, it is "more proper to go to the real truth of the matter than to its imagination";[26] it is more important to consider things as they really happen in this world than to worry about the unknowable "realities" of the other. For Machiavelli, history was a study of human motives and human actions, and not a chronicle of imaginary divine interference in the affairs of the world.

The Renaissance teratologists are very much concerned with history, but when we consider their writings we find that they are still in the shadow of Livy and Obsequens, Augustine, Orosius, and Eusebius. The greatest Renaissance history of monsters and portents, the *Prodigiorum ac Ostentorum Chronicon* (Basel, 1557) of the Alsatian humanist Conradus Lycosthenes, is a year-by-year chronicle of God's violations of the natural order, starting, in medieval fashion, with the year of creation (3959 B.C., according to Lycosthenes) and continuing to the present day. It is a history of God's wrath against sinful mankind, a list of God's marvelous warnings and portents—monsters, comets, earthquakes, rains of blood or frogs or stones, heavenly visions, and so on. But it is not a careful analysis of historical dynamics, even though it was written decades after the death of Machiavelli. The *Chronicon,* in fact, singles out for criticism those few advanced Renaissance thinkers who had begun to look to Aristotle as an authority for the view that all things have rational explanations and that God Himself could not violate natural order; the *Chronicon* is, in short, a medieval work.

It remains to be asked why monsters became such objects of passionate interest in certain epochs. We have seen that monster lore was popular in Babylonian times, in Roman times, to a certain extent in the Middle Ages, and to a large extent in the Renaissance. Part of the explanation must be that in these eras, all things were viewed as reflections of divine reality; the visible world was but the symbol of the invisible. This is the reason that monsters are often interpreted emblematically: they are part of the "Book of Nature."[27] But monsters have been popular in our own time—we've trembled in the cinema before images of Frankenstein and Godzilla; we've closely followed the search for the Abominable Snowman and the Loch Ness monster; we even have popular singing groups that bedeck themselves like creatures from Lycosthenes or Boaistuau. And since we seem to have lost the ability to view material reality as a mass of symbols of a deeper and divine reality, this cannot be the entire explanation.

I have already alluded to part of the explanation, at least as far as the Renaissance and our own age are concerned: the "hypertrophy of the unconscious" that occurs when new media develop, giving mankind freer reign to broadcast his darkest imaginings (think of how television has brought murder and mayhem into nearly every household!). But again, this does not explain it all, for the clay tablets of Mesopotamia and the scrolls and codices of Rome were not media revolutions in quite the same way as print and electronic broadcast were.

The ultimate explanation may lie in the character of the periods in which monsters become popular. The Rome of Livy and Tacitus witnessed countless civil wars, assassinations and power struggles. The late Middle Ages witnessed not only an increase in the corruption and power mania of the Church, but also her split into Rome and Avignon factions. In 1453, Constantinople fell and the Ottoman Turks flooded into the eastern outposts of Christendom. Millenial uprisings broke out, threatening both civil and ecclestiastical authority. It was a time, as Huizinga and others have noted, of profound gloom.[28] Our own era has seen the rise of totalitarianism, of mass genocide, of atomic weaponry, and of total environmental destruction. It is not surprising that these eras have been fascinated by the grotesque and the deformed, by the existence of creatures whose hideous bodies seem to exemplify the discord of the times.

Notes

[1]This article is based, in large part, on the author's doctoral dissertation in Comparative Literature: "Loathly Births Off Nature: A Study of the Lore of the Portentous Monster in the Sixteenth Century," University of Illinois, 1978. Those interested in further readings in teratology I would refer to this work, especially pages 18 and 19. I should mention here, however, Rudolph Wittkower's "Marvels of the East: A Study in the History of Monsters," *The Journal of the Warburg and Courtauld Institutes*, V (1942), 159-97. I should also mention that the world of teratology promises to be greatly enriched upon the publication, hopefully in the not too distant future, of a work by John Block Friedman on the monsters of the Middle Ages. I owe Professor Friedman my deepest appreciation for his encouragement of my own studies of the monsters.

A note about my documentation is in order. In the interests of keeping this article brief and unencumbered with notes, I have dispensed with some of the normal conventions. Familiar works of antiquity I have cited textually, without the customary first note citing the particular text used. In most cases, these texts were from the Loeb Classical Library. When possible, I have used familiar abbreviations, i.e., *Civ. Dei* for *The City of God*, and so on.

[2]Morris Jastrow, "Babylonian-Assyrian Birth Omens," *Religionsgeschichtliche Versuche und Vorarbeiten*, XIV (1914), 29.

[3]Ktesias the Knidian, *Ancient India*, ed. & trans. John W. McCrindle (Calcutta: Thacker, Spink & Co., 1882). Subsequent citations will be made textually.

[4]See Pseudo-Callisthenes, *The Life of Alexander of Macedon*, trans. Elizabeth Hazelton Haight (New York: Longman's Green, 1955). Versions of this work were produced in Arabic, Ethiopic, Syriac, Swedish, Czech, Russian, Italian, German, Hebrew, French, Irish, English, and other languages.

[5]*Table* IV.i, in *The Laws of the Twelve Tables*, vol. III of *Remains of Old Latin*, trans. E.H. Warmington, 3 vols. (Cambridge: Loeb Classical Library, 1938).

[6]A good English translation of this work, with introduction, can be found in vol. XIV of the Loeb Classical Library edition of Livy (Cambridge, 1952-59).

[7]Robert M. Grant, *Miracle and Natural Law in Greco-Roman and Early Christian Thought* (Amsterdam: North Holland Publishing Co., 1952), pp. 153-81. Subsequent citations will be documented in the text.

[8]Harry Elmer Barnes, *A History of Historical Writing*, 2nd revised ed. (New York: Dover Publications, 1963), pp. 46, 50.

[9]Pseudo-Aethicus, Adam of Bremen, Brunetto Latini, Rudolf of Ems, and Gervase of Tilbury, and their relationship with teratology, are discussed in the Wittkower article mentioned in Note 1.

[10]See Florence McCulloch, *Medieval Latin and French Bestiaries*, Univ. of North Carolina Studies in the Romance Languages and Literatures, 33 (1960).

[11]Ms. Bodleian Douce 88, pt. II. fols. 69^7-70^7.

[12]Vincent of Beauvais, *Bibliotheca Mundi Speculum Quadruplex Naturale, Doctrinale, Historiale* (Duaci: V. Belleri, 1624). Cf. *Spec. Hist.* I. xciv; *Spec. Nat.* XXXXi. cxxi.

[13]Pierre Boaistuau, *Histoires prodigieuses* (Paris, 1560), rpt. ed. Yves Florenne (Paris: Club Francais du Livre, 1961), p. 70.

[14]Jacopo Filippo Foresti da Bergame, *Supplementum Chronicarum* (Paris: Apud Galiotum, 1535), fols. 13^j-137^.k

[15]Petrarch, *Rerum Memorandum*, IV.ix.

[16]Raphael Holinshed, *Chronicles* (London, 1807), V, 228.

[17]Jakob Mennel, *De Signis, Portentis, atque Prodigiis* (1503), ms. Vienna N.B. Cod. 4417, fol. 9^7. For a detailed discussion of this monster see Bruno Roy, "Les Races monstrueuses," *Aspects de la Marginalite au Moyen Age: Premier Colloque de l'Institute d'Etudes Medievale* (Montreal: University of Montreal, 1964), p. 65 n.

[18]Marshall McLuhan, *The Gutenberg Galaxy* (New York: Signet, 1969), p. 304.

[19]Rudolph Schenda, Die deutschen Prodigiensammlungen des 16. und 17. Jahrhunderts," *Borsenblatt fur den deutschen Buchandel, Frankfurter Ausgabe*, 77a (Sept. 28, 1961), 1636-37.

[20]I.e., works by Polydor Vergil, Ulisse Aldrovandi, and Fortunio Liceti.

[21]Jakob Mennel, Conradus Lycosthenes, Sebastian Brant, Martin Luther, Caspar Peucer, Jobus Fincelius.

[22]Pierre Boaistuau, Ambrose Pare.

[23]See Hans Fehr, *Massenkunst im 16. Jahrhundert* (Berlin: Herbert Stubenrauch Verlagsbuchhandlung, 1924); and Jean-Pierre Sequin, *L'Information en France avant le periodique* (Paris: Editions G.-P. Maisonneuve et Larose, 1964).

[24]The texts of Melanchthon's and Luther's broadsides on these monsters can be found in vol. 11 of Luther's *Kritische Ausgabe* (Weimar: Hermann Bohlaus Nachfolger, 1900), pp. 375 ff. For a detailed discussion of the monsters, see Konrad Lange's *Der Pabstesel* (Gottingen, 1891).

[25]See Rudolf Wittkower, "Marvels of the East," p. 186 n.; also Rudolph Schenda, "Die franzosische Prodigienliteratur in der zweiten Halfte des 16. Jahrhunderts," *Munchner Romanistische Arbeiten*, XVI (1961), 34.

[26]Niccolo Machiavelli, *The Prince and the Discourses*, ed. Max Lerner (New York: The Modern Library, 1940), p. 56.

[27]The emblematic interpretation of reality has been discussed in such works as George Boas, *The Hierglyphics of Horapollo* (New York: Pantheon Books, 1950); Frances Yates, *Giordano Bruno and the Hermetic Tradition* (Chicago: Univ. of Chicago Press, 1964); Edgar Wind, *Pagan Mysteries in the Renaissance* (New Haven: Yale Univ. Press, 1958); E.H. Gombrich, "*Icones Symbolicae*: The Visual Image in Neo-Platonic Thought," *The Journal of the Warburg and the Courtauld Institutes*, XI (1948), 162-92; Jean Seznec, *The Survival of the Pagan Gods*, trans. Barbara F. Sessions (New York: Pantheon Books, 1953); D.W. Robertson, Jr., *A Preface to Chaucer* (Princeton: Princeton Univ. Press, 1962), esp. pp. 316, 345-46.

[28]Johann Huizinga, *The Waning of the Middle Ages* (Garden City: Doubleday Anchor Books, 1954), pp. 138-51.

Magic Kits

Each of us has wished at some time to send in three box tops and get a magic kit that contains itching powder to give to our enemies, instructions for tricks designed to baffle our friends, and potions to make us more desirable. Exactly so in the Middle Ages. Bruno Roy's delightful essay on medieval do-it-yourself magic reveals the strong popular interest in practical jokes, illusions and tricks. People in the Middle Ages were playful and high-spirited, waiting to entertain and be entertained. The transformative power implicit in the tricks played by jugglers or entertainers appealed to all classes of society; these same jugglers not only dealt in illusory tricks but often used various chemical preparations, giving a "scientific" cast to their pranks. That so many of these tricks were related to the household in terms of the joke itself or the ingredients used suggests the widespread popularity of magic kits, a popularity that today perhaps resides only with the children who save the box tops.

Bruno Roy is professor of medieval studies at the Institute d'etudes medievales, Universite de Montreal, and has published on popular culture in the Middle Ages.

The Household Encyclopedia as Magic Kit: Medieval Popular Interest in Pranks and Illusions*

Bruno Roy

The medieval love of the strange, the mysterious, and the marvelous is by now a commonplace to us. And, indeed, this aspect of the medieval mind has been often remarked on, though usually in a negative sense. For the modern rediscovery of the Middle Ages has been strongly influenced by 19th century romanticism and evolutionist theory, which have accustomed us to see a medieval society composed of credulous, primitive and pre-scientific people. The result has been that several elements of this taste for the strange and marvelous have remained largely unexamined, and none perhaps more than the subject of the present study: popular uses of magic, illusion and practical jokes, illustrated in works on household management.

Let us begin then with a positive view of medieval people, imagining them not as trembling in the face of a universe filled with occult and dangerous forces, but rather as men and women of a lively and playful spirit, fascinated by the inexhaustible riches of nature, whether they be

29

visible or invisible, favorable to mankind or the reverse, serious, or simply light and amusing.

My object in the following pages is to make us aware of some little known and indeed, unlikely repositories for this medieval blend of mystery and fantasy in works of practical knowledge and instruction. We shall see that medieval people had access to do-it-yourself manuals dealing with strange and comic practices, that they knew the great deeds of magicians through the renown of scholar scientists such as Roger Bacon—who were themselves always lightly touched with the brush of the necromancer—and that they frequented sessions of wondrous spectacles staged by the professional entertainers whom for the purposes of this paper I shall call jugglers. Thus there is considerable evidence to show that the public had, at the end of the Middle Ages, access to many secrets hitherto available only to masters of mystery and illusion.

Of the many persons believed to be in touch with invisible powers in the Middle Ages, perhaps the most important for popular culture studies were saints and magicians, who by their mysterious gifts commanded an automatic respect, but whose personalities often showed a playful side which made them human and sympathetic as well. The saint's life is well known, with its large number of miracles and marvels, as an inexhaustible storehouse of white magic, of which a good part served more for simple diversion than for theological instruction.[1] As to medieval magicians, there is an important aspect of their character in literature which has been rather neglected by modern scholars, for they often appear in the epics and romances of the 13th century as comedians who take great pleasure in pranks and practical jokes.[2] The most famous of these men—Merlin—enjoys mocking himself, playing hide and seek, and creating illusions.[3] In the *Roman d'Alexandre* the enchanter Neptanebus is a specialist in illusions, making stones seem to be cheeses, simulating fires, cutting off his head and handing it to a bystander where it immediately takes the form of a snake. Similar tricks are played by the same character in the Middle English *King Alisaunder*. Others, like Barbarin in *Floire et Blanchefleur* and Wistasse in *Wistasse the Monk* amuse themselves by forcing men to undress or fart in church, or give water the appearance of blood.[4]

So too the medieval reverence for marvelous or magical powers created a number of enchanters out of actual people who had no connection with magic. Such, of course, was the fate of Ovid,[5] and especially Virgil, who until well into the 16th century was considered as one of the most powerful magicians of antiquity.[6] One quite popular legend about Virgil in this role concerns the vengeance that he takes upon a woman who has suspended him in a basket in order to mock him. In retaliation, he extinguished by his magic all of the lamps and hearthfires in Rome and the inhabitants could relight their fires only by searching for coals between the thighs of the poor woman, over whom Virgil had thrown a spell.[7]

In the very late Middle Ages there appears an important literary figure who reveals the medieval taste for jokes based upon skill, white magic and mystery. This is Rabelais' Panurge, the companion of Pantagruel, who is presented in the modern idiom as a trickster and a magician of the laboratory. Completely equipped to play his pranks, he fills the 26 pockets of his gown with the tools of his trade, of which some have physical or chemical properties. For example, he goes about equipped with sneezing and itching powders, a bottle of dirty oil to spot peoples' clothes, and some devices to use in sleight of hand and conjuring.[8] The episode of the trick Panurge plays on the woman of Paris who refused his advances Rabelais presents in such a way that he appears as a second Virgil the magician, but times have changed and instead of casting a spell over the lady to punish her as Virgil had done, Panurge amuses himself at biochemistry, concocting a recipe for attracting the unwanted attentions of dogs: pulverize the genitalia of a bitch in heat and sprinkle the powder on the clothes of a man or a woman.[9]

The Panurge who amuses himself in applying some natural law unknown to his victims, and even, perhaps, to himself, resembles in this regard a Virgil touched with the genius of Boyle, but most important, he is a descendant of the medieval entertainers called jugglers. For if the witty enchanters depicted in literature have been so popular, it is because they were in their way a species of super juggler. They are, after all, only carrying to an extreme the jugglers' tricks which everyone had seen at fairs, at celebrations, in the public market, or on the village green. Chaucer had presented this sort of illusion in his *Franklin's Tale,* where he describes the results of the "magyk natureel" used by the entertainers of his day:

> For ofte at feestes have I wel herd seye
> That tregetours, withinnne an halle large,
> Have maad come in a water and a barge,
> And in the halle rowen up and doun.
> Sometyme hath semed come a grym leoun;
> And sometyme floures sprynge as in a mede;
> Sometyme a vyne, and grapes white and rede;
> Sometyme a castel, al of lym and stoon;
> And whan hem lyked, voyded it anon.
> Thus semed it to every mannes sighte.[10]

This passage inspired a 19th-century writer, Joseph Strutt, to a rather typical misinterpretation of medieval illusionism. "The principles of natural philosophy," he notes, "were very little known in these dark ages; and for that reason, the spectators were more readily deceived."[11] It is, in fact, much more likely that the public for these entertainers and wonder workers cared very little about the explanations of the illusions, and that rather they went to see them to be amused and to be "deceived," as quickly as possible.

These entertainers belong to a popular tradition, in the sense that they practice their art before all classes of society. But this was an oral art and was reserved to those who practiced the trade of entertainer. What of a written tradition of popular magic? To be sure, some recipes for prestidigitation can be found in medieval collections; as we shall see shortly, their very rarity even augments their interest for us. But only in the Renaissance do we find written explanations of the main illusions of the minstrel entertainers, ironically, in the works of the self-appointed protectors of the public against the possible abuses of magic.[12] Reginald Scot introduces thirteen chapters on jugglers and their secrets in his *Discoverie of Witchcraft* (1584) by observing that

Now because such occasion is ministered, and the matter so pertinent to my purpose, and also the life of witchcraft and counsenage so manifestlie delivered in the art of juggling; I thought good to discover it, together with the rest of the other deceiptfull arts.[13]

Among the tricks which Scot explains, we find the one practiced by Neptanebus the enchanter, involving a method "to cut off ones head and to laie it in a platter, &c: which the jugglers call the decollation of John Baptist."[14]

This fashion of exposing the secrets of the jugglers, motivated as it was by religious orthodoxy, was far, of course, from bringing about a true democratization of the magic arts; on the contrary, its intention was to make people shun magic, and it was quite in spite of himself that Scot became a source for later writers of books on magic. It would be some years before white magic could be presented openly as a leisure art accessible to all men. The first such treatise appeared in 1612 called *The Art of Iugling or Legerdemaine. Wherin is deciphered, all the conveyances of Legerdemaine and Iugling ... All tending to mirth and recreation, especially for those that desire to have the insight and private practice thereof.*[15] This work was soon recast for a second edition and its new title left nothing to the imagination as regards its popular character: *Hocus Pocus Iunior. The Anatomie of Legerdemaine. Or the Art of Iugling set forth in his proper colors, fully, plainly, and exactly, for than an ignorant person may thereby learn the full perfection of the same, after a little practise.*[16]

Though the secrets of the jugglers which have occupied us thus far are chiefly some tricks of illusion and prestidigitation, these entertainers also used, in order to amuse their public, various chemical preparations and objects with strange properties, such as were found in the pockets of Panurge. As the "scientific" side of Panurge's character suggests, the jugglers were only indirect sources and popularizers of another well known medieval tradition, that of the medieval scholar, whose popular image was based on the great Greek, Arabic and Jewish experimental scientists, as well as on European natural scientists such as Adelard of Bath, Roger Bacon and Albert the Great.[17]

During the period in which medieval science consolidated its gains, the taste for the marvelous did not disappear. And partly as a result of this taste, a particular kind of scientific compilation developed called the *Experimenta.* The vast number of these works and their compositional plasticity, which allowed them to combine very easily with other works of like character, has hindered our understanding of their genesis and purpose.[18] Rarely, moreover, is one of them devoted to experiments in a single discipline, but usually in the same work we find information on chemistry, medicine, cooking, magic, cosmetics, gardening and astrology. Intimately connected with these books were the books of secrets, whose contents were quite similar to those of the *Experimenta;* the main difference was that the books of secrets had an initiatory theme.[19]

This para-scientific literature remains as lively in modern times as it was in the Middle Ages, though the literature of experiments has been almost entirely assimilated to the genre of children's amusement, as we can see in such titles as G.W.S. Piesse's *Chymical, Natural and Physical Magic intended for the instruction and entertainment of Juveniles during the Holiday Vacation*[20] or the enormous *Recreations in Science and Natural Philosophy*, a Victorian translation by Edward Riddle of an 18th-century revision by Montucla of a 17th-century work by Jacques Ozanam.[21] Modern editions of books of secrets, however, address a different segment of the population altogether, which seeks to practice a type of science unknown to or unaccepted by the scientific establishment. Since official knowledge is customarily tied to power, we can see how works of this type are enthusiastically received by many people who seek to overcome their self-perceived isolation from the centers of power. For example, the *Book of Secrets* of Pseudo Albert the Great has recently appeared in France in a popular series bearing the title "Secret Science."[22] And indeed the paradox of this sort of literature is that it is popular precisely because it is secret. Arguing backwards from such contemporary evidence, Louis B. Wright has stated that many of the secret books of the Elizabethans were actually popular and not reserved for a scientific elite. He has concluded that these books were "typical of an enormous literature supplying middle-class readers with information similar to that purveyed by modern magazines that traffic in science and pseudo-science."[23]

But how far can one carry this argument for the medieval period? At first glance, these collections seem rather foreign to popular preoccupations. They are usually equipped with a dedication to an august personage, for example *Libri septem experimentorum ad imperatorem Fridericum*, or they are the work of aristocratic authors, as for example *Experimenta Cancellarii et Cardinalis*, or they are the productions of a scientific elite, *Experienta collecta a magistris Parisiensibus*.[24] Yet certain experiments described in these collections are of such a nature that they are well within the purview of everyone; in them, for example, we learn how to make lamps out of glow worms, how to handle flaming alcohol without burning the hand, and how to make cooked meat appear raw.

Needless to say, the problem of knowing how and in what measure certain medieval collections of experiments found a wide public is complicated by the fact that for the most part these works remain unedited and that few studies have been made of their relation to one another. Thus the present state of our knowledge makes any sweeping *a priori* conclusions about their popular character premature; each collection ought to be the object of a particular examination. Even the minimal results of an investigation of two of the most representative collections, however, can be exceedingly interesting, both for the history of scientific popularization and for the history of social amusements, and can serve as a sort of prolegomenon to the study of the entire subject, though the conclusions I draw from the evidence are naturally limited in scope and ought not to be generalized. The first of these collections occurs in a manuscript of the end of the 15th century[25]; the second has usually been considered an incunabulum but appears to date from the 1540s[26], though a span of forty years does not significantly affect my conclusions.

My belief that these two recipe books can rightly be called popular is based on the two texts considered in their totality and on the public for which they were intended. Since this type of writing is so plastic and various, in the absence of external indications one can determine its audience only from the make-up of the entire work. For example, a book like the *Liber Ignium* is excerpted from military manuals of the period, and its complete title is the *Book of Fires in order to Burn Enemies*, but what is one to think of a collection with a content nearly identical to the *Liber Ignium* but entitled *Some Experiments which King Solomon composed because of his love for and in the imploring of a most excellent queen and they are experiments of nature*? What are the relationships between love and war? In the case of our two collections of recipes, however, they fit best into the category of popular texts for a simple reason: their general content is not that of either orthodox or occult science but rather of domestic economy.

The earlier of the two collections I call for convenience the *Supplement to Solomon*; it consists of twenty seven recipes copied at the end of a volume of experiments called *Solomon's Games of Nature*, itself in turn a French translation of the *Ludi Naturae* or *Experimenta Salomonis missa Sibille sapienti*.[27] The recipes of interest to us are signaled in the work only by the rubric, "here follow several teachings." (Fol. 26R The Latin original exists in several 15th-century manuscripts. As to content, it is similar to other books of experiments using flammable substances such as the *Book of Fire* of Marcus Grecus.[28]

The second of the works, published as *Livre nouveau nomme le Difficile des Receptes* by Jacques Modern at Lyon in 1540/45, contains twenty-four folios of interest to us. This book has two parts, the first containing thirty-two recipes preceded by a table of contents, and the second, without this refinement, signaled thus: "here follow good and useful recipes for all manner of craftsmen and other men who desire to live profitably and virtuously. Included also are several courtesies to make in polite company, the whole extracted and tested by several learned men."[29] It does not appear that the first part of the collection had an independent circulation but that the publisher wished to have one hundred recipes gathered together before bringing out the work.

It may be useful to summarize here the contents of these two treatises. Six of the twenty-seven recipes in the *Supplement* relate to matters of domestic economy, such as struggles against vermin, cleanliness, maintenance of domestic objects, foodstuffs, their production and conservation, while forty-six of the one-hundred recipes in the *Difficile* concern such matters. A similar breakdown appears with respect to bodily health; five of the *Supplement*'s examples concern health and beauty, as do twenty-seven from the *Difficile*. In the category of amusements, fifteen recipes from the *Supplement* concern practical jokes, sleight of hand, illusions and tricks, while twenty-seven recipes from the *Difficile* are devoted to these topics. From this summary we may conclude that the problems addressed in these collections were those common to all households, keeping down vermin, keeping domestic utensils free of rust, obtaining food stuffs and domestic supplies such as vinegar and glue as cheaply as possible, and preserving fresh food. It is worth remarking that cosmetic matter occupies a more important place than bodily health in the *Difficile* and that the recipes are directed to the healthy body, telling the user how to eliminate the facial pitting of small pox, the scars of wounds, and spots on the face. Several are concerned with the ways to obtain beautiful hair. When maladies are mentioned, they are common ones, such as fever, gout and mange, or those such as baldness or cavities in the teeth, which belong to cosmetic care.

The products used in these two collections of recipes are exclusively domestic and ready to hand, such as oil, grease, salt, ashes, clay and certain simples common in medicinal folklore, such as hellbore, camomile and lupin. Other products are those easily obtained at an apothecary's shop such as tartar or salt peter.

In such a domestic context, the high proportion of recipes devoted to amusements becomes very significant; more than a quarter in the *Difficile* and more than half in the *Supplement*. Here are some examples of the recipes relating to amusements with special emphasis on those useful to the amateur magician. Among the guides to the preparation of practical jokes we find directions to make a cooked roast appear bloody by sprinkling it with the blood of a pulverized hare[30]; a similar set will make a raw capon appear cooked.[31] An especially fiendish itch can be caused by sprinkling alum [of lead—a sort of lead wool—] between someone's bed sheets, while a clear water which turns the face black and a dye to make a horse bright green can be prepared by simple chemical processes. To give the impression that a bird is singing in the house, one closes up two frogs in the wall, leaving only a tiny hole before which one places a lighted candle.

For persons interested in sleight of hand, there are recipes which tell how to untie the arms by means of a hidden knife; how to appear to swallow a knife and how to seem to carry fire in a handkerchief without burning it.[32]

Recipes for illusions include invisible writing using the bark of a green ash tree, or onion juice,[33] and directions to make a wine or water which changes into milk.[34] A ring can be made to dance by filling a hollow in it with mercury, and water can be made to rise in a bottle.

Recipes for tricks include schemes to catch fish or birds in the hands using, for the latter, a mixture of grain and bull's gall. One can also learn to make mint grow without planting it in the earth, or to make a white rose red. Some tricks relate to the body, enabling one to see far under water or to prevent dogs from barking as one passes by carrying in the hand the tongue and heart of a dog and bearing a sprig of the herb Dog's tongue in one's slipper.

We can reasonably conclude from our examination of this group of amusing recipes occupying such a large place in a household encyclopedia that medieval people loved to laugh. That this laughter often appears in poor taste is of no importance, because medieval laughter is not always obedient to our standards of the comic.[35] But the high proportion of humorous material and material relating to games in a domestic context gives us a good idea of what the men and women of the Middle Ages considered to be a pleasant household.

This appears all the more significant when we recall that these encyclopediae are in principle open ended—always in flux because of the changing needs of society. Such books have then a special bibliographic status, being very often the single book on the household's shelves. In order to show the universality of this need for laughter in the home, we need only turn to some modern recipe books, such as the well known late Victorian *Everyday Cook Book* written by Miss E. Neil. This collection of 742 recipes has a subtitle which does not appear on the cover, *"and encyclopedia of Practical Recipes, Economical, Reliable and Excellent."* In this book, after chapters on "Invalid Cooking" and "Cosmetics" comes a long section called "Miscellaneous" whose content is very similar to that of our medieval collections: "Stains and Spots, Insects and Vermin, Squeaking Doors, Polish for Boots, Bleeding from the Nose, Excellent Carminative Powder for Flatulent Infants" and the like. After some observations on the "Use of Ammonia," Miss Neil gives several sentences on "Laughter," from which the reader learns that "we do not laugh enough." The author gives the following counsel to marriageable young girls, for whom, apparently, the book is designed. "Laugh heartily, laugh often, girls; not boisterously, but let the gladness of your hearts bubble up once in a while, and overflow in a glad, mirthful laugh.[36] Contrary, however, to the practice of the medieval manuals on this point, Miss Neil does not give her readers a recipe.

As we get closer to our time, however, in these subjects and others like them, we see more and more clearly how they provide us with a window into the lore of earlier times and demonstrate that by and large the subjects humorous to us were also, though perhaps in differing degrees, humorous to people in the Middle Ages. The full extent of this aspect of popular culture—as well as the full range—though surely evidenced must perhaps await fuller examination and generalization.

Notes

[1]See C. Grant Loomis, *White Magic, An Introduction to the Folklore of Christian Legend* (Cambridge, Mass., 1948).

[2]See Robert-Leon Wagner, *Sorcier et magicien. Contribution a l'histoire de la magie* (Paris, 1939), pp.66-100.

[3]See on this point, Philippe Menard, *Le rire et le sourire dans le roman courtois en France au Moyen age* (Geneva, 1969), pp.354-356, 397-398. Merlin derives in part from the medieval wild man, who knows the profound secrets of nature and uses them for grotesque ends. See on this point, Richard Bernheimer, *Wild Men in the Middle Ages,* (Cambridge, Mass., 1952), passim.

[4]On these enchanters, see Menard, *Le rire*, pp.399-403.

[5]See E.K. Rnad, *Ovid and his Influence* (London, 1926), pp.138-141.

[6]See Domenico Comparetti, *Virgilio nel medio evo,* rev. ed. G. Pasquali (Florence, 1955), Vol. II; E.K. Rand, *The Magic Art of Vergil* (Cambridge, 1931); and F.W. Spargo, *Virgil the Necromancer* (Cambridge, 1934).

[7]Spargo, *Virgil,* Chapters, V, VI, X.

[8]Rabelais, *Pantagruel,* in J. Boulanger ed. *Oeuvres Completes* (Paris, 1955), Ch. XVI, p.261.

[9]Ibid., Ch. XXII, pp. 286-89. Rabelais uses in order to designate a bitch, the name of a bitch in the *Eclogues* of Virgil (III.18): Lycisca. His recipe also occurs in a 14th century manuscipt: "Ut canes mingant super vestes alicuius hominis vel mulieris, accipe pinguedinem matricis canicule dum est in amore seu in calore, et sibi unge vestimenta seu calciamenta," Paris, B.N.a.fr. 6539, fol. 97r. This rather impractical recipe seems to result from a confusion between the genitalia of the dog and a plant named by Linneaus *Chenopodium vulvaria* which draws dogs by its odor resembling that of human menstrual blood. See Ruth Winters, *Le Livre des odeurs* (Paris, 1978), p. 57. I am grateful to Madelaine Jeay for this reference.

[10]Chaucer, *The Franklin's Tale* 11. 1143-1151 in F.N. Robinson ed. *The Works of Geoffrey Chaucer* (Cambridge, Mass., 1957). On the backgrounds of these illusions, see Laura H. Loomis,

"Secular Dramatics in the Royal Palace, Paris 1378, 1389, and Chaucer's 'Tragetoures'," *Speculum* 33 (1958), 242-255; Anthony E. Luengo, "Magic and Illusion in the *Franklin's Tale, Journal of English and Germanic Philol.*, 77 (1978), 1-16. See also *House of Fame* III, 1.1260f. One can find similar accounts in Marco Polo, *Mandeville's Travels*, and Froissart, but except for the articles mentioned above, this aspect of the jugglers' art has not been seriously studied, as attention is usually paid chiefly to their literary and musical activities. See, however, Edmond Faral, *Les Jongleurs en France au Moyen age* (Paris, 1910), pp. 272-327; R. Morgan Jr., "Old French 'Jogleor' and Kindred Terms," *Romance Philology* 7 (1953-54), 279-325; and J.D.A. Ogilvy, "*Mimi, Scurrae, Histriones*. Entertainers of the Early Middle Ages," *Speculum* 38 (1963), 603-619.

[11]Joseph Strutt, *The Sports and Pastimes of the People of England* (London, 1834), p. 201.

[12]Criticism of professional entertainers by the Church continued throughout the Middle Ages but focussed on the moral rather than the religious aspect of their art; they were seen as sources of frivolity and dissipation. See on this Faral, *Les Jongleurs*, pp. 26-43 and for a list of councils relating to their activities, Helen Waddell, *The Wandering Scholars* (London, 1934), pp. 244-70.

[13]John Rodker ed. Reginald Scot, *The Discoverie of Witchcraft* (Bungay, 1930), p. 182.

[14]*Ibid.*, p. 198.

[15]Melbourne Christopher, *The Illustrated History of Magic* (London, 1975), p. 23.

[16]See John Ferguson, *Bibliographical Notes on Histories of Inventions and Books of Secrets* (Rp. London, 1959), Suppl. VII, pp. 23-33. One can get an idea of the great popularity of similar books by consulting bibliographies such as those of Sidney W. Clarke and Adolphe Blind, *The Bibliography of Conjuring and Kindred Deceptions* (London, 1920); Trevor H. Hall, *A Bibliography of Books on Conjuring in English from 1580 to 1850* (Minneapolis, 1957); and Edgar Heyl, *A Contribution to Conjuring Bibliography. English Language 1550 to 1850* (Baltimore, 1963).

[17]For the general development of medieval science and discussions of its key figures, see Lynn Thorndike, *A History of Magic and Experimental Science* (N.Y., 1923-58), especially Vols. I-IV; George Sarton, *Introduction to the History of Science* (Baltimore, 1927-47), 3 Vols.; Guy Beaujouan, "La science dans l'occident medieval," in Rene Taton ed. *La science antique et medievale* (Paris, 1957).

[18]Thorndike, *A History*, Vol. II, 770-812.

[19]See Ferguson, *Bibliographical Notes*, and more recently, R. Best and Frank Brightman eds. *The Book of Secrets of Albertus Magnus* (Oxford, 1973), pp. XL-XLVIII.

[20](London, 1858).

[21]See also W. Lietzmann, *Lustiges und Merkwurdiges von Zahlen und Formen* (Breslau, 1930) and W.W.R. Ball, *Mathematical Recreations and Essays* (London, 1939).

[22]Bernard Husson ed. *Le Grand et le Petit Albert* (Paris, 1970).

[23]Louis B. Wright, *Middle-Class Culture in Elizabethan England* (Ithaca, 1935), p. 571.

[24]See Thorndike, *A History*, Vol. II, pp. 802-3.

[25]The work exists in this form in a single example, Paris, B.N., fr. 4046, fols. 26r-28v, paper, after 1472. The contents of the entire MS are fols. 1r-2v *Jeux de nature de Salomon* (18 recipes); fols. 3r-25r, Pierre de Sesson's *Les Vigilles de Job*; fols. 26r-28v, Supplement to the *Jeux de nature*; and fols. 29r-31v fragments of a French morality play. The MS is dated by a superscription on the last leaf, of parchment, but the date is confirmed by the many water marks of the earlier portion. See *Catalogue des nouvelles acquisions de la Bibliotheque Nationale* II, p. 116.

[26]See W.A. Copinger, *Supplement to Hain's Repertorium Bibliographicum saec. XV*, no. 3627; and A.C. Klebs, *Incunabula scientifica et medica* (Brussels, 1938), n. 610. The only known example exists in the Bibliotheque Mazarine, Paris, Catalogue no. 1291. Klebs suggests a date of 1500; the date of 1540/45 comes from a flyleaf signed "J.M." inserted in the Mazarine copy which offers some very convincing support for the later date.

[27]In the absence of an edition and critical study of the *Jeux de nature*, it is difficult to know the exact makeup of the collection because the number of experiments varies from one manuscript to another. The french version is also in the Bibliotheque Nationale, MS fr. 4516, fols. 250v-246v; after nineteen recipes from the *Jeux*, the scribe continues without transition with a portion of the encyclopedia *Sidrac*. There are manuscripts of the *Ludi Nature* in London, British Library MS Harley 2378, p. 353; Ms Sloane 121, fols. 90v-92r; and Paris, B.N. lat. 7105, fols. 155r-161v.

[28]See Thorndike, *A History*, Vol. II, pp. 792-93.

[29]These are fols. 1-8 and 9-24: "S'ensuyvent receptes bonnes et utiles pour toutes gens mecaniques et aultres gens qui desirent a faire leur prouffit et vivre vertueusement. Item aussi plusieurs gentilesses pour faire en toute bonne compaignie: le tout extraict et experimente par

plusieurs gens scavans."

[30]On this recipe, see Thorndike, *A History*, Vol. II, p. 787.

[31]Medieval gastronomy enjoyed these sorts of illusions, except that they must have a "happy ending." See Jerome Pichon ed. *Le Menagier de Paris* (Paris, 1846), II, p. 184 and J. Pichon and G. Vicaire eds. *Viandier de Taillevent* (Rp. Geneva, 1967), pp. 19, 130 for instructions for preparing swans and peacocks so that they have a lifelike appearance even though they are cooked.

[32]See M. Berthelot, *La chimie au Moyen age* (Paris, 1893), Vol. I, pp. 236-46.

[33]On invisible writing, see Thorndike, *A History*, Vol. II, p. 787. Children still make "secret" treasure maps using sap from the pod of the milkweed plant.

[34]See Berthelot, *La chimie*, Vol. I, pp. 17-18 and 164-65.

[35]A farce widely popular in the Middle Ages, *the Boy and the Blind man*, has as a theme the misadventures of a blind beggar who is bullied and robbed by a young man; today we would not find this sort of sadism amusing. On the important component of cruelty in medieval humor, see Lambert C. Porter, "Le rire au Moyen age," *L'esprit createur* 16 (1976), pp. 5-15.

[36](Chicago, 1892), p. 313.

*Grateful acknowledgement is made to John Block Friedman, Professor of English, University of Illinois, Urbana, for the translation of this essay from French to English.

Witchcraft

Present interest in the occult can be seen in the proliferation of horoscopes included in newspapers, in the incredible business of the palm reader, and in the tremendous popularity of books like the Exorcist *or* Rosemary's Baby. *In such interest, the witch has always held a special place, and it should come as no surprise that witches frequently are female. As Elizabeth Tucker points out in her essay, the practice of herbal "magic" was often the task of so-called "wise women" in the Middle Ages, who specialized in "white witchcraft," the cure of disease with herbal mixtures. Such "white witchcraft," however, was not favorably looked upon by the Church fathers; one wonders if the distrust of female practitioners of "magic" had more to do with the fact that they were women who did not, for one reason or another, fit into society. The belief in the dual nature of the witch should not be overlooked; if the witch healed, she could also destroy. That duality remains today in the instructions for witchcraft in such works as Paul Huson's* Mastering Witchcraft.

Elizabeth Tucker, assistant professor of English at SUNY, Binghamton, teaches a seminar in witchcraft and sorcery, and is currently doing research in medieval folklore.

Antecedents of Contemporary Witchcraft in the Middle Ages

Elizabeth Tucker

A composite image of the medieval witch figure has remained current in contemporary witchcraft, on the borderline between folklore and popular culture. The herbs, powders, spell kits, and wands sold in occult supply catalogues, as well as the many "do-it-yourself" manuals, indicate that the tradition of solitary witchcraft is not forgotten. Printed sources from the Middle Ages provide us with enough legends, anecdotes, and descriptions of rituals to demonstrate the conservatism of folk transmission. Although modern attitudes toward witchcraft are not synonymous with those of the Middle Ages, certain key elements in the popular conception of witchcraft have retained a striking similarity to their medieval conterparts.

Among the diverse materials available to today's practitioners of witchcraft, it is possible to discern one common trait: the need for authentication through "ancient" or "medieval" sources. Such allegations are usually not supported by scholarly or even semi-scholarly references.

The *Grimoire of Lady Sheba,* for example, purports to be "the remnant of the ancient Religion as we have it today, fiercely guarded by witches who saved it during the period of persecution."[1] Sybil Leek, one of the best known modern witches, frequently refers to witchcraft as "the Old Religion."[2] Another self-avowed witch, Paul Huson, explains that witches have "preferred simply to practice their arts in the old manner that they inherited from the past, under the banner of the old gods."[3] From these and other statements, it is clear that a venerable origin is essential to the stature of contemporary witchcraft. The opposition levelled against witchcraft by much of our society, in addition to the assumption that witches should not be taken seriously, explains why the quest for authentication has continued.

In spite of the many attempts to establish a direct line of descent from witches of the early Middle Ages to those of the present, no definitive evidence has emerged.[4] Instead, it has been possible to trace the perpetuation of early medieval antecedents in folk tradition. Medieval folklore does not serve the purpose of empirically proving the lineage of modern witches, but it does indicate that popular ideas and stories *about* witches have remained remarkably similar. Other than the trial documents from the late Middle Ages and the Renaissance, there are no testimonies of witches to compare with the ones that circulate so readily today in popular publications.

The need for witches to maintain secrecy is often cited as a reason for the lack of provable documents. Paul Huson, the author of *Mastering Witchcraft,* expresses pride in what he considers to be a long history of artful concealment:

Witch history is steeped in legend, hidden in antiquity. There are few written sources, and those that exist are generally obscure, of an oblique nature, casting light upon rather than informing directly.[5]

Thus, the continuity of folk legends and beliefs has created its own pride of heritage. Belief in the importance of secrecy has led to a renewed credibility; in fact, the lack of empirical evidence seems to have encouraged a particularly strong faith among present-day witches.

There is no lack of hypotheses linking medieval witchcraft with the present. Prominent among these is the "witch cult" theory of the anthropologist Margaret Murray, whose book *The Witch-Cult in Western Europe* was published in 1921. A furor of positive and negative responses followed the book's publication. Murray's controversial argument advocates the recognition of a continuous organization of witches, beginning with Dianic fertility cults. She admits the lack of certain kinds of written records, but emphasizes that "it is contrary to all experience that a cult should die out and leave no trace immediately on the introduction of a new religion."[6] From the early Sabbaths and Esbats, Murray states, have evolved the more recent forms of coven worship.

The witch-cult hypothesis offered a wide range of possibilities to those who brought about the growth of witchcraft groups in the 1950s and 1960s. Gerald Gardner, the author of *Witchcraft Today,* supported the idea of a continuous cultic organization from the Middle Ages to the present. His use of the term "Wicca" as a name for the cult was an innovation that appealed to his followers. Many covens enthusiastically adopted Gardner's interpretation of witchcraft, which included "sky-clad" or naked worship. The premise of a direct line of cultic descent was accepted as the foundation of this interpretation. Anthropologists and medieval historians, however, were not so ready to believe in the medieval witch cult; firm support for the idea simply could not be established. The best authenticated medieval sources have remained those which indicate a solitary rather than a communal form of ritual observance.

The solitary witch of the Middle Ages was known by many names. Some of these, particularly *striga* and *lamia,* denoted vampire-like behavior. Others, notably *divinator, sortilegus,* and *mathematicus,* referred to the practice of divination. The names *veneficus* and *maleficus* were associated with the working of evil magic, usually through spells and potions. As Jeffrey Russell points out in his book *Witchcraft in the Middle Ages,* it is necessary to distinguish between the high magic of divination or alchemy and the lower magic of evil-doing.[8] Nevertheless, some forms of "low magic" do not necessarily involve evil-doing. The *herbaria* or *herbarius,* a gatherer of herbs, was associated with healing as well as with the working of dangerous spells. This figure, the worker of herbal magic, became so well established in medieval folklore that its survival into the twentieth century is not surprising.

As we know from numerous medieval records, the practice of herbal magic was considered to be the domain of certain "wise women" who lived in the villages and towns. These women specialized in the cure of disease through herbal mixtures, incantations, and protective rituals. Although this kind of "white witchcraft" is now known as a beneficial tradition, it was strenuously opposed by the early leaders of the Christian church. In fact, the penalties for herbal healing were sometimes as severe as those for consorting with the devil. The synod of Ankara in 314 A.D. proclaimed that all soothsayers and users of magic healing methods would be threatened with a five-year penance. Later penitential books from about 600 to 900 A.D. declared a variety of punishments for divination, love potions, dream-augury, and the use of incantations or herbal mixtures.

Interestingly enough, these Anglo-Saxon, Frankish, and Roman penitential books identified the prime offenders as women and the clergy. The belief that women were especially vulnerable to evil, later expounded at length in the *Malleus Maleficarum,* had its roots in the early suspicions and punishments of the church. Isidore of Seville, the seventh-century bishop whose writings covered an impressively wide range of subjects, stated emphatically that women were connected with demons.[9] A similar distrust of female practitioners of magic appeared in the civil law of the fifth-century Germanic peoples. The Pactus Alemannorum decreed that all women suspected of being *herbariae* would be put to death by fire. In particular, Germanic civil law stressed that death or severe punishment must be ordained for any woman who caused barrenness, illness, or death by means of herbal potions.[10] From these documents alone, it is evident that the solitary practice of herbal witchcraft by women was a subject of intense concern in the Middle Ages.

Anglo-Saxon and Germanic folk traditions provide us with a great deal of information about the specialized skills of wise women. Some of their elaborate potions and incantations entered general usage, while others remained the province of the wise women themselves. There were charms to heal wounds, to stop the flow of blood, and to expel poison from the sufferer's body. Other remedies helped women through childbirth, prevented miscarriage, cured barrenness, and alleviated the ailments of children. Instead of using herbal mixtures, some mothers put their children into the oven or on the roof to dispel fever; others treated them with earth from the crossroads.[11] It was not uncommon for these varied methods of healing to be combined with the recitation of Christian prayers, particularly the Pater Noster. The spoken and written words of the prayer became magic items, to be used in conjunction with other remedies to cure disease and ward off evil influences. It is noteworthy that prayers for the benediction of herbs were allowed by the church, but other incantations were thought to be potentially evil and dangerous.

Medieval legends sometimes refer to the use of magic potions along with image magic, one of the oldest forms of witchcraft. A case in point is the story of King Duff of Scotland, whose seventh-century reign was marred by witchcraft. According to Charles K. Sharpe, the author of *Witchcraft in Scotland,* the king's health began to deteriorate when several witches combined their efforts: "A company of hags roasted his image made of wax upon a wooden spit, reciting certain words of enchantment, and basting the figure with a poisonous liquor."[12] When they were caught, the women declared that King Duff's body would decay just as fast as the wax image melted. This allegation illustrates the principle of sympathetic magic, by which like follows like in a cause-and-effect relationship. The process did not reach its intended conclusion in this case, however; King Duff destroyed the image, recovered his health, and had the witches burned at Forres in Murray.[13]

In addition to image magic, the custom of dressing up in animal disguises formed a part of the early development of medieval witchcraft. The fifth-and sixth-century ecclesiastical councils of Tours, Auxerre, Narbonne, Rheims, and Rouen all stated their opposition to the festival of the first of January, during which men would dress up as stags or old women.[14] Other records showed that this affinity for wearing animal disguises was an important aspect of the pagan heritage.

In the ninth-century legends of the Witch of Berkeley, we find a modified version of animal masking. By one account, the *Flories Historiarum sub anno 852,* the old witch asked her neighbors to take certain precautions after her death. They were to sew her body up in a stag's hide and put it in a stone sarcophagus, which would be sealed with molten lead, iron, and chains. The repose of her soul was to be assured by many masses, as well as the singing of *Dirige* by fifty priests. In spite of the faithful performance of all of these requests, "a host of demons gathering outside the church, burst open the door which was secured with bolts and bars, and rushing upon the bier broke apart two of the chains binding the coffin, though the third defeated them." On the third night of the vigil, a "devil in gigantic form and of baleful countenance" commanded the witch to come out of her coffin. He flung her over the saddle of his coal-black horse, and "both vanished clean away from the eyes of all that were present."[15]

It is evident from this story that the ritual precaution of wrapping the body in a stag's hide is only one small part of the Witch of Berkeley's futile attempt to resist the devil. By the ninth century, the fear of the devil's power had become so intense that pagan rituals appeared to have little opposing strength. The appeal of this legend was so strong that it continued to be told and written down, in variant versions, through the fifteenth century. The thirteenth-century story of the priest's wife carried off by the devil was derived from the "Witch of Berkeley" pattern: although the woman had four sons, all of whom became priests themselves, none of them could prevent her from being taken away by the foul fiend.[16] The dramatic conclusion of this version made it appropriate for usage as an exemplum, or moralistic story, by preachers. The people who heard the story in church would pass it along to others, with the result that the legend remained popular for a great many years. "The Witch of Berkeley" and similar stories are preserved in two collections of medieval sermons, the *Speculum Laicorum* and the *Alphabetum Narrationem.*[17] Through these sources, it is possible to reconstruct part of the network of sacred and secular storytelling that had such a significant impact upon medieval conceptions of witchraft.

The story of another witch, Dame Alice Kyteler of Kilkenny, became an important segment of Irish folklore. It differed from the "Witch of Berkeley" legends, because there were several authoritative legal documents to which narrators could refer. Alice Kyteler, the daughter of a good Anglo-Norman family, was brought to trial in 1324. Along with several other people, she was accused of missing mass, sacrificing animals to the devil, and offering parts of the animals' bodies to a spirit called "Son of Art." The fifth charge against Dame Alice and her companions made it clear that herbal magic was still included in the accusers' conception of witches' behavior:

In order to arouse feelings of love or hatred, or to inflict death or disease on the bodies of the faithful, they made use of powders, unguents, ointments, and candles of fat, which were compounded as follows. They took the entrails of cocks sacrificed to demons, certain horrible worms, various unspecified herbs, dead men's nails, the hair, brains, and shreds of the cerements of boys who were buried unbaptized, with other abominations, all of which they cooked, with various incantations, over a fire of oak-logs in a vessel made out of the skull of a decapitated thief.[8]

Although the "unspecified herbs" did not seem to comprise a major portion of the evil mixtures, they demonstrated that the arts of the earlier wise women were not forgotten. The growing identification of witchcraft with heresy led to an emphasis upon union with a devil or a demon, resulting in great harm to the innocent. Even more potent than the horror of heretical acts was the fear of children being cooked and devoured by witches. This image of witchlike behavior rose to its high point in the late Middle Ages, when the definitive ecclesiastical treatises were published.

The most authoritative and widely used study of medieval witchcraft was the *Malleus Maleficarum,* also known as the *Hammer of Witches* and *Hexenhammer.* First published in 1486, it served as a manual for those who believed that witches should be sought out and severely punished. The immediate popularity of the book is shown by the fact that there were at least thirteen editions up to the year 1520, and sixteen more between 1574 and 1669.[19] The authors, Jacob Sprenger and Heinrich Kramer, were both Dominicans of a high scholastic reputation. Their work not only brought together church dogma related to witchraft, but also provided an outlet for the considerable corpus of folklore that had become associated with the subject. Legends, anecdotes, beliefs, and practices were liberally interspersed with the statements of ecclesiastical policy, often in an insidiously persuasive fashion.

In reading the *Malleus Maleficarum,* it is important to remember that the authors had deliberately set out to increase the frequency of witch persecution. The papal bull of 1484, which emphatically stated the church's opposition to all forms of witchcraft, was obtained largely through Heinrich Kramer's efforts. In this bull, called the *Summis desiderentes affectibus,* Pope Innocent VIII spoke out against the "many persons of both sexes" who had "slain infants yet in the mother's womb," "blasted the produce of the earth," and perpetrated "the foulest abominations and filthiest excesses to the deadly peril of their own souls."[20] The pope went on to say that Sprenger and Kramer were his deputies in the fight against witchcraft, which would be undertaken with all the strength that the church could muster. In light of this edict, it is understandable that the *Malleus Maleficarum* launched such an intensive period of witch trials.

According to the church dogma expounded in Sprenger's and Kramer's treatise, the crux of witchcraft is heretical connivance with the devil. The two authors place considerable emphasis upon the Satanic pact, by which the soul of the prospective witch is lost forever. In spite of this doctrinal slant, traces of the *herbaria* remain prominent in the view of witchcraft that emerges from the many narratives. One legend from the town of Innsbruck tells of a woman who pretends to be a healer, but actually makes her patient worse while performing strange incantations and ceremonies. When the patient's servant accuses the woman of witchcraft, she receives the response, "You will know in three days whether I am a witch or not." On the third day after this pronouncement, the servant is afflicted with shooting pains, the sensation of having hot coals on her head, and a rash of white pustules. The only remedy for these ailments is the destruction of a loaf of white bread, which contains "some white grains very like the pustules on zthe servant'sD body," with "some seeds and herbs...with the bones of serpents and other animals."[21] Certain aspects of this story are reminiscent of the Marchen or magic tale: the threat of the evil witch, the three-day wait, and the calamity of three separate ailments. Even though the story is told in the first person, its formulaic quality suggests that it is typical of narratives about suspected witches in the late fifteenth century.

The dual nature of healer and destroyer emerges quite clearly from the legend of the Innsbruck witch. On the one hand, she appears to be a beneficent wise woman who does all she can to cure the patient; on the other, she employs her knowledge of the destructive properties of herbs to harm both the patient and her servant. This duality, presented in the dramatic framework of a first-person narrative, is the same as that of the early medieval edicts against workers of herbal magic. Along with the recognition of magical healing comes the realization that the process can be reversed: what can cure can also kill. Thus, the witch figure in the Innsbruck legend conforms to the early medieval pattern of the *herbaria* at work. The evidence of sympathetic magic (white grains producing white pustules on the victim's body) also fits the pattern of cause and effect by the use of a few simple herbs. The only element of the story that obliquely refers to the fifteenth-century preoccupation with heresy is the mention of "bones of serpents," which are at least symbolically associated with the devil. Otherwise, the main concern of the narrative is the discovery of life-threatening objects behind a deceptive facade of herbal healing.

In another story included in the *Malleus Maleficarum,* the ambivalence of herbal magic is further indicated. Just as herbs can serve destructive purposes in the hands of witches, they can protect innocent victims from the witches' designs:

Now it happened in the city of Spires, in the same year that this book was begun, that a certain devout woman held conversation with a suspected witch, and, after the manner of women, they used abusive words to each other. But in the night she wished to put her little suckling child in its cradle, and remembered her encounter that day with the suspected witch. So, fearing some danger to the child, she placed consecrated herbs under it, sprinkled it with Holy Water, put a little Blessed Salt to its lips, signed it with the Sign of the Cross, and diligently secured the cradle. About the middle of the night she heard the child crying, and, as women do, wished to embrace the child, and lift the cradle on to her bed. She lifted the cradle, indeed, but could not embrace the child, because he was not there. The poor woman, in terror, and bitterly weeping for the loss of her child, lit a light, and found the child in a corner under a chair, crying but unhurt.[22]

Both the tone and the content of this story identify it as an exemplum, suitable for the exhortation of parishioners to practice holy ritual. The protective use of holy water, blessed salt, and the sign of the cross comes from the ecclesiastical rite of exorcism, intended for the banishment of devils and other evil spirits. Unlike the elaborate ritual followed in the "Witch of Berkeley" legend, this sequence of protective measures effectively prevents the evil creature from seizing its victim. The difference, of course, lies in the defenselessness of a witch against the devil and the strength of a "devout woman" against the devil's representative. Taken together, the two stories illustrate the principle that holiness can combat evil, but a smaller evil cannot defeat a greater one.

The story of the child in the city of Spires differs from numerous other narratives in the *Malleus Maleficarum* which end with the gruesome deaths of young children at the hands of witches. There is one brief account of a witch who "had killed more than forty children, by sticking a needle through the crowns of their heads into their brains, as they came out from the womb."[23] The moment of birth, like other pivotal points in life, receives special attention in the manual for witch-hunters. This emphasis leads to the conclusion that human beings are especially vulnerable to the evil ministration of witches at times of life-crisis. In particular, Sprenger and Kramer stress the danger of accepting witches as midwives. Like the dualistic healer-witch, the midwife who practices black magic is most dangerous to mothers and children because of her deceptive appearance.

Even before birth, a child's life can be endangered by the introduction of foreign substances into the womb. The legend of the witch of Zabern begins with a pious woman's refusal to accept the services of a certain midwife. Six months after the beginning of her pregnancy, the woman feels intense pain and decides to go on a fast of intercession to the Virgin Mary. Her prayers result in the expulsion of several strange objects from her womb: thorns, bones, bits of wood, and "brambles as long as a palm," as well as "a quantity of other things."[24] Although none of these objects fit the usual category of herbal ingredients, both brambles and thorns are traditionally associated with witches. In this instance of threatened miscarriage, it is logical for the sharp points of plants to represent the pain that the witch has induced. There is little duality in the midwife's behavior; instead, her identity as a witch becomes evident almost at once. Nevertheless, her continued activity as a midwife maintains the secretiveness that is an essential attribute of the medieval with figure.

Other aspects of witchlike behavior are treated in later portions of the *Malleus Maleficarum*. One whole chapter is devoted to various injuries that cattle can incur by witchcraft: plague, disease, inexplicable jumping in the air, and loss of milk. The following chapter describes how witches "stir up hailstorms and tempests, and cause lightning to blast both men and beasts."[25] The tradition of storm-raising is well documented in the penitential books of the earlier Middle Ages, which often list a seven-year penance for causing bad weather.[26] Similarly, there are many accounts of witches' injuries to animals. Both kinds of evil-doing must be accepted as characteristics of medieval witches, at least from the viewpoint of those who feared injury to themselves and their possessions.

Given these facets of medieval witchcraft, how can we perceive the continuing traditions of witches in the twentieth century? It is not difficult to identify the *herbaria* as a prominent figure of the "do-it-yourself" manuals and catalogues. Many self-proclaimed witches state that they only seek to do good by the practice of herbal spells and rituals. The *Grimoire of Lady Sheba,* for example, begins with this 'ancient Wiccan rede': "An it harm none, do what ye will."[27] There is, however, a certain inconsistency in this allegation. Although the book contains a number of recipes for perfume, incense, teas, and medicines, it also features spells to "tie a man to his bed" and "boggle the mind of your enemy."[28] Paul Huson's *Mastering Witchcraft* not only lists love potions of vervain, wormwood, rose petals, honey, and other ingredients, but also tells how to make "martial sachet powders" from wolfbane, dragon's-blood resin, stinging nettles, and death cup mushroom.[29] Clearly, the dual nature of the herb-gatherer has continued to manifest itself among present-day witches.

The viewpoint of non-witches, however, must also be taken into consideration. Rumors and legends about witches of the 1970s often bear a remarkable resemblance to the contents of the *Malleus Maleficarum*. It is not uncommon for a cycle of stories about witches to revive around Halloween, particularly in groups of schoolchildren. One witchcraft scare recently swept two counties of northern Pennsylvania, with stories of animal injuries, graveyard rituals, and plans for the sacrifice of a baby on Halloween.[30] Thus, it seems that our society's fears of witchcraft have not substantially changed since the Middle Ages. The earlier punishments no longer exist, but the awareness of an "outer darkness beyond the flickering

ring of light" is still there.[31]

Notes

[1]*The Grimoire of Lady Sheba* (St. Paul, Minnesota: Llewellyn Publications, 1974), p.96.

[2]One collection of Sybil Leek's writings about "the Old Religion" is *The Best of Sybil Leek*, ed. Glen A. Hilken (New York: Popular Library, 1974).

[3]Paul Huson, *Mastering Witchcraft* (New York: Berkley Windhover Books, 1977), p.17.

[4]Among those who emphatically deny a direct line of descent from a medieval witch cult to the present forms of witchcraft is Rossell Hope Robbins, author of the *Encyclopedia of Witchcraft and Demonology.*

[5]Huson, *op. cit.,* p.9.

[6]Margaret A. Murray, *The Witch-Cult in Western Europe* (Oxford: Oxford University Press, 1921), p.19.

[7]Gerald B. Gardner, *Witchcraft Today* (London: Rider, 1954).

[8]Jeffrey Russell, *Witchcraft in the Middle Ages* (Ithaca: Cornell University Press, 1972), pp.4-7. Russell includes an informative list of names for medieval witch figures on pp.15-16.

[9]Joseph Hansen, *Zauberwan, Inquisition und Hexenprozess im Mittelalter* (Munich: Scientia Verlag Aalen, 1964), pp.40-49.

[10]*Ibid.,* pp.54-56.

[11]George Lyman Kittredge, *Witchcraft in Old and New England* (New York: Russell and Russell, 1929), pp.31-33.

[12]Charles K. Sharpe, *Witchcraft in Scotland* (London: Hamilton, Adams and Co., 1884), p.21.

[13]*Ibid.,* p.21.

[14]Hansen, *op. cit.,* p.42.

[15]This translation of the *Flories Historiarum sub anno 852,* attributed to "an imaginary monk called Matthew of Westminster," is included in Ronald Seth's *Witches and Their Craft* (London: Oldhams Books, 1961), pp.41-42.

[16]Kittredge, *op. cit.,* pp.43-44.

[17]*Ibid.,* p.44.

[18]St. John D. Seymour, *Irish Witchcraft and Demonology* (New York: Causeway Books, 1973), p.28.

[19]Rossell Hope Robbins, *The Encyclopedia of Witchcraft and Demonology* (New York: Crown Publishers, 1959), p.337.

[20]*Malleus Maleficarum,* tr. Montague Summers and ed. Pennethorne Hughes (London: The Folio Society, 1968), p.18.

[21]*Ibid.,* pp. 122-23.

[22]*Ibid.,* p.41.

[23]*Ibid.,* p.128.

[24]*Ibid.*

[25]*Ibid.,* p.6.

[26]Hansen, *op. cit.,* p.45.

[27]*Lady Sheba, op. cit.,* p.vii.

[28]*Ibid.,* pp.64, 67-69.

[29]Huson, *op. cit.,* pp.130, 204.

[30]"Witchcraft Alarm Sweeps Susquehanna," *The Sun-Bulletin* (Binghamton, New York): October 27, 1978, pp.1-3.

[31]Huson, *op. cit.,* p.5.

Feminae Populi

Maureen Fries's essay, although not about witches, expands upon Elizabeth Tucker's paper. The duality of women in the literature examined by Fries show them to be virgin or whore: the woman saint is a model of such desirable qualities as chastity, obedience, and fortitude, while the fabliau woman uses her sexuality for fun and for profit. The literature, in both instances, depicts male values in a male world. Ultimately, the popular image of women can be distilled into the roles of Mary, wholly above feminine weakness, and Eve, who represents the opposite. Possibly the only "mixed" image is that of the Magdalene, who recalls the fallen Eve, but who also is transformed into the virtuous woman. The lack of flexibility, not noted elsewhere in medieval literature, in the perception of medieval women suggests that we need to know more about the society of the Middle Ages and women's place in it.

Maureen Fries, professor of English at SUNY, Fredonia, has written many articles on medieval literature; her current work-in-progress is Mirrors, Ribs and Vessels: Women in Late Medieval British Literature.

Feminae Populi:
Popular Images of Women in Medieval Literature

Maureen Fries

Courtly images of women in medieval literature are familiar from their origins in the female archetypes of the Provencal and Stilnovisti poets. One archetype is the Lady who comes as close to perfection as can any human being, typified by Dante's Beatrice: physically beautiful, admirably chaste, she draws men to goodness from the heights to which her poet has raised her. Dead, and hence no longer disturbingly fleshly as in the earlier poems she inspired, Beatrice in the *Commedia* leads Dante to union with Divine Knowledge through human love. But there is another, negative archetype of the Courtly Lady, the also beautiful, also inspirational, but ultimately destructive unchaste woman, best exemplified by Guinevere in the *Prose Vulgate* and Malory. Although she encourages Lancelot to earthly greatness, her sensuality incites him to abandon his Grail Quest vow to foresake her, and she is the ultimate occasion of his break with Arthur which triggers the downfall of the Round Table and its potential for spiritual greatness. Like all Christian archetypes, the Courtly Lady reflects

Divine Consciousness in human life, either as the illumination of Wisdom teaching us to grasp and love the Good, or as the darkening of the image of God through folly and/or satanic guile teaching us to shun Evil.[1] As Frederick Goldin has demonstrated, the composite Courtly Lady is a mixed mirror of matter and spirit, the ambivalent *speculum* in which the aristocratic male may picture his own potential for moral achievement or failure, an essentially passive figure.[2] This tenuous and dual figure may serve as a touchstone against which to measure the more diverse popular images of women which are the subject of this paper.

Like the courtly images, the popular conceptions of women not only tend to the dualistic but also derive from the two prime archetypes of Christian thought, the Blessed Virgin and Eve. While Adam is assigned equal blame with Eve in the Genesis text of the Fall, biblical exegesis in the hands of the celibate Fathers of the Church tended to excuse Adam and to make Eve the sole source and symbol of Original Sin. Like her successors such as Delilah, Bathsheba, and Potiphar's wife, she represented lust and the dangers of the Flesh to man, while Adam represented Reason drawn awry by her influence. Opposed to Eve and her tribe was the influential but unfortunately unique archetype of the Blessed Virgin Mary, who had achieved the highly desirable condition of motherhood without the questionable act of sexual intercourse. Mary Magdalene constituted a mixed archetype of great popularity, perhaps because her career as Christ's most prominent female disciple represented the necessity for all women except the Virgin to reform. That same necessity led to the stereotypes by which first the Fathers and after them more popular moralists categorized all women. As daughters of Eve, women were said to tend naturally to disobedience, vanity, cupiditas, indeed to all sin. Because of Adam's failure properly to guide his (properly) weak and inferior wife, all women should be obedient and submissive; because the Fall had brought about the necessity for sexual intercourse (which Augustine, for instance, thought would have been asexual in Paradise) and because of the example of the Virgin (however impossible of imitation), all women should be impeccably chaste.[3] St. Thomas Aquinas, while recognizing the differences in human personalities in body as well as in soul, can nevertheless conclude that differences between male and female are substantive rather than accidental; that woman is inferior to man, the only form-giving procreator; and that woman, unlike a slave, is *by nature* the servant of another, man (italics mine).[4] Such learned teachings were reinforced by ancient and medieval science, and canon and civil law, and found their way into such popular writings as the standard sermon collections, marriage manuals, penitentials, instructions for wives and children and even into the third book of that prime manual on courtly behavior, Andreas Capellanus' *De arte honeste amandi.*

But to counteract this misogynistic tradition there was another group of learned writings, the Christian personification allegories, where—from classical precedent and probably classical grammar—writers represented abstract ideas as usually feminine. In the decisive work of this tradition, Prudentius' *Psychomachia,* both the virtues and the vices are pictured as females and their relative strength and weakness are not sex-linked but dependent on the characteristics of the abstract idea which they figure forth: Superbia is a valiant warrior, for instance, but Patience reluctant to fight (she only wins when Wrath perishes by her own hand).[5] In the allegories of Boethius, Martianus Capella, and Alanus de Insulis which followed, women also appear as forces for good as well as for evil—often in balanced pairs, as with Boethius' Lady Philosophy and Dame Fortune. Marriage, treated negatively by the Fathers, becomes with these writers "a metaphor for the reconciliation of opposites."[6] Allegory was thus potentially a non-sexist genre, although as Jean de Meun was to demonstrate it could also become antifeminist. In the late fourteenth-century popular poem, *Piers Plowman,* unfortunately too long to consider here, this thriving tradition of female potential for good and for evil continues in the figures of Lady Holichurch and Lady Mede, and may help to explain the striking paucity of misogyny in Langland's work.[7] Unfortunately, the evidence indicates far greater bulk of the misogynistic tradition in sources which inspired popular writers than of the more positive one.

Prime in notoriety among negative female images I want to discuss is the woman of the fabliau.[8] In these short, comic tales which turn either upon sexuality or excrement, or both, the vanity, cupiditas, and disobedience ascribed to all women in the misogynistic tradition emerge in the stark and often cruel actions of the female characters. A typical fabliau plot involves an attractive and lecherous wife more or less willingly with a cunning seducer, usually a cleric, in the deceit of a dull, jealous, and usually old husband. The quick-thinking, sensual, and materialistic female of the fabliau, even when she is technically a lady as in Guerin's "Berenger of the Long Arse," never behaves like one but always like a whore. As a maiden, she does not display that concern for her virginity so demanded by her male dominant society: in both "De Gombert de des II clers: and "Le Meunier et les II clers" (sources for Chaucer's "Miller's Tale"), the miller's daughter trades her maidenhead willingly for a worthless ring from a household appliance. As a wife, she is usually so greedy as to deserve the punishment of "The Lover's Gift Regained" in that most widespread and worldwide of fabliau plots in which the lover borrows from the husband to pay for the wife's favors and then contrives to make it appear he has left the husband's repayment with the wife.[9] Even beyond the age of and opportunity for profitable sexuality, the fabliau woman cannot operate outside its frame of reference: like "Dame Sirith" of the only English fabliau before Chaucer, she turns clever bawd in order to help (for money) a clever clerical seducer deceive an exceptionally gullible and putatively virtuous young wife.[10]

If the fabliau woman is thus distorted from reality into stereotype, the same may be said of the woman of the saint's legend, whether sacred or secular. In contrast to the dreaded female vices depicted in the fabliau, the woman saint is a model of the desirable virtues, especially chastity, obedience, and fortitude. The combined roles of virgin and Christian virago were especially appealing, and appear in the lives of Sts. Catharine, Margaret, Juliana and the extremely popular St. Cecelia. Their union of "maidenly purity and flaming audacity" toward the enemies of Christ and their virginity were irresistible,[11] combining an imitation of the Virgin and of the "good" figures of Christian personification allegory. Defying suitors and judges alike, preaching like men under God's inspiration, resisting as a rule several efforts to put them to death, these legendary women inspired secular avatars in works often called romances which can be better considered as legends of secular saints. English romance, coming late and as a rule a "popular debasement" of the earlier French achievement,[12] is especially rich in such images of the female. The most numerous examples involve an innocent, usually royal wife in a false accusation of adultery (usually made by the ubiquitous villain of popular romance, the seneschal and/or the mother-in-law), which the husband believes whether because of faked evidence or even if there is no evidence at all. Obediently going into exile, sometimes with a child, the wife's prime subsequent function is to prove her chastity by constantly defending it against all comers.[13] She is rewarded for this virtue by divine aid, either through a miraculous voyage (Emare), a judicial combat (the Empress in *The Erle of Toulous),* *thaumaturgical skill (Florence of Rome)* and also by either reunion with her penitent husband or (if he has conveniently died) a prosperous new marriage. So important is the virtue of chastity that the woman exemplifying it does not even need a name: sold by her husband for a small sum, wed to a king with whom she manages a celibate marriage for many years and after his death contriving to get her husband named his successor, the heroine of *Sir Isumbras* is known throughout the romance bearing *his* name only as "the wife of Sir Isumbras."

Besides chastity the other important virtue for wives in popular romance is obedience, and its prime exemplar is that Patient Griselda renowned throughout Europe in the Middle Ages and written of eventually by such courtly authors as Petrarch, Boccaccio and Chaucer. Griselda's unflagging endurance of every sort of trial put upon her by a patently unjust husband is echoed by other popular heroines. Belisaunt in *Amis and Amiloun,* also a widespread European tale, not only does not object to her husband's killing their children to obtain their blood for the healing sworn brother but is quick to remind him they may have other children.[14] The pregnant Queen in *Athelston,* kicked by the King as she begs mercy for his innocent sworn brother, aborts her child without uttering any reproach to her husband. The unnamed wife in *Sir Amadace* urges on her reluctant husband when he hesitates to keep his rash vow to the White Knight to divide herself and her child physically with him. Such obedience is rewarded, respectively, by the miraculous rebirth of the children, the timely arrival of the infant St. Edmond to replace the King's dead heir, and the White Knight's generous (?) refusal to claim his promised reward. But the important lesson of wifely submission is seen, as in the case of Griselda, as the condition upon which any such release from male testing may be won; and sworn brotherhood concomitantly takes precedence over the marriage vow and responsibility to one's children for the male.

The polar opposites of the unchaste, disobedient fabliau woman and the obedient and chaste female saint, whether sacred or secular, appear side by side in popular lyric and dramatic traditions. In popular lyric, the Virgin is the favored female speaker and/or subject, especially in English literature. Her planctus exhorts her hearers to meditate upon her role in the central

Christian drama of Christ's career. Meek accepter of her asexual role as virgin mother of God, patient sufferer of separation from Him and of His Death, often firm admonisher to other, more fortunate females as well, she is a constant reminder of her own uniqueness and the inability of other women to share her experience. Complaints of other women tend to display their contrastive inferiority, particularly those in the carol tradition which were sung in a ring-dance in both France and England. The distance between the sexual gullibility of a young girl and the exceptional cunning of her clerical seducer appear in two of these. The refrain of one, "Kyrie, so kyrie," underlines both the woman's blasphemy in conducting a flirtation at Mass and the ultimate irony of her praise of God since her adventure results in "Alas! I go with childe." A like result follows the adventure of the speaker of "Thought I on no gile," a refrain which stresses hypocrisy in the female who reveals herself as a willing cooperator in her defloration, an attitude summed up in the relish of the line, "the murgest night that ever I cam inne." Similar sensuality and passivity informs those songs for an absent male friend called *cantigas de amigo* in Spanish and *winileodas* in German: the latter early caused such scandal that Charlemagne forbade abbesses to continue writing them. There are exceptions to this generally negative picture of most women, such as the striking "Alison" with its brown-haired, black-eyed love-object so different from the stereotyped pink-and-white blonde of courtly tradition, and "Now springes the spray." But both of these are spoken by males; and when the listener reports in the latter the first line of the "litel may," "'the clot him clinge!'" we are reminded of the lack of decorous diction in woman speakers in popular poetry, where males usually retain some vestige of it even if they are not themselves nobly born. The simplemindness and real or pretended naivete of women speakers in lyric all over Europe reinforces the stereotype of the female's dependence upon the male and her lack of reason and even common sense. This is reiterated by the passage into the lyric tradition of the folk-song competition of the holly and the ivy, in which the sturdy evergreen stands for the male and the vine lacking self-support for the female.

A similar war between the sexes, the most stereotyped of medieval domestic scenes: the struggle for "maistrie" between Noah and his wife, finds its most enduring representation in the Corpus Christi dramatic cycles, although it had earlier appeared in medieval art and folktale. While there were two traditions about Noah's wife (who in the Bible has only a walk-on part) in medieval learned and subsequently popular sources, one of which depicted her as a type of Mary (and a rare one[15]), the other as one of Eve, three out of four of the extant English cycle plays on the subject portray her as disobedient and immoderate: a type of the shrew (which had not at this time narrowed its meaning to encompass only the female). Whether she merely complains of Noah's faults as a breadwinner as in the Townley/Wakefield version, or refuses to leave off drinking Malmsey with the gossips she wants Noah to save as in the Chester, Uxor delays the departure of the Elect and invariably comes to blows with her spouse before she is finally and reluctantly dragged aboard the Ark. Since the Ark represents the true Church, the Wife who must be saved only with much effort came to represent the recalcitrant and hard-hearted sinner—a deliberate distortion of the original biblical role of Noah's spouse, who only in the N Town Cycle remains pious and obedient. As might be expected, Eve is also much blamed in the cycle plays, displaying a weakness and perversity similar to Noah's wife; according to the Chester play, even the serpent has "a maidens face" as was true in rabbinic tradition and in medieval art. The contrary image to these "bad" women is, as in the lyric, that of the humble and submissive Mary, whose New Testament "Magnificat" is the basis of her original appearance in the "Annunciation" play. But her very conception of Jesus was not totally sacred to medieval dramatists, who tend to devote the remainder of the play to Joseph's Trouble about Mary (whose child he knows he has not fathered). In opposition to the dignified treatment of the same theme in "The Cherry Tree Carol," medieval playwrights dramatize Joseph's conflict in fabliau terms: an old, impotent and jealous husband's suspicions of his young wife. In Towneley/Wakefield he broods, " ' I wote well, for I am unwelde; / Som othere has she tane.' " In the (authentic) Coventry "Annunciation," he presents himself as an example for all old bridegrooms and accuses Mary of being in sin. Yet in all versions Mary's meek and untroubled responses—she carefully calls Joseph "Sir" in replying to his unwarranted accusations in both Towneley and Coventry—leave her as untarnished as does the treatment of the Nativity in the "Second Shepherd's Play." Any comparison with Gill, Mak's deceitful wife in the latter, only emphasizes the Virgin's uniqueness once again: "antifeminist humor and bawdry allow the audience to laugh at typical [i.e., female] failings and yet perceive that Mary is wholly above feminine weakness."[16] The most interesting elaboration of New Testament female portraits, in the play of "The Woman Taken in Adultery" (mentioned only in John 8:1-11, but treated in three out of the four English cycles) attempts to combine the themes of feminine weakness and the possibility of conversion as in the career of Mary Magdalene, with whom the heroine of this story was often conflated.[17] Like the Magdalene, "the adulterous woman recalls Eve as fallen woman, and yet by her dignity in the face of oppression she also reminds us of the Virgin Mary bravely facing her detractors"[18]—and, we might add, of the Christian virago. The Magdalene herself becomes a Christian virago in the "Mary Magdalene" of the Digby MS, a long play incorporating many of the events of the Corpus Christi cycle in which (as in the elaborate biography constructed by the earlier learned writers) her travels, especially to Marseilles, and her achievement of miracles through the grace of a chaste conversion, make her resemble strikingly the secular saints of romance.[19] Since medieval drama had revived the *Quem quaeritis* trope of the Easter service, in which she was a leading actor, Mary Magdalene is, next to the Virgin, the most popular female image for medieval playwrights.

Popular images of women, then, had a range similar to courtly ones, encompassing a positive ideal archetype in the Virgin; a negative opposite depicted as Eve only in the cycle plays but appearing in various avatars in fabliaux, lyric and dramatic traditions; and a mixed form best expressed in the career of the Magdalene. But such a similar range does not imply a similarity of actual image. Popular images are both more diverse and more contradictory than the courtly ones. The fabiliau woman is given a wit and resourcefulness usually denied by the exegetes to women; but she uses it to repeat Eve's sins of disobedience and especially cupiditas. Women in the saint's legend, who on a spectrum ranging from "good" to "bad" would appear very near but not quite equal to the Virgin since no one else could be both Virgin and Mother of Christ, confound their judges with their logic and wit but only at the sacrifice of their sexuality and their lives. Their secular successors in popular romance must suffer unjust accusations, painful exiles, repeated assaults from lechers, all for a chastity which they have never really violated; or, if obedience is required, Griselda and her sisters must choose between a blind and submissive wifehood and a threatened motherhood. Women in the lyric, particularly the carol, exhibit a sexual and rational weakness undoubtedly pleasing to their lovers, but punished not only by abandonment and/or pregnancy but by its contrast, on the one hand, with the proper chastity and obedience of the Virgin, and, on the other, with the *daunger* and virtues of the lady of the courtly lyric. Medieval drama, bound as it was to Christian history, gives us the most stereotyped versions of women in such portraits as those of Eve and Noah's wife; but it is also the only form to suggest the perfectibility (insofar as a non-Virgin could be perfect) of a sinning woman,[20] even if only in single plays. Such isolated efforts were not enough; there was in popular literature no more than elsewhere in medieval society no attempt to "shape a countervision of women" to the prevailingly misogynistic one. Carroly Erickson has noted: "when it came to women, medieval perception lost its flexibility," a quality it retained elsewhere.[21] That loss of flexibility provides us with the provocative but tantalizingly incomplete and mostly unassimilable popular images of women I have here examined.

Notes

[1] On archetype, see Sister Ritamary Bradley, "Backgrounds of the Title *Speculum* in Mediaeval Literature," *Speculum* 29 (1954), 100-115; and her unpublished paper read at the Midwest Modern Language Association Meeting, Oct., 1972, "A Schema for the Study of the Characterization of Women in Medieval Literature."

[2] *The Mirror of Narcissus in the Courtly Love Lyric* (Ithaca: Cornell Univ. Press, 1967).

[3] For example, Paul, 1 Timothy 2:11-14; Augustine, Sermon 51, *De concordia evangelistarum Matthaei et Lucae in Generationibus Domini* 2 (*PL* 38, 334-335); Bonaventura, *Opera Omnia* IV (Quarrachi, Italy: Collegium S. Bonaventurae, 1882-1902), IV. Sent., 760 B.

[4] *Summa Theologica* I, q. 92, a. 1; q. 99, a. 2 ad. 1; q. 115, a. 3 ad. 4; q. 115, a. 2 ad. 3; *In III Sent.*, 3. 2.

[5] Prudentius, tr. *en face* H.J. Thompson, Loeb Classical Library (Cambridge, Mass.: Harvard Univ. Press, 1949-1953), vv. 178 ff., vv. 109 ff.

[6] Joan Ferrante, *Woman as Image in Medieval Literature: From the Twelfth Century to Dante* (New York: Columbia, 1975), p. 43.

[7] I discuss Piers Plowman at length in a book-in-progress, *Mirrors, Ribs and Vessels: Women in Late Medieval British Literature*.

[8] There has been much recent discussion as to authorship of the fabliau; but whether authorship was bourgeois or aristocratic, we must recognize that it is a popular genre in essence: "the taste for this sort of literature has never been restricted to any one class," as Larry D. Benson and Theodore M. Andersson note in *The Literary Context of Chaucer's Fabliaux* (Indianapolis: Bobbs-Merrill, 1971), p. 10.

[9] The tale-type has been discussed by J.W. Spargo, "Chaucer's Shipman's Tale: The Lover's Gift Regained," *FF Communications*, No. 91 (Helsinki, 1930), and forms the basis for Chaucer's most sophisticated fabliau.

[10]That even Chaucer could not overcome the limitations of the fabliau form, in spite of his obvious sympathy for women, is proven in Arlyn Diamond's "Chaucer's Women and Women's Chaucer," *The Authority of Experience: Essays in Feminist Criticism* (Amherst: Univ. of Massachusetts Press, 1977), pp.60-83.

[11]The phrase is Gordon Hall Gerould's, *Saints' Legends* (Boston: Houghton Mifflin, 1916), p.211.

[12]So the well-documented opinion of Charles Muscatine, *Chaucer and the French Tradition: A Study in Style and Meaning* (Berkeley: Univ. of California Press, 1969), p.12.

[13]This type of romance has been studied in detail by Margaret Schlauch, *Chaucer's Constance and Accused Queens* (1927: rpt. New York: Gordian, 1969).

[14]I am indebted here and in the following three sentences to Margaret Gist, *Love and War in the Middle English Romance* (Philadelphia: Univ. of Pennsylvania Press, 1947), but the conclusion is my own.

[15]See Ferrante, Ch. One, "Exegesis," for the rarity of positive (i.e., Marian) types, the frequency of negative (i.e., Evian) types, and the extent to which biblical females were "neutered" into neither.

[16]David Bevington, ed., *Medieval Drama* (Boston: Houghton Mifflin, 1975), p.356.

[17]She was also conflated with all other New Testament Marys except the Virgin, e.g., Mary of Bethany, sister of Lazarus, and with the sinful woman who washed Christ's feet with her tears (as Mary of Bethany had with ointment). A good recent study is Marjorie M. Malvern's *Venus in Sackcloth: The Magdalene's Origins and Metamorphoses* (Carbondale: Southern Illinois Univ. Press, 1975). While she had avatars in saint's legend such as Mary of Egypt, I have not discussed them here because the Magdalene is a more limited type than the Christian virago—she did not noticeably influence romance, for instance—whose chief importance seems to be for the drama.

[18]Bevington, p.460.

[19]Morton W. Bllomfield, "Episodic Motivation and Marvels in Epic and Romance," in *Essays and Explorations: Studies in Ideas, Language and Literature* (Cambridge, Mass.: Harvard Univ. Press, 1970), pp.97-128, explores the influence of fairy tale and saint's life upon romance.

[20]This is one of the differences between courtly and popular literature which might be explored: all the "mixed" courtly women, such as Isolde and Guinevere, effect in their own lives and those of their lovers a trajectory from good to bad; only the medieval drama, in the twin images of Magdalen and Woman Taken in Adultery, offers the reverse.

[21]*The Medieval Vision: Essays in History and Perception* (New York: Oxford Univ. Press, 1976), p.211.

Popular Views of Medieval Women

Shirley Marchalonis' essay suggests that it is not always so easy to define the medieval attitude toward women in such clear-cut terms as the virgin or the whore. Nonetheless, Marchalonis admits that the courtly lady of the romances comes awfully close to the passivity of the Virgin Mary. The courtly lady in the romances plays only a minor role in many instances; she is the prize, more often than not, of the hero at the end of the story. At best, she is a vehicle of passive virture, acted upon rather than acting. Obviously such a role is admired: the woman stays within her boundaries, which are defined by men, and so is respected and desired. One of the popular images of women, in the medieval world at least, is one of dependence; women exist as complements to men.

Shirley Marchalonis, an associate professor of English at the Pennsylvania State University, Wilkes Barre, has published on medieval literature, folklore, and popular literature.

Above Rubies:
Popular Views of Medieval Women
Shirley Marchalonis

Scholars of the literature and history of the Middle Ages will be quick to tell us that the medieval attitude toward women was curiously but definably split: worship of Mary and the courtly love lady on one hand and the clerical anti-feminist tradition so delightfully used by the Wife of Bath on the other.

It is always comforting to be able to label something neatly and then never have to think about it again, as I think, many scholars have done. Certainly it is easy to discover what St. Jerome and the clerics who followed him felt about women; in my opinion, it is completely impossible to know what Chaucer thought about them. If we want to know what the ordinary citizen of the Middle Ages thought about women—and about many other things—we need to turn away from the great or the patristic writing of the time and turn instead to the popular literature—in this case, the Middle English metrical romances.

The metrical romances are a group of sixty-five rhymed stories dealing, for the most part, with the exploits of chivalric heroes.[1] The written copies in existence date from 1225 to late fifteenth century. Their length varies, but in general they are much shorter than the Arthurian prose cycles, and, as literary critics insist, much inferior because of their jangling rhymes and episodic, repetitive plots. They are either ignored by scholars or dismissed as bad literature; Chaucer made fun of them and so do Chaucerians.

Although the romances can be dismissed as having slight literary worth, they cannot be overlooked as indicators of popular taste. Any popular literature (or art) reflects the day-to-day values of its society far more accurately than does the "great" literature produced at the same time. The romances were enormously popular, and their audience seems to have been a wide and varying one, ranging from nobleman's hall to village tavern or square. The minstrels who performed the romances provided entertainment and were rewarded according to the success of their performance. Obviously when we read the romances today we miss a large part of what they are: stories to be acted out to a responsive audience, not poems to be read in solitude. They demand the actor-audience-text relationship just as a play does.

The members of the audience, whether baron or peasant, had one thing in common: they were illiterate, or, at best, functionally literate. There was, of course, a tiny percentage of the population who read and wrote what we now call medieval literature. Most people, however, *heard* stories—as folktales, sermon exempla, or as romances.

The strong oral-aural aspect of medieval life is too often overlooked. Certainly it shapes the romances, and it allows us to draw some conclusions about the attitudes and values of the people who listened.

The romances are linear and episodic and tell the life and the adventures of a single hero.[2] The hero is either a young man in the process of establishing his knighthood or an older knight being tested for his chivalric virtues.[3] Adventures occur one after another, so the plot is a series of episodes that sometimes seem to be interchangeable: one battle with a dragon is much like another battle with a dragon. The hero's goal is always the same: marry the princess, live happily ever after, and rule the kingdom well.

The basic structure of the romances is the initiation process; the testing of the hero results in his return as a stable, responsible member of his society. This structure, of course, is also the basis of the folktales in the Aarne-Thompson 300-749[4] classification and parallels the prevailing literary-religious metaphor of life as journey, quest, or pilgrimage, with the notable difference that the tested and proven romance hero takes his place in the world rather than his departure from it.

Since the stories reached their audiences' minds through ears rather than eyes, those audiences must have been skilled listeners. Nevertheless, there are certain restrictions that an orally-performed, aurally-received work imposes upon itself. Everything must be clear and fairly unsubtle; the listener cannot pause to ponder a point, nor can he turn back to check something he might have missed. There is no room for the things on which modern literature is judged: plot complexity, skill in characterization, psychological insight, use of symbolism. There is, in fact, no place for anything that might distract the audience from the adventures of the hero.

The hero functions according to the values of his society. Because he is a knight, his job is to fight, and he fights against evil in tangible forms (dragons, Saracens, evil stewards, giants). Good and evil are polarized, and by the behavior of "good" and "evil" characters, as well as the ideas and beliefs that are simply taken for granted, a whole set of values and attitudes are revealed. Examination allows us to identify with much security those beliefs and attitudes that were accepted without question as basic assumptions and expectations. We can tell how the vast majority of medieval people felt about the importance of duty, the concept of station, the inevitable triumph of virtue, and necessity of order, the definition of good kingship, and the active concern of a personal deity in the affairs of men.

Certainly the romances reveal attitudes and beliefs about women, although these attitudes are neither the awed worship of the courtly love poets nor the anti-feminist tirades of St. Jerome and Clerk Jankyn. It is not surprising that in all but two of the romances (those with female protagonists) women are of minor importance. All the characters except the hero are of minor importance in these single-strand romances; furthermore, the world of chivalry was, in fact as well as in story, a man's world.

Nevertheless, women are part of the romances, and their treatment and role are often revealing. To generalize, the women in the romances are the princesses or ladies that the heroes marry at the end. They are important for what they represent rather than what they do. The typical romance lady is a ruler or the heiress of a ruler; she has inherited or will inherit her father's kingdom because she is his only child. But she does not rule the estate; she merely transmits it. The situation is implicit in most cases, but is spelled out in the romance of *Ipomedon*.[5] The Princess of Calabria has inherited her father's kingdom. Her barons come to her to suggest that she marry and get an heir for the good of the kingdom. When she says she will not marry yet, they go to her uncle, her closest relative. He is blunt in his advice to her:

> ..."Dere cosyn, here my wille:
> An husband must ye take you tylle,
> The whiche may of this land be kynge,
> And gouerne it in all thynge;
> For no woman may take on hand
> Wele to gouerne suche a land." (512-17)

She promptly agrees, only stipulating that a tournament be called to determine whom she should marry. Her uncle is simply reminding her of a fact that everyone knows: it simply is not a woman's place to rule and there is no more to be said about it.

There is more to the romance lady's role, however, than just presenting the hero with a kingdom. She is, of course, beautiful and virtuous; if she seems to the reader to be a flat character, so is everyone else in the romances. She represents the hero's reward: in exchange for his proven knightly prowess and the successful completion of his quest, she brings beauty, virtue, a kingdom, and her ability to bear children. In short, stability, virtue, and the end of adventure.

Several years ago a *New Yorker* cartoon showed a knight and lady sitting in the baronial hall. Over the vast fireplace is a stuffed and mounted dragon head. The lady holds a rather fretful-looking infant; both knight and lady seem to be bored to extinction. But that is a 20th-century view of the end of the quest, not a medieval one. The marriage established a family unit, a good ruler who met his responsibilities, a personal, social and political order. In that sense the heroine is essential.

She is even, occasionally, essential to the plot. The hero of *Havelok the Dane* claims and restores order in two kingdoms, Denmark and England. The heroine's wicked usurping uncle forces her to marry the unknown youth who turns out to be the heir to the Danish throne. Through the marriage Havelok gets the support he needs to claim and restore both kingdoms. The heroine of *Sir Gowther*, one of the few romances heavy with symbolism,[6] acts as a direct messenger of God's will. One of the few ladies with a personality, and one of the few whose name is frequently used, is Rymenhild, the heroine of *King Horn*. Rymenhild has what amounts to an hysterical outburst, which leads to a mutual declaration of love; more important, it leads to the knighting that Horn needs before he can begin his quest. He tells her quite bluntly that if she will arrange to have him knighted he will marry her when he completes his task and regains his rightful kingdom.

In the two romances with female heroes, *Emaré* and *Lai le Freine*, the women, like the chivalric heroes, are tested, but for a far different set of qualities. Women do not have to prove their worth as fighters or their loyalties to the class. Feminine virtue is passive; women, it seems, must endure rather than act.

The heroine of *Emare*, a version of the story that Chaucer used in the Man of Law's Tale, refuses her father's attempt to marry her and in punishment is set adrift in an open boat. Eventually she lands on a strange coast, is rescued by a local nobleman, and, having demonstrated her courtesy and graciousness, as well as her beauty, she is married to the King. All goes well (although she never tells him her background) until the King has to go away just before her child is born. The messenger who goes to tell the King about the birth of his son is waylaid by the wicked mother-in-law, who substitutes letters saying that the Queen has given birth to a monster. The King sends back a letter saying that the Queen is to be cared for, but again the mother-in-law changes the letters and Emaré is put in the boat again. When the King finds out what has happened, he has his mother executed, but Emaré and her child are gone. Again she is brought safely to shore, and several years later she is reunited with her husband and then with her father.

Lai le Freine begins when a lady accuses the wife of a neighboring knight of having had a lover because she gave birth to twins. Later the lady herself gives birth to twin girls; in order to avoid disgrace or the alternative of having to apologize to the slandered lady, she has one of the twins smuggled out of the castle and left on the doorstep of a convent. The child, Freine, is reared by the Abbess as her niece. When she is a beautiful young lady, a neighboring knight, Sir Guroun, falls in love with her and wins her love. She goes to live with him in his castle, where she is soon loved by everyone. The knight, however, is under pressure to marry and have an heir, and of course he cannot marry a nameless foundling. A marriage is arranged with a neighboring landowner's daughter who, to no reader's surprise, turns out to be Freine's twin sister.

The lady and her family come to Sir Guroun's castle, where the marriage is to be held. Just before the wedding Freine sees that the marriage bed looks rather drab, and decorates it with her mantle. Her mother recognizes it, explanations are made, Freine's parentage is established, and she and Guroun are able to marry.

Both Emaré and Freine are acted upon rather than acting; they are what Vladimir Propp calls victim heroes.[7] There are similarities in their upbringing. The motherless Emare is reared by a lady of the court called Abro:

> She taught hyt curtesye and thewe,
> Gold and sylke for to sewe
> Amonge maydenes moo.
> Abro tawghte thys mayden small
> Nortur that men useden in sale,
> Whyle she was in her bowre.
> She was curtays in all thynge,
> Both to olde and to yynge,
> And whyte as lylye flowre.
> Of her hondes she was slye;
> All her loved that her sye,
> With menske and mychyl honour. (58-69)

Freine is brought up by the abbess; when she is twelve years old, "In al Inglond there was non/ A fairer maiden than hye was on" (239-40). When Guroun, who has heard of her, goes to see her,

> The abbesse and the nones alle
> Fair him gret in the gest-halle;
> And damisel Frein, so hende of mouthe,
> Get him faire, as hye wele couthe.
> And swithe wele he gan devise
> Her semblaunt and hir gentrise,
> Her lovesum eiyen, her rode so bright,
> And comenced to love her anon right.... (263-70)

Both are beautiful and courteous, two essential qualities for medieval heroines; both are tested for virtues beyond beauty and courtesy.

Emare's only "act" is her total rejection of her father's incestuous desire to marry her.[8] Her refusal is really a reaction rather than an act, based on her knowledge that such a union is forbidden by God. She appears to accept a hierarchy of authority over her: God's will comes first and she will take the consequences of following it and therefore of disobeying her father. She does not protest her father's authority, and later what appears to be her husband's, even though they seem to be sending her to certain death in spite of her own innocence. She endures her hardships without complaining (a moan or two, perhaps, but no action), and she continues to love her husband and father, even though she does not know that the former is guiltless and the latter has repented his temporary madness. Eventually she brings about their reunion, although she allows her son to be the active participant in her plans. In the versions by Chaucer and Gower her religious faith is more overt, but even in the romance it is clear that what makes her act as she does is her acceptance of God's (and man's) will.

Freine's first action is sinful: she runs away from the convent and goes to live with Sir Guroun. Although they love each other, there is no possibility of marriage; when Guroun's knights urge him to marry and get an heir,

> And seyd him wer wel more feir
> In wedlok to geten him an air
> Than lede his liif with swich on
> Of was [whose] kin he knewe non. (316-19)

It is not Freine or even the fact that she and Guroun are not married that the knights object to; it is the fact that Freine has no identity, even though the poem tells us earlier that "al his meyne loved her wel" (306) and "al her loved" (308). No one protests, no one objects, even though Freine is saddened and Guroun reluctant. She does not expect to be able to marry; she accepts the codes of her society. She not only endures the pain (like Griselda but without Griselda's one mildly human, small outburst in which she suggests that Walter treat his tender young wife-to-be with a little more kindness), she goes beyond it. Her decoration of the marriage bed with her own cherished mantle is an act of love and generosity that is almost stunning. Her act of devotion apparently cancels out her sin; she is rewarded with an identity, the husband she loves, and the stability and safety of marriage.

I do not wish to make comparisons with the Chaucerian analogues to these two tales except to point out that Chaucer's heroines are far more real. We know what Constance and Griselda are feeling; we have to assume that Emaré and Freine think and feel, but we must not assume too much. The romances are concerned with plot rather than character analysis. All the indications in the texts suggest, however, that these women do not question, protest, or resent what is done to them. They endure, they are patient and loving and kind against all odds, and they are rewarded with love, security, and a stable family unit.

Obviously in all the romances women are complementary to men. Men are active: fighters, seekers, doers; women receive, accept, remain faithful. Their virtues are patience, endurance, submission, fidelity, forgiveness, love, generosity, trust in God. They are in themselves the reward, or, like Emare and Freine, they are rewarded by marriage.

There is little indication of courtly love attitudes in the romances, and no sign of anti-feminism. In fact, these women are admired. As their roles are defined, they are important parts of their communities.

Guy of Warwick is one of the longest and most popular of the metrical romances, so long that it is really three separate romances using some of the same characters. In the first part, the young hero, Guy, loves his lord's daughter, Felice. He sets out to prove his worth and eventually wins the lady and the estate. In the second part, after fifty days of marriage Guy decides that he has been selfish in fighting only for his own worldly glory; now he will fight for God. He leaves his pregnant wife in charge of the estate and goes off on pilgrimage. Years later, when he can fight no more, he becomes a hermit; he and Felice do not meet again until he is dying. The emphasis is all on the hero's adventures, not on the fact that Felice is back home bringing up their son (who is the hero of the third part of the romance) and running the kingdom. She is not made to seem in any way unusual or more capable than other women; historically, in spite of the Princess of Calabria's uncle, it was fairly common for the lady of the manor to be left in charge while her husband went off to battle or court. Felice does not complain.

The image of women as presented by the romances is certainly not anti-feminist, nor does it present the lady as an exalted being too rarefied to be touched. The lady is valuable; she contributed to the stability and order so prized by the Middle Ages. She reaffirms social values. She is important and respected.

There is, however, a reverse side, for it would seem that the lady is respected and admired as long as she stays within her boundaries. None of these ladies has the power to act independently; in fact, the only romance lady who has control over her own actions and destiny is the fairy mistress in *Sir Launfal*, and she, of course, is a supernatural being. What all this seems to indicate is that the popular attitudes reflected by the romances avoid the extremes; women were not independent, but they were respected and admired as long as they stayed in their places. It is true, of course, that in the medieval view of the universe everyone, not just women, had a place and was expected to stay in it. The idea of "place" should not surprise us, given the intellectual background of the time, but it is clear that woman's place was defined by men.

The romances depict a world in which the place and role of both men and women are sharply and clearly defined. The world is a masculine one. Biblical, and especially Pauline, concepts shape the role: a good woman is above rubies, but wives, submit yourselves to your husbands.[9] Women exist in this world as complements to men; they should adorn the establishment of the male to whom they belong and they should inspire, assist and reward him. In an orderly Medieval world, man acts and woman endures.

Notes

[1] For technical information concerning the metrical romances, see J. Burke Severs, *A Manual of the Writings in Middle English 1050-1500*, I, Romances (New Haven: The Connecticut Academy of Arts and Sciences, 1967).

[2] Axel Olrik, "Epic Laws of Folk Narrative," in *The Study of Folklore*, ed. Alan R. Dundes (Englewood Cliffs, N.J.: Prentice-Hall, 1965), pp. 129-41.

[3] Shirley Marchalonis, "The Chivalric Ethos and the Structure of the Middle English Metrical Romances," unpublished dissertation, Penn State, 1972.

[4] Aarne, Antti and Stith Thompson, *The Types of the Folktale* (Helsinki: Suomalainen Tiedeakatemia Academia Scientiarum Fennica, 1973).

[5] Texts for the romances quoted and referred to in this paper are as follows: *King Horn, Sir Gowther, Havelok the Dane*, and *Sir Launfal*, are found in *Middle English Metrical Romances*, ed. Walter Hoyt French and Charles Brockway Hale (New York: Russell & Russell, 1964); *Emare* and *Lai le Freine* in *The Breton Lays in Middle English*, ed. Thomas C. Rumble (Detroit: Wayne State University, 1965); *Guy of Warwick*, ed. Julius Zupitza, *EETS* 25-26 (London: N. Trubner, 1875-76); *Ipomedon, Metrical Romances of the Thirteenth, Fourteenth and Fifteenth Centuries: Published from Ancient Manuscripts*, ed. Henry Weber, Esq. (Edinburgh: Archibald Constable and Co., 1810).

[6] Shirley Marchalonis, "*Sir Gowther*: The Process of a Romance," *Chaucer Review*, 6 (1971), pp. 14-29.

[7] Vladimir Propp, *The Morphology of the Folktale*, trans. Laurence Scott (Austin: Univ. of Texas Press, 1970).

[8] The subject of the incest theme in Medieval Literature is examined in Margaret Schlauch, *Chaucer's Constance and Accused Queens* (New York: New York Univ. Press, 1927).

[9] Proverbs 31:10 ff; Ephesians 5:22-23. See also First Corinthians 7, 11.

Woman as Mediator

The two previous essays by Maureen Fries and Shirley Marchalonis are further elaborated on by Caroline Eckhardt in her analysis of one of the most popular medieval images of women—that of mediator. This image of women has a long and complex history and remains with us today, as evidenced in Marina Warner's Alone of All Her Sex. *The link between the image of the Virgin Mary as mediatrix and women in medieval romances is a strong one, and, as Eckhardt points out, may provide us with a reasonable hypothesis of audience taste and response to the romances. If women comprised a goodly proportion of the audience, and it is likely that they did, the image of women presented to them affirmed the life-nurturing functions in a heightened fashion; at the same time it maintained the established and accepted relationships between men and women. In the role of intercessor, women might act, but within carefully accepted limits.*

Caroline D. Eckhardt is an associate professor of English and Comparative Literature at the Pennsylvania State University and has published on medieval literature.

Woman as Mediator in the Middle English Romances
Caroline D. Eckhardt

In the fourteenth-century English poem known as the *Alliterative Morte Arthure,* King Arthur and his army are pressing the siege of the city of Metz to its conclusion. The city is about to fall. Arthur has assembled his knights for the final assault; the moveable towers are being brought up against the walls; missiles flung over the walls by the catapults are battering down the buildings inside—monasteries, hospitals, churches, inns. The people inside the city are desperate: "The pyne of the pople was pete for to here."[1]

On the words *pyne* (pain) and *peté* (pity) the whole perspective of the scene shifts. We are no longer watching the siege of Metz from the viewpoint of the conquering army, whose victory we will applaud. Showing here (as elsewhere) his capacity for widely distributed human sympathy, the poet turns away from the triumphant Arthur to focus our attention instead on those who are defeated and terrified. Significantly, it will be a woman who will mediate between victor and vanquished.

63

Than the Duchez hire dyghte with damesels ryche,
The Cowntas of Crasyn, with hir clere maydyns,
Knelis down in the kyrnelles thare the Kyng houede,
On a couerede horse comlyli arayede.
They knewe hym by contenaunce and criede full lowde,
"Kyng crownede of kynde, take kepe to these wordes!
We beseke 3ow, Sir, as soueraynge and lorde,
That 3e safe vs todaye, for sake of 3oure Criste;
Send vs some socoure and saughte with the pople,
Or the cete be sodaynly with assawte wonnen." (3044-53)

The appeal works. Arthur lifts his visor to see the supplicants more clearly, considers for a moment, and then—speaking to the Duchess in particular— tells her "with full meke wordes" that no member of his army will harm either her, her chief maidens, the children of the city, its clergy, or its chivalrous knights. The only person to whom Arthur does not extend a "chartire of pes," in fact, is the Duke himself. The king then immediately issues an order to cease the assault. The city is saved from destruction; its inhabitants (with that one exception) are protected from harm.

In Malory's *Morte Darthur,* a prose work of about 1470, King Arthur, who is facing the last of his battles, is visited in dream by the spirit of his dead nephew Gawain. Arthur is touchingly glad to see Gawain again: " 'Wellcom, my systers sonne, I wende ye had bene dede! And now I se the on lyve, much am I beholdyn unto Allmyghty Jesu."[2] And Gawain is anxious to warn Arthur against fighting Mordred on the morrow. The opportunity to speak together is thus regarded by both of them as a marvelous gift. It has been achieved through the mediation of women. As Gawain explains, answering Arthur's inquiry about the "number of fayre ladyes" who accompany him,

"all thes be ladyes for whom I have foughten for, whan I was man lyvynge. And all thes are tho that I ded batayle fore in ryghteuous quarrels, and God hath gyvyn hem that grace at their grete prayer...that they shulde brynge me hydder unto you." (3.1234)

To leave aside the Arthurian tradition, in the thirteenth- or fourteenth-century verse romance *Floris and Blancheflour,* the king proposes to kill the maiden Blancheflour because he does not approve of his son's infatuation with her. It is the queen who intervenes. She agrees that the lad's affections should be directed elsewhere, but objects that it is not necessary to kill the girl: all they need to do is make their son *think* that she is dead.

"Dame," he [the king] saide, "I tell thee my reed:
I will that Blanchefloure be do to deed."

The Quene answerede then and said,
And thought with hur reed
Save the maide fro the deed.

"Who so might reve that maide clene
That she were brought to deth bidene,
Hit were muche more honour
Than slee that maide Blancheflour."[3]

Rather grudgingly, the king accepts her plan to send Blancheflour away, build a tomb for her, and tell their son that she is dead. They do so. Rather than forgetting about her, however, Prince Floris persists in mourning and finally is about to stab himself on her grave. His mother rushes in, grabs the knife away, and thus saves "there the childes lif" (196). She hastily appeals to the king, saying that it would be far better for Floris to marry Blancheflour after all than to die of grief.

Forth the Queene ranne, all weeping,
Till she come to the King.
Than saide the good lady,
"For Goddes love, sir, mercy!
Of twelve children have we noon
On live now but this oon;
And better it were she were his make
Than he were deed for hur sake." (297-304)

The king (again somewhat unwillingly—"Sen it may noon other be," 306) once again accepts the queen's assessment, upon which she runs back to the lad and explains that Blancheflour is not dead at all. Much of the remainder of the romance is concerned with Floris' search for her and their eventual reunion.

In Chaucer's "Wife of Bath's Tale," a knight who has raped a maiden faces death for that crime. The queen and her ladies intercede on his behalf:

the queene and othere ladyes mo
So longe preyeden the kyng of grace
Til he his lyf hym graunted in the place,
And yaf hym to the queene...[4]

The queen proposes to remit all punishment if the knight can tell her what it is that women desire most, and if he cannot answer the question now, she will give him a year in which to do so. The year passes. The knight, who has no confidence in the many answers that have been given him, is turning sadly homewards when he encounters an ugly old woman who hints that she can help him.

"Tel me what that ye seken, by youre fey.
Paraventure it may the bettre be;
Thise olde folk kan muchel thyng," quod she. (III.1002-04)

When the knight explains his predicament, the old woman assures him that she has the right answer. She tells him what it is, exacting a promise that he will honor a request from her when she chooses to make it. The answer she supplies (that women most desire mastery, or, as we would say, dominance) is correct, and his life is saved. In addition, by insisting that the knight honor her request—which is that he marry her—the old woman is making available to him a further benefit. Once he agrees to give her mastery, she becomes young and beautiful and will also be, she pledges, true and good. At the end of the tale, this rather undeserving rapist finds himself, through the good offices of women, in a comfortable situation indeed.

For joye he hente hire [his wife] in his armes two.
His herte bathed in a bath of blisse,
A thousand tyme a-rewe he gan hire kisse,
And she obeyed hym in every thyng
That myghte doon hym plesance or likyng.
  And thus they lyve unto hir lyves ende
In parfit joye.   (III.1252-58)

Similarly, in the fourteenth-century romance of *Sir Launfal,* the knight Launfal—who is so impoverished that he cannot go to church for want of stockings, shoes, clean breeches, and a shirt—encounters two maidens who bring him to their lady, Dame Tryamour. This fairy princess, like the ugly woman in Chaucer's tale, promises to solve the knight's problems if he will accept her love. Launfal delightedly does so and is supplied with silver, gold, rich clothes, armor, and so forth. He becomes quite the rich lord, giving splendid feasts and delivering prisoners and supplying clothing for jesters. When he fails to abide by the fairy lady's one requirement (that he not mention her) and is under sentence of death, she again rescues him from his predicament. This time she takes him away to the fairy country: "Sethe saw him in this lond no man."[5]

These five examples may be permitted to represent an element in Middle English romance so widespread as to be reasonably called a convention: the role of woman as intercessor—as mediator between the forces of death or denial, and the forces of life or affirmation.[6] In many different narrative contexts, it is woman who attempts to halt (or prevent) the bloodshed of battle, to soften the violence of wilfulness or revenge, to call upon mercy rather than justice and so gain pardon or privilege for the undeserving. The action thus performed is at once pragmatic and emotional. On the one hand, it takes the form of practical intervention; on the other, it seems to be based upon what we would recognize as a fundamental emotional or instinctive urge to nourish and preserve life. At the siege of Metz, the duchess carefully dresses herself and goes out to kneel on the battlements, accompanied by her maidens: her conduct and posture are calculated, although her plan is born of desperation. The souls of the maidens who have intervened on behalf of Gawain have apparently undertaken a joint appeal to God. Floris' mother—thinking fast—offers a complicated scheme to replace her husband's simple plan of killing Blancheflour. The old woman in Chaucer's tale proposes a careful bargain (twice), with the goal being not only to save the knight's life, but also to revivify her own. Dame Tryamour arranges to meet Launfal's every financial, social, and personal need. The convention at which we are looking depicts woman not only as the protector of life in a sentimental way, but also as the designer (and sometimes executor) of saving actions. It is a positive role in the sense that the poets themselves endorse the woman's intervention, often by such devices as sympathetically shifting our attention to it, as in the *Alliterative Morte Arthure.* It is an active role, even when the action in a literal sense consists only of conversation. The woman knows to whom to appeal and with what arguments to persuade.

The narrative function of the role varies considerably. In some cases (as in the scenes from the *Alliterative Morte Arthure* and Malory's *Morte*

Darthur) it makes only a minor contribution to the plot as such, helping to get an episode explained or completed. In other cases (as in *Floris and Blancheflour,* the "Wife of Bath's Tale," and *Sir Launfal)* it makes a central contribution to the plot, causing a fundamental re-direction. The affective function of the role seems to be more constant. It provides often-intense evidence of the desire to live; sometimes, by inversion, concentrating on the vocabulary of weeping at the prospect of death. Thus the role supplies an opportunity for the emotions of pity and fear to come to the surface, although in a mode we would call more pathetic or sentimental than tragic.

II

What traditions or assumptions does this role of woman as intercessor reflect? Can it be taken to represent one aspect of the re-assessment of women in late medieval popular thought in England? The romances were intended at least partially for popular audiences, and can therefore be seen as responding to certain expectations in those audiences' minds.[7] In fourteenth- and fifteenth-century England, as has often been pointed out, women, or at least women of what we call the middle class, enjoyed a considerable amount of personal freedom. The wife of Bath, exemplar and exponent of female individualism, is a weaver (self-employed?) who directs her own affairs, travels about as she pleases, and initiates and manages her personal relationships with men. She also affirms the pleasures of life in unblushing terms. Behind her extraordinary example one can assume that there stand the paler figures of her sisters, nourishing and protective of the life-forces in the traditional fashion, yet tending more than did their ancestors to take charge of the conduct of events, even if only in the sense of manipulating their menfolk to do what they want. As for the role of woman as intercessor, the fifteenth-century *Paston Letters,* which provide a rare glimpse into the human relationships of an actual late-medieval family, show Margaret Paston repeatedly mediating between the members of her household and the forces that threaten them. She cajoles, persuades, insists, explains, threatens, argues, and assumes the postures of submission—by turns, as the situation requires. For example, Margaret intervenes to protect her husband's servant Jamys Gloys, whom her husband's enemy Wymdham or Wymondham wants to kill. Margaret first tries to make Wymdham look beyond his anger of the moment to see that he would feel sorry afterwards; then she tries to frighten him off by warning him that Gloys' death would eventually have to be paid for by his own. These two tactics in combination were apparently successful, at least for the moment. She describes the episode in a letter to her husband:

Qwhan Wymdham seyd that Jamys xuld dy I seyd to hum that I soposyd that he xuld repent hym jf he schlow hym or dede to hym any bodyly harm; and he seyd nay, he xuld never repent hym ner have a ferdyng wurth of harm thow he kelyd 3w and hym bothe. And I seyd 3y, and he sclow the lest chylde that longyth to 3wr kechyn, and jf he dede he were lyke, I sopose, to dy for him.[8]

Seventeen years later (for example), she intercedes with her husband on behalf of their son, who has incurred his father's displeasure.

For Godys sake, ser, a pety on hym and remembre yow it hathe be a long season syn he had owt of you to helpe hym wyth, and he hathe obeyed him to yow and wolle do at all tymis, and wolle do that he can or may to have your good faderhood. And at the reuerence of God, be ye hys good fader and have a faderly hert to hym. And I hope he shall euer knowe hym-selff the better her-after and be more ware to exchewe suche thyngys as shuld dysplease you, and for to take hed at that shuld please you. (8 April 1465; p. 293)

Particularly intersting about this appeal is the fact that Margaret does not argue the merits of the quarrel that has taken place between her husband and her son. She does not attempt to prove that her husband's anger is without justice. Instead, she appeals to pity, to the length of time that the estrangement has persisted, to her son's general good character towards his father—a sequence of emotional appeals concentrating upon the concept of an ideal father-son relationship and placed within a Christian context ("at the reuerence of God, by ye hys good fader"). It would not be appropriate to seek the stylistic subtleties of a literary artist in Margaret Paston's letter to her husband, yet perhaps it is not accidental that its language suggests an analogy between the forgiveness of God the father toward His wayward but repentant children, and what she hopes will be John Paston's fatherly forgiveness of his now-obedient son.

Margaret Paston is no heroine of medieval romance. Her preoccupations are with family feuds, property disputes, local politics, and the minutiae of daily life, not with the wars of legendary kings (the Arthur tales) or with the fate of flower-maidens (Blancheflour) or with universal psychological truths ("What do women desire most?"). Nevertheless, the components of her behavior as mediator show a remarkable resemblance to those of the women who function as mediators in the romances.

Yet there are factors that should caution us against assuming that the role of woman as intercessor in the Middle English romances derives from the cultural fact (or perception) of woman as fulfilling this role in actual life. One of these cautionary factors is the existence of a long antecedent tradition of woman as intercessor in continental romance. It is possible that the English romances reflect that European tradition rather than a contemporary English reality. In fact, in four of the five Middle English works cited as examples above, the episodes in which woman acts as a mediator are derived from the known literary sources of those works. The exception is the *Alliterative Morte Arthure,* the known sources of which do not seem to include the appeal made by the Duchess of Metz.[9] It is possible, as has been pointed out (see Krishna, pp.19-22), that in this work the emotional Duchess episode—like the Gawain-Priamus episode adjacent to it in the text—represents the intentional admixture of romance material in a narrative that is otherwise primarily epic. If so, the Duchess' function as mediator may have been intended to capture for the poem the emotional values of a romance convention.

The case of the maidens who intercede on behalf of Gawain, toward the close of Malory's *Morte Darthur,* offers a valuable example of the development of the convention of woman as intecessor. In the thirteenth-century French prose romance *La Mort le roi Artu,* Gawain is accompanied by a group of poor people:

"Rois Artus, nos avons conquestee la meson Dieu a ués monseigneur Gauvain vostre neveu por les granz biens qu'il nos a feiz; et fei aussi comme il a fet, si feras que sages."[10]
(King Arthur, we have prevailed in the house of God on behalf of Milord Gawain, your nephew, because of the great goodnesses that he has done for us; and you should do as he has done, if you would do what is wise.)

Similarly, in the English *Stanzaic Morte Arthur,* Gawain is accompanied by a crowd—"mo folk than men can neven."[11] These people are, he explains, the souls of those whom he had served in earthly life.

Lordes they were, and ladies hende
    This worldes life than han forlorn;
While I was man on life to lende,
    Against their fon I fought them forn;

They asked leve with me to wend,
    To meet with you upon this morn. (3208-11, 14-15)

Malory, who was working from both the *Mort le roi Artu* and the *Stanzaic Morte Arthur* (see Vinaver, 3.1615-25), chose to heighten the emotional impact of this scene by making Gawain's companions specifically a group of ladies. He also emphasized their role as intercessors. In the sources, the accompanying souls seem simply to have appealed for Gawain, or simply to accompany him, but in Malory's version, cited above, Gawain explains that the women have been given grace, at their "grete prayer," is "brynge me hydder unto you." Evidently it is only by means of their guidance or conveyance that he is able to come. The accompanying souls thus appear to be more active participants in the event—perhaps even its initiators—and all of them are women.

In the known sources or analogues of *Floris and Blancheflour,* of the "Wife of Bath's Tale," and of *Sir Launfal,* the role of woman as mediator is also apparent.[12] Sometimes, as with the example of Gawain's companion souls, there are important revisions or heightenings in the English versions, but it is clear in general that the presence of the mediating woman in these works derives from the previous romance tradition. And the same is true of many other Middle English romances. The vast majority of the extant corpus of works in this genre consists of translations, more or less modified, of antecedent French texts.[13] Hence the conventional role of the mediating woman in romance is an international phenomenon, one that reaches back to the development of the romance genre in twelfth-century France (cf. the interceding fairy in Marie de France's *Lanval*). Its development cannot be attributed to a desire to reflect late-medieval English realities.

If one looks at medieval literature beyond the romances, it is immediately apparent that the convention has a considerably longer and broader history yet. Several of the obvious examples belong to the genre of vision-literature, a highly popular form of medieval narrative in which an individual undergoes an illuminating experience. Whether or not he physically travels, he is led to understand such fundamental concepts as the nature of free will and the place of human beings in the overall world order. The first major and widely influential work of this sort in the Western medieval tradition is the sixth-century *De consolatione philosophiae* (The Consolation of Philosophy) of Boethius. Its narrator, imprisoned and under sentence of death for a crime he did not commit, is at first utterly estranged from the divine will. He is visited in his prison cell by an impersonation of Philosophy, who extends to him both merciful understanding and firm guidance. By the end of the visionary experience, Boethius is reconciled to his situation—or, more accurately, his individual situation has ceased to be of importance. The impersonation of Philosophy is a woman. (It has been suggested that this is because the Latin word *philosophia* is of feminine gender, yet there may well be other and less coincidental reasons for Boethius' choice.) The persona of Philosophy, a woman at once comforting and commanding, is the means by which the narrator is led towards metaphysical wisdom. The woman, who takes the initiative throughout the work, intercedes between the narrator and what would have otherwise been his fate, death in a state of despair and resentment.[14] Although she does not physically save his life, she achieves for him something that is regarded as infinitely more important, the recognition of his immortality.

The tradition of Boethius was very productive in medieval literature. The *De consolatione* was translated into English by King Alfred and by Chaucer; it was a prolifically influential work.[15] In the *De planctu naturae* (The Complaint of Nature) of Alanus de Insulis, for example, a female personification of Nature, manifestly indebted to Boethius' female Philosophy, leads the narrator both physically and intellectually towards his goal. She takes the initiative, interposing herself between the searcher and the exterior world, and serves as his guide, companion, and teacher. (The heirs of Alanus' female Nature include, among others, the Nature personifications in Chaucer's "Parlement of Foules" and in the "Mutabilitie Cantos" of Spenser's *Faerie Queene*.)

Dante's *Commedia,* a work of far greater aesthetic importance than the *De planctu,* similarly includes the role of the mediating woman—here Dante's beloved Beatrice, who plays such a variety of roles that it is patently insufficient to look at her in this function only, and it is only for convenience that I do so. Beatrice, like Boethius' Lady Philosophy, functions as a guide in the narrator's journey from ignorance to wisdom. It is, in fact, the mediating efforts of three feminine personae in sequence that initially make Dante's visionary journey possible. First Mary alerts Lucia (Light or Grace), who appeals to Beatrice, who secures Vergil's help in saving Dante. The specific bond between Dante and Beatrice is love. "Amor mi mosse," "Love moved me," explains Beatrice to Vergil. Similarly, Dante's love for her is recognized, as when Lucia urges her to aid him: "Chè non soccorri quei che t'amò tanto?"—"Why do you not help the one who loved you so much?"[16] Because of their love (a theme much expanded from the affectionateness of Boethius' Philosophy), Beatrice functions as the intermediary between Dante and the entire visionary world. She is his link, though he must learn to relinquish her; she calls forth in him earthly passions, though he must learn how to substitute for them the divine passions; she explicates, though he must learn how to articulate his experience himself. She is the means by which he arrives at a mystical understanding of the divine mysteries. She thus performs the highest role of which woman as mediator is capable.

Let us return to England and to the fourteenth century. The English poem *Pearl* also incorporates the Boethian tradition of woman as intercessor. In this vision too, a narrator, a man, is guided towards divine truth by a woman who (like Dante's Beatrice) takes part of her strength from her affective value, the personal emotional bond between herself and the narrator. It is again the link through love that enables her to join her mind to his. In this case, the interceding persona is the soul of the dreamer's daughter, who apparently died in early childhood. Like Beatrice, she leads the narrator to a vision of the heavenly city. Again, it is she who takes the initiative, she who has the knowledge to offer, she who manages his progress from one psychological and epistemological step to the next, she who has obtained for him the privilege of a glimpse of the holy city.[17]

"thu may not enter with-inne hys tor,
Bot of the lombe I haue the aquylde
For a sy3 ther-of thur3 gret fauor."[18]

("You may not enter within his tower, / But I have obtained for you from the Lamb / a sight of it, through [His] great favor.")

The female personification here, as in Boethius and Dante, is the means through which an understanding of immortality is achieved.

In the Boethian tradition of vision-literature, then, the role of woman as intercessor extends in an unbroken line from the fourth century to the fourteenth and onwards. It coincides, at the later end of this line of development, with the period in which the romance as a genre evolved its own literary conventions. It is therefore quite possible that the romance's use of the role owes something to the Boethian tradition. Chaucer, for example, wrote both romances and dream-visions; the *Gawain*-poet too practiced both forms; presumably other romance-writers did also. One work in which romance and Boethian traditions are clearly merged—and a work highly influential on the subsequent development of romance—is the thirteenth-century *Roman de la Rose,* again a dream-vision in which a narrator is guided by personifications, including not one but several female characters. Some of them oppose his progress, but others enact the conventional role at which we have been looking: they intercede on his behalf; they affirm the life-forces, here centering on his desire to bring a love affair to successful concluson; they manage the course of events, even if only by manipulating the behavior of male characters. Two such female figures, Nature and Reason, are of special importance. This work too was very well known in the later medieval period; like Boethius' Consolation, it (or part of it) was translated by Chaucer.

There is yet a third literary tradition in which the figure of woman as mediator, intervening to forestall disaster or to facilitate success, is a standard convention. This is a tradition of hagiography (saint's-life biography), specifically the hagiographical narratives about Mary. The function of Mary as intercessor in narrative is part of the general medieval conceptualization of her as the merciful Mother of God, willing to intervene on behalf of sinners.[19] The term *mediatrix* was applied to Mary, in its Greek form, by the eighth century or before. The title *Maria mediatrix* was popularized in the Latin Church by St. Bernard in the twelfth century; slightly before, the prayer that we know as the Hail Mary became popular (although the form below was apparently not finalized until the sixteenth century).

> Ave Maria, gratia plena,
> Dominus tecum,
> benedicta tu in mulieribus,
> et benedictus fructus ventris tui, Jesus.
> Sancta Maria, Mater Dei,
> ora pro nobis peccatoribus,
> nunc et in hora mortis nostrae.

(Hail Mary, full of grace; the Lord is with thee; blessed art thou among women, and blessed the fruit of your loins, Jesus. Holy Mary, Mother of God, pray for us sinners, now and in the hour of our death.)

Reflecting various facets of the *Maria mediatrix* figure, St. Anselm says that the sinner flees from the just God to the good mother of the merciful God; a Franciscan exemplum instructs sinners that "when we have offended Christ we should first go to the queen of heaven" and offer her our repentance so that she will "come between" us and "Christ, the father who wishes to beat us, and she will throw the cloak of her mercy between the rod of punishment and us."[20] Hoccleve sees her as mediator both between man and God and between man and the devil:

Betwixt God and man is shee mediatrice
For oure offenses mercy to purchace.
Shee is our seur sheeld ageyn the malice
Of the feend...[21]

Chaucer's afflicted Constance, set adrift on the sea, puts it both more pathetically and more beautifully:

Now lady bright, to whom al woful cryen,
Thou glorie of womanhede, thou faire may,
Thou haven of refut...(*CT* II.850-52)

"Haven of refuge" is exactly the role that *Maria mediatrix* fulfills in the many medieval miracle-narratives told of her. Like her secular counterparts in the romances, Mary intervenes on behalf of those who are threatened, devises plans to save them from their enemies, and represents simultaneously an active, pragmatic approach and the traditional forgiving warmth of motherhood. Some of these stories are amusing to us in their *fabliau* overtones. In one (to choose from among a great many examples), an abbess who has fallen into sin with her page becomes pregnant, and her sister nuns denounce her to the bishop. Upon being asked for help, the Virgin miraculously removes the child, and it is the tattle-tale nuns who are rebuked.[22] In another, a jealous woman gives credence to false tales of her husband's sexual infidelity and kills herself and their children;

the Virgin intervenes to restore them to life.[23] Again and again *Maria mediatrix* intervenes on what we might generally call the side of life. She protects people from physical harm, she permits them to escape punishment for enjoying worldly goods and worldly escapades, she applies mercy rather than justice as the criterion of judgment. By a combination of practical schemes and emotional appeals she always succeeds in her purpose, which is to save those who resort to her help.

The narratives of Mary's miracles, in which we can easily recognize folktale ingredients, were very popular in medieval England. One by one or in collections called *mariales,* they circulated in Latin, in Anglo-Norman, and in English.[24] In structure, these miracle-narratives are quite similar to secular tales, and the figure of *Maria mediatrix* could comfortably move from one context to the other. For a specific instance, one miracle-tale is remarkably similar in its overall plot to the siege of Metz episode in the *Alliterative Morte Arthure,* the work with which this paper began. Again we focus on a city under siege and upon the desperation of its inhabitants.

> Of socour thei seyen non other won
> But yelden the city or elles ben slon.[25]

The bishop of the city appeals to Mary, who miraculously causes the enemy soldiers to become blind and helpless, so that the citizens, issuing bravely out, are easily able to kill or capture them; the city is saved. The author of the miracle-tale says that his source is a *Brut* chronicle ("Bruit the Chronicle witnesset wel," 1.27), a fact that explicitly links this Mary story to the secular tradition, since the *Brut* chronicles are intimately associated with many versions of Arthurian romance.

III

Maria mediatrix; Lady Philosophy and her (dream-) vision daughters; the continental elder sisters who underlie the accompanying ladies in the *Morte Darthur,* the interceding queen in *Florio and Blanchoflour,* the helpful fays in the "Wife of Bath's Tale" and *Sir Launfal:* from the narrative traditions of hagiography, vision-literature, and French romance derive many of the components of the conventional woman-as-mediator role in Middle English romance. We must see the origin and background of that convention as literary, then, and as pan-European; not as "real-life" or as specifically English. Despite the resemblance between the romances' mediating woman and Margaret Paston, it would not be legitimate in this case to use the romances as social documents. They cannot safely be assumed to give testimony about the real lives of women in late-medieval England. (It is possible, of course, that other conventional roles that the English romances attribute to women—or to men or to children—do in fact originate in contemporary English reality; each ingredient of the romances needs to be examined on its own.)

The caution that we should not use the Middle English romances as social documents in this case leaves an alternative direction, and a fruitful one: the romances are valuable as *literary* documents. That is, in addition to their aesthetic value to modern readers, they provide information about the literary tastes of the medieval audiences. Although the role of woman as mediator may have originated in European literary traditions rather than in English realities, the role's continuing vitality shows that it remained functional, that it responded to some literary need or desire or expectation. I have suggested above that this function had to do not so much with plot—since the ways that the role aids in the development of plot are quite variable—as with the emotional or affective quality of the stories; the role of woman as mediator permitted the emotions of pity and fear to be expressed in a pathetic context.

It is possible to speculate a little further. Nobody knows to what extent the audiences of the romances consisted of women, and it is not likely that this information will ever become available. However, we can certainly assume that women composed some significant fraction of the audiences; and they might have found the role of woman as mediator a particularly attractive one. In showing women behaving with heightened courage and inventiveness, and receiving recognition for doing so, it would have satisfied a woman's desire to admire a finer, more exciting version of herself. Yet it would have been emotionally acceptable, safe rather than threatening, because its basis was still in the socially sanctioned "feminine" functions of sustaining and protecting life, and because it was often presented with the familiar rhetorical emphasis upon the "feminine" qualities of beauty, fine clothing, delicacy, and actions such as kneeling and weeping. Thus the role would have extended, without violating, women's normal expectations of themselves. (A few other roles assigned to women in the romances did, in fact, violate normal expectations and may have functioned to provide a thrill of horror and denial instead.[26] The same typical "feminine" ingredients—the beauty, the actions and gestures, the life-nurturing functions—might have made the role acceptable to the male audiences of the romances too, particularly since the role of woman as mediator is invariably subordinated to one or another male role. The predominant point of view of the romances is always male, in the sense that it is a male character's adventures that the narrator follows. The *Alliterative Morte Darthur* is Arthur's story, although for a moment our attention is deflected to the Duchess of Metz; the interceding ladies who accompany Gawain are there to promote his cause, not theirs; in *Floris and Blancheflour,* the "wife of Bath's Tale," and *Sir Launfal* it is clearly the knight's career that predominates. To male members of the audience, then, the role of woman as mediator may have functioned almost as it did for female members of the audience, since it provided a heightening of normal expectations without threatening any fundamental principle of the established relationships between men and women. Even the Wife of Bath's helpful hag, having unconventionally obtained mastery, uses it only to increase the happiness of her husband.

Such interpretations of the ways in which members of the audience might have responded to the role of woman as mediator are, as I have indicated, speculations only. They seem to me reasonable, but I certainly would not insist upon their correctness. In any case, they are not essential to the main purpose of this paper, which has been to call attention to the conventional role of woman as mediator in the Middle English romances and to explore the background of that conventional role. This inquiry reaffirms the international nature of Middle English romance, since in this convention, as in many others, it clearly shares the literary traditions of continental Europe, some of them reaching back into the Roman period, some of them incorporating widespread folktale ingredients. Indeed, it may someday be worthwhile to question whether there exists a separate body of romance that is "Middle English" in anything but language, so pervasive are the general similarities between the extant romances in that language and the extant romances in continental languages. That, however, is an issue far too large to be determined here.

Notes

[1] *The Alliterative Morte Arthure,* ed. Valerie Krishna (New York: Burt Franklin, 1976), 1.0343.

[2] *The Works of Sir Thomas Malory,* ed. Eugène Vinaver, 2nd ed. (Oxford: Clarendon Press, 1967), 3.1233.

[3] *Floris and Blancheflour,* in *Middle English Verse Romances,* ed. Donald B. Sands (New York: Holt, Rinehart & Winston, 1966), 11. 45-46, 52-54, 59-62.

[4] *The Complete Poetry and Prose of Geoffrey Chaucer,* ed. John H. Fisher (New York: Holt, Rinehart & Winston, 1977), *Canterbury Tales* III. 894-97.

[5] *Sir Launfal,* in *Middle English Verse Romances,* ed. Sands, 1. 1036.

[6] To my knowledge, the episodes in which this conventional role occurs have not previously been brought together. In Gerald Bordman's *Motif-Index of the English Metrical Romances,* one might consult such headings as H1233.1.1 Old woman helps on quest; P21.2. Queen intervenes on behalf of king's falsely accused sworn brother; P231.9. Mother tries to arbitrate dispute between sons; P.252.9. Helpful sister, R.52.4 Captor's wife frees prisoners; etc. The *Motif-Index* is *FF Communicatons* 190 (1963).

[7] The best recent work on this subject, and one that links the Middle English romances as popular literature with various modern forms of popular literature, is Velma Bourgeois Richmond's *The Popularity of Middle English Romance* (Bowling Green, Ohio: Bowling Green University Popular Press, 1975). See also John Stevens, *Medieval Romance: Themes and Approaches* (New York: Norton, 1973), especially the chapter "The Pervasiveness of Romance"; and Dieter Mehl, *The Middle English Romances of the Thirteenth and Fourteenth Centuries* (London: Routledge & Kegan Paul, 1968), who cautions that the concept of a "popular" audience should not be limited to an uncritical, illiterate level of society: "The popular character of the romances, generally taken for granted by scholars,...implies above all that they catered for people of wide interests and from many walks of life, but it does not mean that they were only designed for the illiterate" (p.13). The whole concept of "popular literature" needs to be used very carefully, since for the medieval period it should not suggest—as it does now—a body of literature separate from that read or heard by educated people.

[8] Margaret Paston to John Paston, 19 May 1448, in *Paston Letters and Papers of the Fifteenth Century,* ed. Norman Davis, I (Oxford: Clarendon Press, 1971), p.225.

[9] On the sources of the episode of the siege of Metz, see William Matthews, *The Tragedy of Arthur* (Berkeley: University of California Press, 1960), pp.44-51.

[10] *La Mort le roi Artu, roman du xiii siècle,* ed. Jean Frappier (Geneva: Droz, Textes littéraires français, 1956), p.225.

[11] *The Stanzaic Morte Arthur,* in *King Arthur's Death,* ed. Larry D. Benson (New York: Bobbs-Merrill, 1974), 1. 3197.

[12] See *Floire et Blancheflour,* ed. W. Wirtz, Frankfurter Quellen und Forschungen, Heft 15 (Frankfurt, 1937), and *Floire et Blancheflour,* ed. M. Pelan, Publication de la Faculté des Lettres de l' université de Strasbourg, Textes d'études (Paris 1e ed., 1956); W.F. Bryan and Germaine Dempster, eds., *Sources and Analogues of Chaucer's Canterbury Tales* (Chicago: Univ. of Chicago Press, 1941), and the further bibliography in Fisher, pp.999-1000; A.J. Bliss, *Sir Launfal* (London: Nelson, 1960).

[13] "Most of them are based upon French originals.... The Middle English romances adhere faithfully to their French models; many an English author seems to have worked with the French

text before him. Others adapt more freely, or reproduce the sources from memory." Helaine Newstead, "Romances: General," in J. Burke Severs, *A Manual of the Writings in Middle English*, 1 (New Haven: Conn. Academy of Arts & Sciences, 1967), pp.11-12.

[14]On Philosophy's presentation as *mulier,* woman, see Elaine Scarry, "The Well-Rounded Sphere," in *Essays in the Numerical Criticism of Medieval Literature,* ed. Caroline D. Eckhardt (Lewisburg, Pa.: Bucknell Univ. Press, 1980).

[15]A useful brief sketch of the Boethian tradition, especially as an influence upon later medieval dream-vision poetry, is provided by A.C. Spearing, *Medieval Dream-Poetry* (Cambridge: Cambridge University Press, 1976), pp.18-40.

[16]Dante Alighieri, *La Divina Commedia,* I, *Inferno,* ed. Louis Biancoll (New York: Washington Square Press, 1966), canto 2.72, 102. Spearing (among others) points out that the *Commedia* is not properly classed as a dream-vision, since the narrator does not fall asleep. However, it is clearly a work in the Boethian visionary tradition.

[17]Cf. "Through the intercession of the maiden, the dreamer's vision gradually improves"; his vision is his ability to see truth (Alan Metcalf, "Gawain's Number," in *Essays in the Numerical Criticism of Medieval Literature,* ed. Eckhardt).

[18]*The Pearl,* in *Early English Alliterative Poems,* ed. Richard Morris, EETS, OS, 1 (1869; rpt. Oxford: Oxford Univ. Press, 1965), lines 966-68.

[19]On Mary as *mediatrix,* see the *New Catholic Encyclopedia* (New York: McGraw-Hill, 1967), 6.898, 9.223,570; and Marina Warner, *Alone of All Her Sex* (New York: Knopf, 1976), Part V, "Intercessor" (pp.273-331).

[20]These examples are cited by Warner, pp.315 and 285.

[21]Thomas Hoccleve, "The Monk and Our Lady's Sleeves," in *The Middle English Miracles of the Virgin,* ed. Beverly Boyd (San Marino, Ca.: Huntington Library, 1964), lines 7-11.

[22]See Warner, p.277.

[23]"The Good Knight and His Jealous Wife," in *Middle English Miracles,* ed. Boyd.

[24]For a brief introduction to the Mary miracles in Middle English, see Boyd, pp.3-10.

[25]"How Chartres Was Saved," in *Middle English Miracles,* ed. Boyd, lines 41-42.

[26]*Amis and Amiloun* and *Sir Amadace,* for example, depict women willing to participate in the murder of their children in order to satisfy a promise their husbands have made.

Popular Fable Tradition in the Middle Ages

Evelyn S. Newlyn's essay is concerned with two issues: the popularity of the fable tradition and Henryson's use of it to comment on various social and political ills. The fable has a long history as a form of literature designed not only to entertain but to instruct, and Henryson's creativity with the form is evidenced in his use of it to address social issues, as well as to incorporate moral instruction with entertainment. The popular representation of various social classes, with all their follies, and the hard-nosed look at the failure of certain institutions such as the law and the Church, reveal Henryson's awareness of reality as he perceives it.

Evelyn S. Newlyn is assistant professor of English at Virginia Polytechnic Institute and State University. Her current work-in-progress is "The Artistry of Robert Henryson."

Robert Henryson and the Popular Fable Tradition in the Middle Ages

Evelyn S. Newlyn

In the Middle Ages, the fable was a popular literary form; medieval preachers often used the Aesopic and Reynardian tales as exampla, and medieval teachers used fables as subjects for language study as well as a means for conveying moral instruction. Medieval poets also used the fable for artistic purposes, and the Middle Scots poet Robert Henryson, writing in the latter part of the fifteenth century, explains in the prologue[1] to his collection of fables that even though the primary purpose of the fable may be to instruct, it is also possible and desirable that the fable entertain. Henryson adds a further function, however, in using the fable not just to instruct the individual, but to comment upon popular issues, and to point to social ills which need correction. A study of Henryson's adaptation of the genre's traditional form and content to suit his own age and purpose can help to provide a clearer understanding of the fable's function as popular literature in the Middle Ages.

Henryson begins the prologue to his fables by explaining that even though fables may not be grounded entirely in truth, they are nevertheless pleasing to the human ear. Henryson also states that the beast fable is particularly suited to his purpose because, while Aesop has told how animals are like humans, able to speak, reason, and make logical conclusions, humans are also like animals when they habitually live carnal and sinful lives which are ungoverned by a capacity for shame. In further defense of the fable as allegory, Henryson states that, like a nutshell which

77

is hard and tough but which holds within itself a sweet and delectable kernel, a fable similarly contains a wise doctrine, full of nourishment. The reader, however, must make an effort to obtain the doctrine; just as flowers and corn sprout from the earth when it is cultivated, so does a moral message spring from poetry for those who will seek it. Yet, while Henryson emphasizes the moral function of the fable, he simultaneously insists that learning is best accomplished when made as pleasant as possible; he compares the mind which always studies to the bow which, when it is always bent, becomes weak and dull. Surely it is the voice of Henryson the schoolmaster, speaking from personal experience with reluctant if not fractious young scholars, who acknowledges that it is wise and beneficial "to mix with sad matters some merriment."

We thus find in Henryson's prologue those elements which, combined, define a medieval beast fable. First of all, we learn that a fable is a story, an imaginary creation wherein animals behave as humans. Second, a fable is both entertaining and aesthetically satisfying, since its content is interesting and its form pleasing. Third, a fable has a moral, a message from which human beings can benefit if they are receptive to it. However, for Henryson the fable is also a vehicle for social commentary, a means by which he can call attention to societal ills which plague the lives of ordinary people.

In his use of the fable form, Henryson is working in an ancient tradition. It is impossible to trace the genre to a single source, or to a first writer, but we do know that the fable tradition existed in the Arabic and the Indian cultures as well as in the culture of ancient Greece. Although there were in the Middle Ages many variant forms of the fables—in poetry and in prose, and in many languages such as French, German, Latin, and English—many of the medieval beast fables are traceable, ultimately, to the Aesopic tradition by means of such redactors as Demetrius Phalereus, Phaedrus, Babrius, Avianus, and Gualterus Anglicus. Whether Aesop actually is responsible for all the fables attributed to him—or, for that matter, any of them—cannot, of course, be finally determined, but we do know that the tradition of the beast fable places Aesop near the beginning of the genre in Greece. By the time of the Middle Ages, Aesopian fables were a popular form of literature, and were even used in medieval schools as exercises in grammar and composition. Although it seems likely that Henryson had access to some collection of fables, he may also have known some of the tales because of their use by medieval preachers as exempla, or because of the tales' pervasiveness in the oral tradition. Whatever his sources, however, Henryson's creativity is evident in his own use of the conventional fable material. By assigning new particularity, local details, and homely representations to traditional forms and subjects, he makes those forms and subjects freshly pertinent and interesting to his audience. He therefore not only preserves the heritage from the past by using it, but he also revitalizes it as he recreates and reforms the ancient material to suit his present purposes. In using inherited material to address current issues, and in combining moral instruction with entertainment, Henryson's fables are particularly representative of popular literature in the Middle Ages.

In dealing thus with contemporary medieval conditions, the fables reveal the poet's concern for the failure of the individual as well as for the failure of society. He uses the fable form to convey instruction; to point a moral; to satirize political, social, or ecclesiastical error; and to condemn the breakdown of morality at all levels and in all institutions, but particularly in the individual. There are underlying rules in Henryson's world and many of his poems deal with the misfortune that comes to those who do not observe the rules, whether it be the sheep who pretends he is a dog, the birds who will not heed the warning of the swallow, or the fox who trifles with the sacrament of confession. Yet the poet's sympathy for his characters is ever present. Although he disapproves of social disruption, materialism, and human error of many kinds, he understands those who are foolish or misled. Those who are deliberately evil, however, receive his greatest scorn, and his severest criticism is reserved for those faulty institutions which fail in their duty to protect the innocent. The plight of those innocent who suffer and are oppressed on all sides is, in fact, a frequent concern of Henryson's, and many of his fables seem to express a *Weltanschauung* which sees humanity, in the form of anthropomorphic animals, struggling against nature and fate. In fact, it is that very world view which surely engendered much of the poet's art, and which is probably also responsible for the conflict which occasionally arises in the poems when the poet's attempts at theodicy appear in striking juxtaposition with his attempts to portray life realistically.

As is typical of much medieval poetry, and of the beast fable tradition in particular, Henryson's fables have several layers of meaning and can always be read on at least two levels. On the allegorical or instructional level are represented human beings, their follies and their graces, their willfulness and their weakness; the wise reader is one who applies to himself the lesson which they illustrate. On the surface level, however, live small creatures who strive and complain, who suffer and repent, who are noble and foolish, and who amuse us with their disputations. Henryson seems always to be aware of the people in his audience and, while his intent on the allegorical level is to teach, his intent on the surface of his poetry is also to delight.

Although Henryson uses the traditional form of the fable to treat a broad range of contemporary concerns, certain themes tend to recur frequently in his fables. One typical theme concerns the failure of the individual who unwisely chooses to satisfy his bodily appetites rather than his spiritual and intellectual needs. His fable of "The Cock and the Jasp"[2] most vividly illustrates this theme. The fable centers on the cock's discovery, as he scratches for his dinner in a dunghill, of a beautiful precious stone. In spite of this great discovery, however, his immediate and urgent problem is that he is hungry; he needs such things as corn, or worms, or snails, to fill his empty stomach. Yet he recognizes, as indicated by his apostrophe to the jewel, that this is a very valuable stone: "O, beautiful gem, O rich and noble thing...thou art a jewel for any wordly king...so valuable and good." On a practical level, however, he knows also that the jewel, since it will not feed his stomach, is of no real use to him in spite of its great value. The cock does not, however, reject the jewel without careful thought. He even acknowledges the irony that a gem of such value should be found by a poor preoccupied creature like himself. Although the jewel is indeed a thing of virtue and beauty, he is not able to make use of it; he pointedly reminds us, in a statement with which we can hardly argue, that "hungry men cannot live on beauty." Henryson thus calls our attention to the difficult life of those who suffer from such social ills as hunger, those whose lives are entirely preoccupied with fulfilling basic physical needs. The cock is not, furthermore, extravagant in his desires; he does not ask for delicacies, but for the simplest fare: "had I dry bread, I would keep no cooks."

The cock therefore presents himself to us as a sensible creature of simple tastes; he is also sufficiently intelligent and perceptive to regret that he is unable to make use of this precious stone, and that the gem should have come to be in such a place. He concludes his address to the jewel by telling it to rise out of the dungheap and go to its proper place, since he and the jewel are not suited to each other. This statement has a peculiar effect on the reader, who knows perfectly well that the jewel will not rise and pass to its proper place; on the other hand, we can hardly find fault with the cock, for the narrator has indicated rather strongly that the cock is faced with a most urgent need which he is not able to ignore. The reader at this point in the poem feels that the cock is right in his judgment, that he has taken the only sensible course; after all, one's physical needs must be satisfied before one can appreciate things which satisfy only the spirit. Yet, there is created in the reader a sense of discomfort, an uneasiness, because we know, and the cock knows, that the gem is valuable, and we suspect that the cock could appreciate it, if only he could somehow manage to get his stomach filled first. At this point the narrator enters the fable to end the tale; the cock, we are told, left the jewel upon the ground and went off somewhere to look for food. Although the narrator claims not to know what happened to the jasp, he does intend to follow the example of his author, Aesop, and tell of the inner meaning of this fable, which he does in the *Moralitas* which follows.

We find immediately in the *Moralitas* that not only has the cock erred gravely in casting aside the stone, but we, too, have erred in thinking him right to do so. The *Moralitas* tells us that the Jasp has wonderful properties; the stone signifies prudence and cunning, which make a man strong, victorious, safe and happy, and which enable him to rule honorably and resist vice. The stone is, in fact, "science," or education, which is "eternal meat" to the human soul. The cock, concentrating only on his earthly meat, is therefore like the fool who scorns knowledge and will not learn, or like the sow, in whose trough are cast precious stones. In fact, the narrator tells us, the jewel which is knowledge is now lost; we, being content instead with riches, do not even seek the jewel. There is, therefore, no point in his talking further, since to do so simply "wastes wind."

The fable thus operates on at least two discernible levels. On the literal level, the cock, apparently with good common sense, ignores something which seems to be of no real use to him. However, since both the narrator and the cock have indicated the worth of the jasp, the cock's behavior makes the reader uneasy; this uneasiness occurs because there is, in fact, another level of meaning. The cock also symbolizes the ignorant man who errs because of faulty perception and misunderstanding, the man who is so caught up with consideration of his physical life that he fails to see the importance of attending to his spiritual or intellectual life. The poem thus creates a tension between the level of "popular" common sense, which declares the stone of no use, and the level upon which one recognizes the stone's spiritual significance. The cock, nonetheless, can hardly be faulted for his choice; Henryson has made clear that he is a victim of his social and economic condition and is thereby prevented from attending to things of spiritual importance. The level at which the cock could appreciate things of transcendent spiritual merit is, in fact, closed to him, because of his poverty and social position. However, although the cock can never benefit from the jewel, the reader can; the wise reader will follow the narrator's symbolically-stated advice and "go seek the jasp."

Certainly one of Henryson's intentions in "The Cock and the Jewel" is to call to our attention the difficult plight of the individual whose social status obliges him to focus his life on needs physical rather than spiritual. A corollary concern is explored in his fable of "The Two Mice,"[3] which typifies a second recurring theme in Henryson's fables. In this fable and others are embodied Henryson's praise of the simple life and its virtues, and his warnings against the dangers inherent in materialism. The fable tells of two sisters whose lives have taken different paths. The elder mouse lives in town as a guild member and free burgess, going wherever she pleases "among the cheese and meal in boxes and chests." Meanwhile, the younger mouse lives in the country like an outlaw, sometimes under bushes and briars and sometimes in the corn, often enduring cold and distress. The conflict in the poem arises when each mouse attempts to lead the same life as the other.

Much of the aesthetic satisfaction the reader finds in the tale is attributable to the characterization of the mice, which, combining animal and human qualities, not only adds color to the tale but provides a vehicle for social commentary. That the mice are sisters makes their differing social positions and attitudes more pointed, and allows the narrator the opportunity to comment upon those who, dissatisfied with their humble station, "climb up most high." The characterization of the mice therefore has at least three functions within the fable: the creatures are mice, that live on the literal level of the poem; they are representatives of differing social classes, the peasant and the burgess; they are also, of course, allegorical symbols for erring and misguided humans. The younger mouse, that is more favorably presented, is clearly of the lowest class, while the elder sister is represented as a social climber, symbolic of the growing middle class which Henryson deplores as committed to materialistic pursuits. The characters of the two sisters are revealed indirectly, through dialogue and through their actions.

The younger mouse is delighted at her city sister's visit, and their reunion is one of Henryson's most charming scenes. However, when the younger sister brings forth from her buttery her best food, nuts and peas, the city mouse scorns this coarse food, explaining patronizingly that her stomach is accustomed to food as good as any lord's. In a most tactless manner she both belittles her country sister's hospitality and establishes herself as a creature that has risen above their common humble origins and developed finer tastes: "these withered peas and nuts.../ will break my teeth and make my stomach slender/which was accustomed before to meats most tender." The country mouse defends her modest dishes by pointing out that, although they are simple, they are served with good cheer, which should make them tender, sweet and good, since a moderate portion of food served with good will and a gentle heart is much more pleasant than many spiced dishes served with a sour face or a frowning brow. The city mouse is not, however, persuaded. She announces that she has food of much better quality in the city, where she also has a house where there is no danger of cat or trap.

When her younger sister, with some timidity, agrees to visit her elder sister's residence in town, she finds that the promises concerning food are true: they find cheese, butter, fish, meat and sacks of meal. Personal safety, however, is another matter. No sooner has the narrator warned us that "after joy often comes care/and trouble after great prosperity," than a servant comes in and surprises the mice at their dinner. The city mouse immediately heads for a safe hole, but the poor country mouse, not knowing where to go, faints dead away. Even though the servant has no time to chase them, the country mouse is frightened half to death and lies prostrate on the floor, her heart pounding and her feet and hands trembling. Although the city sister comforts her, the country mouse is so terrified that she declares she would rather fast forty days on water soup than have a feast in such fear. She has barely calmed down from the servant's visit when the cat appears; this time, the country mouse is not so lucky. For several agonizing moments the cat plays with her, tossing her from paw to paw and playing hide-and-seek with her under the straw. When the poor mouse is finally able to escape, she fervently declares her disenchantment with city life, where rich and abundant food is soured by the threat of danger. Once at home, the country mouse finds her den as warm as wool, even if it is not luxurious; more important, however, is the fact that she has enough to eat of peas, nuts, beans and wheat, and that she eats in peace without fear.

On the literal level of the poem, then, we learn, with the mice, that the inconveniences and evils with which we are familiar are the easiest to live with. In the *Moralitas*, however, the narrator clarifies additional layers of meaning. While it is true that no station in life is free of adversity, yet trouble and vexation may especially plague those who climb high, those who are not content with a simple life. In an echo of the Beatitudes, the narrator explains the allegorical significance of the poem: "Blessed is the simple life without fear; / Blessed is food eaten in peace; / Whoever has enough needs no more than that." Finally, on the tropological level, the narrator warns the gluttonous man who makes a god of his stomach. The narrator then concludes the *Moralitas* by reiterating his belief that a simple and unmaterialistic life is the best way to achieve earthly happiness.

The message of the *Moralitas*, however, is more than just a paean to the humble way of life; the narrator also draws upon the narrative to make statements about social climbers who become proud and deny their background, about the shallowness which results from an overemphasis on physical comforts, and about the true value of peace of mind. As Henryson presents them, the two adult sisters represent both the lower class, which lives simply, humbly and close to the earth, and the middle class, which pursues materialism and physical comforts, and which lives in town. Although the two sisters had the same parents and the same modest upbringing, they differ greatly as adults because of their newly dissimilar stations in life. While the growth of the middle class may have had the desirable social effect of ending the sharp dichotomy between the aristocratic and the peasant classes, yet, for Henryson, there were dangers inherent in the values held by that middle class, dangers to the characters of individual people. The city mouse, having moved away from her rustic background, attempts to deny her simple origins and presents herself as a superior creature of worldliness and refined sensibility in comparison to her rural sister. Henryson's characterization of the city mouse, however, is not favorable, since he protrays her as a thoughtless, self-centered, proud and materialistic creature, while her country sister is generous, kind, noble and properly keeps the custom of her parents. Henryson thus uses the characterization of the two mice to point up some of the undesirable effects of social mobility, and particularly of the move to the richer and more sophisticated life in town. The fable therefore serves as a vehicle for Henryson's commentary on contemporary social change, while it also enchants us with its charming story of the tiny sisters. In this fable, particularly, the relation of the narrative and *Moralitas* is close to that of exemplum and sermon,[4] and the reader comes away feeling perhaps as did the audience which heard a medieval preacher—both educated and entertained.

The fable of "The Sheep and the Dog"[5] may be less entertaining on the literal level than other Henrysonian fables, but it is certainly one of his most powerful. In its attack on the corruption not only in the ecclesiastical and civil courts but in the world at large, it also reflects a final thematic concern of Henryson's fables. And since it questions, ultimately, the Christian paradox which justifies the slaughter of the innocent, it provides an intriguing and explicit example of the conflict in Henryson between theodicy and reality.

In the narrative, Henryson concentrates on injustice done to the individual in the "consistory" or ecclesiastical court; in the *Moralitas* he widens his scope to include the civil court, which similarly abuses the innocent; and, finally, he comes to consider the reality of widespread human suffering in the world, and to wonder why God permits it. To complete his tripartite analogy, however, would establish God as a third element, along with the ecclesiastical and civil courts, which causes or permits people to suffer undeservedly. The poem thus presents an interesting conflict; the realism of the narrative and most of the *Moralitas* is juxtaposed strikingly with the narrator's abrupt attempt at theodicy in the last stanza, when he seems suddenly to become aware of the direction of his analogy. At that point he quickly explains that of course God permits humankind to suffer "because of our great offense," because we are sinners.

This hasty attempt at recovery, however, hardly outweighs the evidence which the poet amasses in the fable as he depicts a world where poor people are at the mercy of the evildoers, and where the systems which have been established to protect the poor and the innocent from the evil and the powerful are proven wholly inadequate. This failure of the ecclesiastical court to do justice, which Henryson portrays in the narrative, represents the failure of the civil court; and the failure of these earthly systems is additionally symptomatic of a greater and more all-encompassing social disarray which indicates that God has drawn his attention from the world's affairs, thus permitting evil to rule unchecked. Consequently, many poor people have no recourse but to submit to the will of their oppressors and to hope for something better in an after-life.

Yet there is a conflict in the narrator's mind between his awareness of life's harshness and injustice and his personal conviction that there does exist a just and benevolent God. He attempts a partial justification in his statement that these social evils are visited upon us because of our great sinfulness, but his relegation of this attempt at theodicy to the last few lines of his poem makes the effort somewhat less than convincing. Further, the narrator's withdrawal from the *Moralitas* and his assertion that he only reports what the sheep has said is evidence of his desire to distance himself from the sheep's harsh criticism; clearly, the narrator is unwilling to be a participant as the sheep criticizes not only the religious and legal systems, but even the condition of God's world, and God's governance of it.

All of this theological questioning and social commentary are built upon the central conflict of the narrative, which tells us of a dog that goes before a wolf-judge and falsely claims that a sheep owes him a loaf of bread. The dog's claim, of course, is fraudulent, but the judge is dishonest and biased, a natural enemy of the sheep, and he permits injustice to be accomplished under the sanction of the ecclesiastical court. After this rapid introduction, Henryson sets the stage with animals that have traditional characteristics that help to convey an overwhelming impression of corruption and injustice within the legal system.

The wolf, of course, was generally considered a rapacious beast of prey, but Christianity added to that image further characteristics of deception, treachery and murderous intent. In addition to drawing upon these traditions, the narrator puts in the wolf's mouth a claim to the very qualities which are opposite to his traditional nature: the wolf describes himself as "never guilty of fraud or deception." We are thus reminded of the customary view of the wolf by his claim that he is the opposite; Henryson uses this technique of verbal irony throughout this fable.

The rest of the court is similarly described. The apparitor, or summoner, is Sir Corby Raven, which has "picked many a sheep's eye." The court clerk and notary for the case is the fox, which had, in the Middle Ages, a long association with craftiness and treachery. Legal experts for the court are the gled and grip, scavenger birds, that band together to support the dog's false plea against the sheep. The narrator explains, in a direct and explicit condemnation of these birds, "Though the charge is false, they have no conscience."

The poet thus creates, through the animal images which he employs, a setting for his fable which indicates that the defendant is surrounded by evil, malice and injustice. Although the atmosphere of a court should reassure the innocent that justice will be done, Henryson portrays for us a court where justice is clearly not a possibility, where all the judicial authorities are corrupt. He underscores that corruption by choosing for his fable animals which have traditional imagery immediately indicating that the sheep will be judged by officials that are cruel, dishonest and malicious. In his portrayal of the sheep Henryson similarly draws upon the sheep's traditional image, but he adds to that image characteristics which strengthen his point that the innocent, even if they are intelligent and courageous, are no match for the evildoers of the world.

When the trial begins the sheep stands alone, not just without legal assistance but also alone in his purity, honesty and courage. Although he quite properly objects to appearing before a judge who is suspect and a biased court at a time and place which are clearly illegal, he is no match for his enemies, and the court directs him to pay the dog in either silver or bread. The sheep, cast in the role of sacrificial beast, is obliged to sell his fleece in order to buy bread for the dog. The narrative ends with a description of the sheep, naked, without his wool covering, going sadly into the country.

Having, in the narrative, thoroughly denounced the ecclesiastical court, in the *Moralitas* Henryson wides his scope to include the civil court. On the allegorical level the sheep represents poor people, who are oppressed by tyrants seeking to prosper by false means. The wolf-judge of the fable is comparable to the real sheriff of the civil court who obtains a false decree or summons and then charges poor men wrongly. The raven-apparitor is like a false coroner in the real world who has a roll of offenders, but who is perfectly willing "to scratch out 'John' and write in 'Will'," and so exact bribes from both.

The narrator then moves to the third part of his analogy, where the sheep is seen as a figural representation of suffering humanity. Although it is customary for the narrator to speak in the *Moralitas*, in this poem the narrator withdraws, claiming that he will simply repeat the sorrowful lament of the sheep, which he heard as he passed by. The narrator's departure from the poem is not surprising in view of the content of the rest of the *Moralitas*; it is one thing to point out how ecclesiastical and civil courts abuse poor folk, but it is quite another to imply that God is similarly at fault for permitting innocent humankind to suffer. It is perhaps understandable that the poet decides to put these words in the mouth of the sheep, which is sharply critical as he calls God's attention to the disordered state of the world. Just as the sheep suffered wrongly as a result of the proceedings of the ecclesiastical court, and just as the innocent poor suffer at the hands of the civil court, so, finally, does humanity suffer because of the evils which seem to exist unchecked in the world. Casting his eyes up to heaven the sheep asks for an explanation of this injustice:[6]

> Oh, Lord, why sleepest thou so long?
> Walk, and observe my case, which is true.
> Look how I am by fraud, wrongful force, and deceit
> Peeled naked, and so is many a one ...
> See how the cursed sin of greed
> Has overcome love, loyalty, and law.
> Now few or none will execute justice:
> Therefore, the poor man is overcome...
> Do you not see, Lord, this world is overturned?

> Now simony is considered to be no sin...
> Kindness is dead, and pity is no more.
> Alas, Lord God, why do you permit it?

The sheep, like many of Henryson's animals, is possessed of some high rhetorical skills. Superimposed upon the underlying structure of the repeated exhortation to God is a gradual widening of the sheep's concern from his particular case to other poor folk, and finally to the broader shortcomings of society when he bemoans the lack of kindness and pity. Within these structural frames, the sheep's denunciation of society's flaws and God's apparent inattention grows increasingly bitter and pointed as it moves outward from himself to "many a one" who also suffers.

Suddenly, however, the poem reverses itself as the sheep ceases to question God and attempts to justify humanity's dreadful condition. He states that God sends us such troubles as plagues, hunger, famine, war and disease because few sinners will amend their lives. Poor people, in consequence, can do little more than pray. This stanza attempts to resolve the Christian paradox that a loving God permits the innocent to suffer, but the fable seems to say that the innocent poor suffer doubly on earth: God sends trouble to humans as a signal to mend their evil lives, but the innocent seem to suffer more from these afflictions than do the guilty. At the same time, the innocent are also the victims of sinners, and the victims also of institutions which should provide some earthly justice but which are, in fact, corrupt. The last three lines of the poem convey a sense of hopelessness concerning earthly existence, a hopelessness mitigated only by the possibilty of a heavenly reward:

> We poor people, therefore, may do no more
> than pray to thee, since we are thus oppressed
> upon this earth. Grant us in heaven good rest.

Thematically, then, the poem is about a sheep that is persecuted wrongly by a dog in a judicial process which was intended to insure justice; the poem is also about poor folk who suffer from wrong-doing by their leaders and their social systems; and, finally, it is about bewildered Christians who see sinners prosper while the innocent are beset on all sides by evil and misery. Thus the poem, while it concerns social corruption, also reflects a central conflict between the poet's religious faith and his awareness of reality. There seem to be two mutually exclusive truths in Henryson's world, truths which he attempts to reconcile in the last stanza of the poem: the first truth is that poor people suffer from a great many social ills, and the second, that a benign God governs the world's affairs. In essence, as he addresses this issue Henryson questions divine wisdom—but only to a degree. Even though he is tormented by the world's oppressed people, Henryson ultimately must assume that there is a reason for that oppression; God's benignity cannot really be questioned, although the realism reflected in his fable surely points to a conflict in the poet's own mind concerning God's methodology.

That conflict between the poet's portrayal of realism and his attempts at theodicy makes the poem especially interesting within the medieval context. The poem is also noteworthy, however, for the irony of opposition which the poet uses as he manipulates traditional animal imagery to create a negative, ironic tone. In a similar manner, the poet uses legal details, phrases and customs to indicate and underscore the illegality which governs the proceedings. The paradoxical situations created by his use of such oppositions seem to parallel that Christian paradox which is at the center of the poem: the suffering of the innocent. The narrator seems to find few convincing and logical explanations for these anomalies, so at the end he draws upon Christian *sententiae*; the naked, shivering sheep can only pray and hope for a better life in heaven.

These three fables are typical of Henryson's use of the fable genre and of his thematic concerns. Although most of his fables have as their basis relatively short Aesopic tales, Henryson has, in all cases, widened the fable's application so that various levels of meaning are available to the reader. Henryson uses the fable to provide moral instruction and to convey social commentary, but also to entertain; it is, perhaps, not difficult to understand why the beast fable was one of the most popular types of literature in the Middle Ages.

Notes

[1] All references are to my translation which is based upon *The Bannatyne Manuscript*, Vol. IV, W. Tod Ritchie, ed., Publications of the Scottish Text Society, new series vol. 26 (Edinburgh and London: William Blackwood, 1930).

[2] "The Cock and the Jewell" is found in *The Bannatyne Manuscript*, " 208-11.

[3] "The Twa Mys" is found in *The Bannatyne Manuscript*, pp. 217-15.

[4] This fable was, in fact, used as an exemplum in medieval sermons. Compare the exemplum numbered CLVII in *The Exempla of Jacques de Vitry*, in Thomas F. Crane, ed. (London: David Nutt, 1890), p. 69.

[5] "The Dog, the Scheip and the Wolff" is found in *The Bannatyne Manuscript*, pp. 225-31.

[6] Compare Psalm 44:23.

Surnames and Medieval Popular Culture

The answer to the question "What's in a name?" is plenty, according to W.F.H. Nicolaisen in his essay on Scottish surnames and what they can tell us of medieval popular culture. Place names, for example, often provide information about prehistoric strata and come to be equivalent in significance to material items which provide archeological insight into cultures. Surnames, when tied to place names, can give us information on migrations, while other types of names reveal occupational histories and patterns of kinship. The very act of naming has both communal and personal importance and can yield significant socio-cultural data.

W.F.H. Nicolainsen, assistant professor of English at SUNY-Binghamton, has been a Carnegie Research Fellow at the University of Aberdeen for the past year and has been a professor of English and folklore.

Tension and Extension:
Thoughts on Scottish Surnames and Medieval Popular Culture

W.F.H. Nicolaisen

Our names preserve a record of the
government, industries, habits, beliefs,
and fancies of our ancestors.
Donald Mackinnon (1887).[1]

Names are initially, one might even say primarily, linguistic items. When first given they usually mean in the way in which words mean, and when used they are embedded in linguistic contexts—phonologically, morphologically, syntactically. It is therefore fair to expect them to yield, when studied, chiefly linguistic information. As markers of different strata in linguistic history, for example, and of the relative chronology of that stratified history, they have provided invaluable evidence, especially in countries with a long and diversified sequence of immigrant languages as, let us say, Scotland.[2] Place names have proved to be particularly instructive material in this respect, supplying, most as names of major water courses, information about early, prehistoric strata for which no written record of any other kind is available. In such forays into linguistic prehistory they have become equivalent in significance and expressive force to the surviving items of material culture which are the archaeologist's sources of information and objects of research.

Although perhaps less dramatically, place names have also served well the student of medieval matters linguistic in Scotland, helping effectively to determine the extent of Scandinavian linguistic (and political) domination of the Scottish north and west, to chart the gradual progress of Gaelic in the kingdom of Strathclyde, and to reconstruct some of the aspects of the ousting of Pictish, to cite but three important examples.[3] In all three instances, the history of the languages involved and the settlement of the speakers of these languages are so intertwined that it is practically impossible, and probably also undesirable, to separate them. A large variety of extra-linguistic information is, it appears, readily available in toponymic evidence, as long as one knows how to extract it and, equally important, as long as the limitations of that evidence, as well as its scope, are recognized.

Our knowledge of medieval popular culture is not only likely to benefit from such evidence, but it can be expected to be one of the chief beneficiaries, for the act of naming and the use of names are, after all, first and foremost aspects of culture-bound behavior on a "popular" level, in the broadest sense of that term. Whether we give names to places or persons, or call them by their names, this will only in a small number of instances involve official decrees or sanctions: naming and using names is an essential privilege of the people. With the help of place names people turn a threatening wilderness into a habitable landscape; with the aid of personal names people transform the perplexing human environment into a structured society. The investigation of naming strategies and of the employment of names consequently will of necessity throw light on several aspects of popular culture, the medieval period being eminently suited for the task.

II

Through a systematic scrutiny of the appropriate specifics, or defining elements, in compound place names, for instance, it is possible to reconstruct a fairly accurate, though because of the survival factor and the "accidental" nature of names, by no means comprehensive picture of animal husbandry or other noteworthy agricultural and pastoral practices. The island of Lewis, northernmost part of the Outer Hebrides, like the rest of the Western and Northern Isles of Scotland, and the adjacent mainland, under Scandinavian domination from the 9th to the 13th century, abounds in Scandinavian place names of both manmade and natural geographical features. A careful perusal of these names provides some intriguing and instructive facts[4]: Names like *Quier* 'cattle-folds,' *Croigary* 'pasture of the cattle-fold,' and *Garrabost* 'enclosed farm' indicate the keeping of cattle and the consequent necessity for enclosed pasture and fields. *Rossal* 'horse-field,' *Hestaval* 'horse-hill,' *Hestam* 'horse-islet,' and *Roisnish* 'horse-headland' inform us that horses were also kept and that there must have been special grazing grounds for them. Some of them seem to have been pastured on islands for at least part of the year, and there appear to have been other islands which were primarily used for the pasturing of sheep (*Soay*), lams (*Lampay, Lamalum*) he-goats (*Haversay*), and calves (*Calva*), although the latter name is also applied metaphorically to small islands situated close to a larger one. Besides *Hestaval*, there are *Soval* 'sheep-hill' and *Neidalt* 'rough hill ground for cattle,' supplying further evidence for the practice of transhumance in Scandinavian Lewis, and in the Hebrides in general. Certain farms seem to have specialized in the keeping and breeding of certain animals, like *Geshader* 'goat-farm' and *Galson* and *Griosamul*, both referring to a pre-occupation with pigs. Other farms concentrated the growing of corn (*Cornabus*) or flax (*Linshader*); there is also the name *Lionel* 'flax-field.' The economic and culinary importance of fishing in both river and sea is reflected in such names as *Laxay* 'salmon-river' and *Shiltenish* 'herring-promontory.' Other names comment on the presence of fortifications (*Borve, boreray*), of a bridge (*Brue*) and of ecclesiastical buildings (*Kirkebost, Kirkipul*); others again convey a notion of personal ownership of permanent farms, as *Swanibost* 'Sveini's farm,' *Tolsta* 'Tholf's farm,' *Grimshader* 'Grim's farm,' and others. *Eoropie* 'Jorunn's farm' speaks of female ownership. Considering the paucity of our documentary evidence for Lewis and other Hebridean islands during the early Middle Ages, this toponymic information is a welcome and quite detailed addition. Naturally, it is possible to reconstruct similar pictures for other parts of the country.

The gap between place names and personal names is bridged by surnames derived from the names of locations, including fully-fledged place names. Hereditary surnames (about which more below) came into being in lowland Scotland mostly in the 13th and 14th centuries, while the Highlands followed suit much later.[5] When counted individually as names, this group of local surnames is much larger than any of the other three surname categories,[6] but undoubtedly the proportions would change if the individual bearers of all types of surnames were to be counted instead. It is significant in this respect that in both a list of tenants of the lordship of Fermartyne of 1382 and a list of members of the Guild of Ayr, *circa* 1431, surnames of relationship (the so-called "patronyumics") are the most numerous.[7] This change in emphasis does not, however, detract from the fact that in the Middle Ages many people were identified by an indication of their place of origin, like *Abercorn, Aberdour, Amisfield, Belhelvie, Colston, Eshiels, Fenwick, Glendochart, Hangingshaw, Kilconquhar, Middleton,* etc. Almost invariably, and certainly not surprisingly, persons bearing such names are mostly on record in places other than the ones from which they originated, according to their surnames, whether they were actually born there or had only lived there for a while.[8] For this reason, local surnames can be exploited as raw material for research on two topics about which otherwise there is very little known, i.e., the medieval hinterlands of some of the big cities and the degree and range of mobility exhibited by medieval people. Obviously, also, persons bearing surnames belonging to one of the other three classes—patronymics, occupational surnames and nicknames—did not necessarily remain stationary but, for one reason or another, changed their places of residence; the picture is therefore incomplete because their movements are not as directly traceable. It is, on the other hand, unlikely that their patterns and degree of mobility were very different from those of the sample group that carries their status as strangers or newcomers in their communities on their anthroponymic sleeves, so to speak. It is by implication the volume of movement, rather than the range, which eludes the name scholar, as long as the assumption is correct that persons bearing local surnames in the 13th, or perhaps even

14th or 15th centuries, had either themselves comes from the places indicated or had recent forebears who had left those localities, more often than not small places, both in size and importance.

A preliminary investigation of the hinterlands of the cities of Edinburgh and Aberdeen, as demonstrated by the presence of medieval bearers of local surnames, has shown that these are not terribly extensive and easily restricted by sizable natural barriers such as river estuaries or hill ranges.[9] Cities or big towns, according to this evidence, were clearly more attractive to those living in their vicinities, and their reputation as desirable places of work and residence for those with certain skills and inclinations did not usually outweigh the reluctance to travel long distances and leave one's familiar social environment behind. It should be possible to corroborate this conclusion by tests examining the occurrence of local surnames in terms of distance from their locations of origin,[10] but this is not an easy task to accomplish because of the skimpiness of the Scottish evidence.

The record is flawed in quite a number of ways, and consequently the demonstrable occurrence of surnames which can reliably be ascribed to definite localities of origin is sporadic with regard to the general populus before 1500. A major obfuscating factor is the recorded presence of many persons having surnames derived from the lands they own or the titles they bear. Since members of this "upper," frequently aristocratic, layer of society tend to hold military, political or ecclesiastical office, they are also found to be travelling or employed much farther afield, but without losing their direct links with the eponymous piece of land they own or which gave them their titles. Their presence at the royal court or at an important religious house hundreds of miles away from home does therefore not throw any light on the question of popular mobility. The record becomes much fuller after 1500, but whether this is to be attributed to the much larger number of documents available or a genuine scarcity of non-aristocratic surnames of local origin before the end of the 15th century is, at present, difficult to say. Only a systematic and comprehensive survey of the surnames of Scotland will tell.[10] Until the results of such a vast undertaking are available, one has to be content with meagre and spotty medieval evidence and with the projection of such observations, as the distinct regionality of certain modern surnames with toponymic affiliations, to the Middle Ages. After all, the distribution of such surnames is not likely to have been less restricted then that now, but rather more so.

We are on much less controversial ground in the assessment of surnames derived from a particular trade, occupation or office; name scholars and medieval historians alike have seized upon this extensive category as a potential source for the study of certain facets of medieval society.[12] Two issues in particular have attracted scholarly attention: the survival, in the form of surnames, of numerous medieval occupations which have ceased to exist as the result of industrialization and changing commercial practices, on the one hand; and "the surprising variety and specialised nature of medieval occupations,"[13] on the other.

In the former category, the name *Barker* (Patrick Barcar 1200)[14] recalls the now obsolete occupation of bark-stripper who produced and prepared an important ingredient for the process of tanning. *Bellman* (Gilbert Belman 1398) makes reference to the office of town-crier whose significance in the system of communications of a medieval town was considerable, putting official announcements against rumor rampant. Somebody would be called *Blindseil* (William Blindcele 1398), if he had the special job of sealing, or covering, the eyes of falcons used in hawking. A *Boyter* (Andrew Boytour 1510) would make "boxes," a *Buckler* (Robert Buklar 1402) "buckles," a *Challoner* (Robert Chaloner 1472) "chalons," i.e., coverlets for beds, a *Cordiner* or *Cordwayner* (Thomas Cordonar 1442) "shoes of goat-skin leather," a *Cutler* (Matthew de Coteleir 1296) "knives," a *Horner* (Nicholas Horner late 15th cent.) "horn-spoons," a *Lorimer* (Matthew Lorimer 1463) "bits, spurs, stirrup-irons, etc.," a *Naesmith* (Adam Nasmith 1420) "knives," a *Patternmaker* (Henry Patynmakar 1427) "patterns," i.e., "clogs," etc., etc. A *Brander* had the task of "branding" (fish) barrels. Hay was put up in "cocks" by a *Cocker* (Alexander Cokker 1363), and charcoal burned by a *Collier* (John Colzear 1582). The list of such obsolete or obsolescent occupations, as represented by modern surnames, is obviously much longer, but even from this brief example it becomes clear that it is of no consequence in this context whether a name is still semantically transparent (*Barker, Bellman, Buckler, Cutler, Brander*), merely suggestive as to its original meaning (*Naesmith, Cocker, Collier*), or totally opaque (*Boyter, Challoner, Cordinar, Lorimer*). As a record of medieval life they all carry equal weight, just as hereditary surnames, they are now all equally detached from their primary lexical meaning, despite a high instance of transparency or suggestiveness in quite a few examples.

In certain respects the list of names just paraded has already been illustrative of the second extraordinary phenomenon which has given scholars something to write about—the remarkable degree of specialization in medieval occupations, resulting in a wide terminological spectrum with fine distinctions and nuances and, subsequently, in a large variety of surnames originating from that finely shaded terminology. The brief catalogue of names derived from nouns depicting objects of manufacture (*Buckler, Challoner, Cordiner*, etc.) is a case in point; a full inventory of such names would naturally be even more persuasive. A similarly diversified background in the "making" of things has given us the many different kinds of names ending in —*smith* "a worker mostly in metal" and —*wright* "a worker mostly in wood." In addition to the simple names *Smith* (Robert the smith c. 1199) and *Wright* (Rauf le Wrighte 1296), we have compounds such as *Goldsmith* (Walter the goldsmith 1296), *Locksmith* (Robert lokessmyth 1214) "maker of locks," *Naesmith* (Adam Naesmith 1420) "knife-maker," *Shearsmith* (Andrew Schiersmythe 1479) "maker of shears," *Whitesmith* "worker in white metals," and *Wildsmith* (John Wyldesmyth 1259) "wheel-smith," as well as *Glasenwright* (Johannes Glasinwricht 1406) "glazier," *Plewright* (William Plewryght 1649) "plough-maker", *Sawright* (John Sawright 1570) "saw-maker," *Sievewright* (William Suffwricht 1512) "sieve-maker," and *Slaywrock* (Metylda Slaywrock 1348) "slay-maker" (Slaywright?), and *Wheelwright* (Johannes Quwelwrycht 1361—65) "maker of wheels and wheel-carriages."[15] In addition, a detailed analysis of the medieval surnames of neighboring

England has produced 99 compounds of —*maker*. The same studies have collected 40 names ending in —*monger*, reflecting an almost corresponding specialization in the handling of saleable commodities; often, of course, the maker, seller and mender of particular items was the same person.

When considering individual trades or industries, the degree of differentiation which emerges from an examination of documented surnames is even more astonishing. In England, as many as 165 medieval surnames refer to the cloth industry, names connected with weaving and dyeing being especially numerous; according to Reaney, "there are 18 different surnames denoting makers or sellers of hats, caps, hoods, etc."[16] It is worth noting in this connection that the output of cloth for export was highest at the end of the late 15th and the beginning of the 16th centuries,[17] so that a large and varied labor force was required in that particular industry. Other occupations and services well represented by surnames are the metal trades (108) and the provision dealers (107).[18]

Specialization was, however, not merely an urban trait in medieval society, as the various "herdsmen" in the personal nomenclature indicate: *Bulman* (Stephen Bulman 1662) "bull herd (?)," *Calvert* (Johannes Calfhyrd c. 1350) "calf-herd," *Coltart* "colt-herd," *Femister* (Alexander Feemaister 1458) "flock-master," *Gosman* "tender of geese," *Hird* (W. dictus Hyrd 1328) "herdsman, shepherd," *Hoggart* (Henry Hoggart 1525) "one in charge of hogs, i.e., young sheep," *Pastor* (William and Walter Pastor 1262) "shepherd, also clergyman," *Shepherd* (Henricuv Scyphard 1363), *Stoddard* (David Stodhirde 1376) "stot-herd," i.e., herder of bullocks," *Storrar* (William Sturor 1534) "in charge of flocks or herds," and *Wetherherd* (Thomas dictus Wethyrhyrde c. 1200) "wether-herd." Apparently bulls, calves, colts, geese, hogs, sheep, bullocks and wethers required their own herdsmen with special expertise concerning the animals in their keeping and, of course, separate pastures.[19] At the other end, some of the major products of these herding activities, meat and hides, were handled by correspondingly specialized slaughterers and a large number of occupations associated with tanning and the manufacture of leather goods. The processing of wool obviously became part of the cloth industry (see above).

An intriguing sidelight is thrown on occupations likely to have been carried out by women, by a small morphological group of names ending in - *ster*: *Baxter* (Reginald Baxter 1200—1240) "female baker," *Brewster* (Thomas le Breuester 1296) "female brewer," *Dempster* (Andrew Dempster 1360) "judex," *Litster* (Pieres le litstere 1296) "female dyer," *Sangster* (James Sankster 1452) "(female) chorister," *Walkster* (William Walkster 1739) "female fuller," *Webster* (Malcolm Wobstare 1436) "female cloth-weaver." The medieval evidence, and certainly that afforded by our surnames, is by no means unambiguous, insofar as even Old English -*estre* was sometimes used to designate male persons. The suffix was, however, the most productive of the very few derivative endings available to distinguish women, and it has been shown that there are at least thirty-eight Old English examples in which -*estre* is esclusively a feminine suffix,[20] like *keppestre* "saleswoman," *webbestre* "female weaver," *hoppystre* "female dancer," and *hearpestre* "female harper." Since many occupations could be carried out by both men and women, the suffix became neutral with regard to the indication of sex, in the early Middle Ages, and certainly names like *Dempster* and *Sangster* cannot be said to refer to women in our context. The other names, however, significantly denote tasks performed around the home—baking, brewing, dyeing, fulling, weaving—as part of the production of food and clothing,[21] an extremely limited and limiting circle of activities. In this respect, it is also worth recalling that *-estre* appears to have been created, in most cases, as the feminine equivalent of masculine agent nouns in *-ere* (Modern English *-er*), so that we have *Baxter* besides *Baker*, *Brewster* and *Brewer*, *Walkster* and *Walker*, *Webster* and *Webber*, but also the English *Dyster* and *Dexter* besides *Dyer*.[22] An enlightening glance at the world of medieval woman through the telescope of surnames!

III

Whether one seeks information about agricultural and pastoral activities in a Hebridean island under Norse rule, the hinterland of medieval Scottish cities, the mobility of Scottish persons in the Middle Ages, the occupational composition of medieval Scottish society, or the tasks performed by women in that society, names provide important clues, if sensitively and sensibly utilized. There are also numerous other aspects of popular culture in medieval Scotland for the elucidation of which names might be similarly and appropriately employed. Indeed, in all these pursuits, onomastics [the study of names] plays a handmaiden role, supportive of other disciplines, especially medieval social history, but also linguistics, archaeology, geography, ecclesiastical history and others. Because of the effectiveness of secondary extra-onomastic results achieved through the study of names, it is easily forgotten that, above all, names should be studied as *names* and should therefore be expected to have something to say about the act of naming and of name usage, both of which are, as we have already seen, processes involving most directly and essentially the "people" themselves.

Any essay trying to put into words some so-called "thoughts" concerning the significance of surnames in the popular culture of medieval Scotland would consequently have to be considered severely deficient if it neglected to pay any attention to these peculiarly onomastic properties and functions of names. In fact, everything said so far (especially since it cannot be claimed to be truly "new," except as a personal synthesis) can only act as a focussing device that will give selective substance and direction to the ideas and notions which are expressed in the following. Otherwise these reflections are bound to lose their most telling dimension.

As must have become apparent in the previous discussion, the various extra-onomastic conclusions, arrived at on the basis of onomastic evidence, without exception rely on, indeed require, the prior competent etymologization of the names in question, i.e., the successful reduction of these names to the words they once were and the disclosure of their embeddedness in the lexicon. Without this rediscovery of lexical meaning and the corresponding re-allocation of a slot in a live and meaningful vocabulary, the semantic opacity of a fair proportion of the evidence would prevent a convincing presentation and acceptance of such conclusions. If one extends Reaney's dictum that "occupational surnames originally denoted the actual occupation followed by the individual,"[23] to the other three categories of surnames, by stating that "surnames of relationship originally denoted the actual (paternal) parent whose child the individual was," that "local surnames denoted the actual place from which an individual had come," and that "nicknames referred to an actual characteristic of the individual so named," then this retrospective identification of name and word is, of course, justified. It is, however, necessary to stress in this context that these actual circumstances which gave rise to recorded surnames, regardless of whether they have survived or not, obtained only at that time when these very surnames were first created, i.e., when they became hereditary. At that time, as it had been for generations before, a person called *Crocker* was a *crocker* (or potter), a person called *Aberdour* had come from *Aberdour* in Fife or in Aberdeenshire, a person called *Thomson* had a father called *Thom(as)*, and a person called *Thin* was indeed of slender build.

Such lexically meaningful *by*-names or *to*-names were added to a comparatively small number of *font*-names, i.e., names given in baptism, that were, with few exceptions, no longer transparent semantically, having frequently entered English naming traditions from other languages, in quite a few instances through Biblical influence. In a manner of speaking, they were all *Nick*names (*eke*-names "additional names") needed to identify individuals in a society which had largely lost the knack of creative first-naming. Naming as the deictic act of identification was, however, not an isolating process, but one which placed the name bearer in a complexly structured societal setting. This was, of course, only possible if an identifying name was not only knowable but understandable. This excluded not only opacity but also privacy and secretiveness, and the facts from which recognizable characteristics were selected had to be publically discernible.

This need probably also accounts for the comparative lack of offensive nicknames in the surname network. Most of these would be used behind the individuals' backs or in their absence and would not be known to them; this would give them a semi-privacy which practically excluded them from ubiquitous, public knowability. Otherwise the four major categories of potential surnames are excellently suited for this purpose, and it is not surprising that one eminent modern name scholar calls the division into these "four broad classes ... the only sure ground" of surname lexicography.[24] One's genealogical links, one's place of birth or origin, one's occupation or office, and one's physical, sartorial and behavioral qualities are, in a sense, "outward" attributes which allow others to name and identify, and through the use of such names to re-identify, an individual. While the first three categories, if applied competently and correctly, contain factual information which permits no choice on the part of the outside names giver and names user, the fourth class—the so-called nicknames proper—admits of a certain degree of spontaneity and chance. After all, somebody may be *Brown, Thin, Little, Swift, Wise,* and a

Makepiece at the same time, and other things besides. It is by no means predictable what will strike his neighbors as his most noticeable peculiarity. Not unexpectedly, however, the number of nicknames in the Scottish surname repertoire is much smaller than that of any of the other three categories which are based on indisputable fact and not on imaginative interpretation of, or emotional response to, someone's visible nature.[25]

The act of lexically meaningful naming, then, puts the identified and identifiable individual into a social context. A person called *Aberdour* may thus be labelled as an incomer and be accorded stranger value and suspicion in Kirkcaldy and Aberdeen; an individual onomastically depicted as *Thomas(s)-son* is primarily seen as his father's offspring and made conscious of his family ties with the past; a man named *Goldsmith* may be associated with the excellence of the craft and the reputation of the guild. Thus names do not exist in a vacuum, have no real significance on their own, but function in contrast to other names, just as their bearers live in competition with and contrast to other persons. As a socio-cultural item, the meaningful by-name (the proto-surname), has its existence in the tensions of the lexical field in which the word from which it derives has its structural slot. A name locates an individual in society, not just in a geographical sense, as in the case of surnames derived from actual place names or from vague topographical ascriptions like *Hill, Wood, Milne,* or *Shaw.* Location through genealogical or occupational associations is just as common and just as valid. Quite apart from one's identification as a social individual, society itself is given, on this level and in this respect, a structure and cohesion, not easily reflected in any other linguistic manner. In this setting, naming reinforces identity in the context of socio-cultural relationships.

The changes triggered in the anthroponymic system—the havoc wrought is perhaps a more appropriate phrase—by the introduction of hereditary surnames can hardly be overestimated. This is not the place to present the apparent reasons for their introduction, except to say that they seem to have been Anglo-Norman rather than Germanic in origin, and that they were brought into being by the needs of administrators and officialdom rather than by a change of attitude among the people themselves. Although their development was gradual, beginning with the land-owning clases in the 12th century, the repercussions were nothing short of revolutionary and are most poignantly epitomized by an entry in the Royal Burgh Records of Stirling of 1525 in which *Agnes Beltmakar* is described as a *kaikbakstar!*[26] Two or three hundred years earlier she would clearly have been a "maker of belts and girdles," not a "baker of cakes."

As this example shows, the hereditary principle had some major consequences: the surname became detached from its lexical etymon and, even if word meaning was accessible as in the case of *Beltmakar*, ceased to function within the tensions of a current semantic field. In addition to many meaningless font-names, people were also more and more beginning to bear meaningless surnames. This increasing semantic opacity or irrelevance eliminated the surname as a viable locating device placing identified individuals in their rightful slots in contemporary society. Seeming contradictions like the one mentioned above no longer disrupt when the surname is no longer expected to mean as a word. Somebody called *Aberdour* may now have been born in Kirkcaldy, somebody named *Thomson* may have Peter as a father, and somebody bearing the name of *Little* may be of considerable physical stature. When the very occupations denoted by surnames have perished or decayed (*Barker, Gosman, Cordiner*, etc.), then the surname becomes nothing but a linguistic fossil useful perhaps in the reconstruction of medieval popular culture but without much direct relevance to the contemporary scene.

Instead of the semantic tension of fields of lexically meaningful surnames, we now find an extension of the genealogical principle of the *Thomson* and *Macdonald* variety, by which an individual is not so much identified in the present as in the past. All surnames have become surnames of relationship, and are, metaphorically speaking, "patronymics." In the chapter on "Scotland before the Reformation" in her book *Life in Scotland*, Rosalind Mitchison makes the following observation: "A kinship society...will be a status-dominated society with the key to that status, family, lying in the past. Not for nothing did most highland clans use as surname some filial derivative. A man's lineage was what mattered most to him."[27] Without wishing to stretch this point too far, one might argue that the introduction of hereditary surnames effectively turned medieval popular society into a kinship-oriented one.[28]

In such a situation, surnames function on an onomastic, albeit intra-cultural, level only; etymological strategies are no longer capable of revealing their meaning; and their knowability is not dependent upon their understandability. Their contents instead depends chiefly on what other individuals know about the bearer. Consequently, competence in name usage has much to do with the scope and intimacy of that name knowledge. Identification of individuals through surnames, hinging greatly on filial and uxorial links, is achieved almost exclusively through extra-linguistic processes. Administrative necessity has destroyed, or at least considerably affected and distorted, the denotation of individuality through multifaceted locatory devices. The knowledge that John is the son of Thom, comes from Aberdour, works as a beltmaker, and is small in size, is not conveyed by his hereditary surname *Smith*, or even by a less ubiquitous name like *Latimer*. To "know" the person John Smith or Latimer, such information has to be obtained independent of the lexically opaque onomastic evidence. In the later Middle Ages, therefore, onomastic fields no longer function in conjunction with the corresponding lexical fields, but only as a reflection of the socio-cultural constellation of their bearers, in relationship to each other. The onomastic revolution, caused by the introduction of hereditary surnames, has produced a new concept of self by abandoning the old language-bound devices of social location. It has also shifted the locus of identity and knowability from the name of a kinship-dominated system of linguistically opaque signs and ultimately to the labelled individuals themselves. The function of surnames as sanctuaries and reservoirs of identity has become quite circumscribed. A new era has begun.

Notes

[1](Donald) Mackinnon, "Place Names and Personal Names in Argyll. V. Archaic Words and Forms," *The Scotsman,* Nov. 29, 1887, p. 7.

[2]For details see W.F.H. Nicolaisen, *Scottish Place-Names* (London: B.T. Batsford, 1976).

[3]See the appropriate maps and text in *An Historical Atlas of Scotland c. 4000—c. 1600.* Eds. Peter McNeill and Ranald Nicholson (St. Andrews, Trustees of the Conference of Scottish Medievalists, 1975); also Nicolaisen, *loc. cit.*

[4]See Nicolaisen, "Life in Scandinavian Lewis," *The Scots Magazine* 78, No. 4 (Jan. 1963), p. 329; also *Scottish Place-Names,* pp. 97-98.

[5]"Surnames were rare in the Highlands till the sixteenth and seventeenth centuries when the younger and minor clans escaped the tutelage of the Island lords and the 'lieutenancies' of Huntly and Argyll. Individuals were designated by a string of ancestors, ending usually with the name of the croft or farm occupied, such as: — John MacHamish vic Aonas vic Allister Reoch *in* Ballachroan (1679). After the '45 matters rapidly changed; movements and expeditions to the Lowlands necessitated surnames; and these were adopted either from the clan to which the individual really belonged or to which he attached himself, or from the name of the district or place of origin. It has been a common thing for the smaller septs to sink their real surname in the bigger tribal or clan name." Alexander Macbain, "The Study of Highland Personal Names." *Celtic Review* 2 (1905-06), p. 63.

[6]According to P.H. Reaney, *A Dictionary of British Surnames* (London: Routledge & Kegan Paul, 1958), p. xv. See also Basil Cottle, *The Penguin Dictionary of Surnames.* Second Edition (London: Allen Land, 1978), p. 18.

[7]The exact figures are given by George F. Black, *The Surnames of Scotland: Their Origin, Meaning, and History* (New York: The New York Public Library, 1946), pp. xxiii—xxiv.

[8]See Cottle, p. 19; also P.H. Reaney, *The Origin of English Surnames* (London: Routledge & Kegan Paul, 1967), p. 36.

[9]The studies are still in progress and therefore not yet available in published form. As models might serve Rolf Bergmann, "Ein Kölner Namenverzeichnis aus der Zeit Erzbischof Hermanns I." *Rheinische Vierteljahrsblätter* 29 (1964), pp. 168-74; Rudolf Schützeichel, "Köln und das Niederland (Groningen: J.B. Wolters, 1963); "Die Kölner Namenliste des Londoner Ms. Harley 2805." *Namenforschung—Festschrift für Adolf Bach (Heidelberg: Carl Winter, 1965), pp. 97-126.*

[10]Some interesting facts and observations on this topic are contained in Gillis Kristensson, *Studies on the Early 14th-century Population of Lindsey (Lincolnshire). Scripta Minora Regiae Societatis Humaniorum Litterarum Lundensis* 1976-1977: 2 (Lund: W.K. Gleerup, 1977). See especially pp. 6-12.

[11]There is at present no surname equivalent to the Scottish Place-Name Survey of the School of Scottish Studies in the University of Edinburgh, and George Black's *Dictionary* (see note 7) remains the only extensive collection of Scottish surnames and their early recorded forms. David Dorward, *Scottish Surnames* (Edinburgh: William Blackwood, 1978) is a popular presentation of familiar names and their background.

[12]G. Fransson, *Medieval English Surnames of Occupation, 1100-1350* (Lund: C.W.K. Gleerup 1950); B. Sundby, "Some Middle English Occupational Terms." *English Studies* 33 (1952), pp. 18-20; M.M. Postan, *The Medieval Economy and Society: An Economic History of Britain in the Middle Ages* (Harmondsworth: Penguin Books, 1975), pp. 226-227.

[13]Reaney, *Dictionary,* p. xxxviii.

[14]Early documentation, when given, is from Black, s.v.

[15]These lists can be considerably expanded by the inclusion of complementary evidence from England, for which see, for example, Reaney, *Origin,* pp. 204-08. See also Elsdon, C. Smith, *The Book of Smith* (New York: Nellen, 1978).

[16]Fransson, p. 30, and Reaney, *Origin,* pp. xxxviii and 181.

[17]Postan, p. 227.

[18]Reaney, *Origin,* p. xxxviii (after Fransson).

[19]From England we might add *Coward, Eweart, Gathard, Geldart, Lambert, Nothard, Oxnard,* and *Swinard* (Reaney, *ibid.,* p. 177).

[20]Bogislav von Lindheim, "Die weiblichen Genussuffixe im Altenglischen." *Anglia* 76 (1958), p. 500.

[21]*Spinster* besides *spinner* would also belong here but does not seem to have resulted in a

surname. The Modern English word has, of course, undergone a semantic shift.

[22]Reaney, *Origin*, p. 356.

[23]Reaney, *Dictionary*, p. xxxviii.

[24]Cottle, p. 9.

[25]Most nicknames appear to be based on eye-judgments, but some moral and mental characteristics are also singled out.

[26]Black, p. 68.

[27]Rosalind Mitchison, *Life in Scotland* (London: B.T. Batsford, 1978), p. 15. See also note 5 above.

[28]One curious side-effect has been that modern surname lexicographers have been forced to emphasize expressly that "the purpose of a Dictionary of Surnames is to explain the meaning of names, not to treat Genealogy and family history" (Reaney, *Dictionary*, p. x), or that "names, not their bearers, are the characters" in such a compendium (Cottle, p. 10).

Medieval Pilgrims

Although the differences between medieval pilgrimage and twentieth-century tourism are perhaps obvious, the similarities between the two deserve closer scrutiny. This John M. Theilmann provides in a witty and insightful analysis of medieval pilgrimage.

By concentrating on the development of pilgrimage in medieval England, it is possible to examine not only the motives that first set people on the road but also the attendant social pressures as well. Medieval England was a society in which geographic and social mobility was extremely limited. The process of participating in a pilgrimage provided an acceptable means for leaving a local community for a time; moreover, the group fellowship for such pilgrimages often cut across social lines—as Chaucer's pilgrims delightfully demonstrate.

Pilgrimages were carried out for a number of reasons in medieval England—many for spiritual reasons, of course, but others for secular ones. Often the motives were completed mixed. The examination of both sets of motives—as well as examples of pilgrim behavior—helps to explain the origins of tourism in England and by extension in the western world.

John M. Theilmann is an assistant professor of History and Political Science at Converse College, Spartansburg, S.C. His research interests are in later medieval England and the history of popular belief systems.

Medieval Pilgrims and the Origins of Tourism

John M. Theilmann

Today, tourism is an accepted part of life in the western world with family weekends in the country and summer vacations. In the past this was not the case. Governments in western Europe severely limited peasant mobility in the 16th, 17th, and 18th centuries. In England, for example, laborers without a job could be whipped and returned to the parish of their origin. If society in the past took such a dim view of lower class mobility, when did tourism become a way of life in England? A facile answer would be the 19th century with a weakening of the bonds of society and increasingly cheaper transportation. A more convincing origin for present-day tourism centers around medieval pilgrimages.

There are differences between pilgrimage and tourism. One is a religious and the other a secular activity. Yet, pilgrims enjoyed seeing the sights and tourists claim educational and even spiritual benefits from their travels. By concentrating on the development of pilgrimage in medieval England, it is possible to examine some of the motives that set people on the road and some of the societal pressures surrounding pilgrimages.

Medieval England was a society in which spatial mobility was extremely limited. Serfdom (until its decline in the 14th and 15th centuries) bound peasants to the land, and even free peasants had their mobility circumscribed by law and custom. Yet, the process of taking part in a pilgrimage, often to a saint's tomb, provided an acceptable means for peasants to leave the local community for a time. Pilgrimages were carried out for several reasons in medieval England—many for religious reasons, but others for secular ones or a mixture of the two. Both sets of motives help to explain the origins of tourism in England, and by extension in the western world.

Pilgrimage played an important role in the religious life of medieval England.[1] Throughout the Middle Ages people participated in pilgrimage as a means of venerating the memory of the saints. Saints' cults took many forms, from the internationally known ones of St. James at Santiago de Compostella in Spain or St. Thomas Becket at Canterbury to the unofficial cults that grew up around little William of Norwich in the 12th century or King Edward II in the 14th century. The Church expected that people would improve their spiritual conduct through learning about the saints, and pilgrimages provided a ready means for accomplishing this goal. Some pilgrims, however, expected more from the saint whose tomb they visited. Some people traveled to saints' tombs seeking an intermediary with God in solving personal problems—perhaps a twisted leg or even a lost cow—or to commemorate successful cures. The Church accepted and even encouraged the medical motivation for pilgrimage, and canonization processes included miracle lists as evidence of the saint's miracle working abilities. Not all pilgrims set off voluntarily; some were forced to go on a pilgrimage as penance for their spiritual or secular sins. Both lay and ecclesiastical authorities encouraged penitential pilgrimage in part because malefactors were forced to depart from the community, often for extended periods of time.

Heretofore the reasons for pilgrimage were acceptable to the clerical and secular authorities. Some pilgrims had very unreligious motives. Thieves, cutpurses, and bawds all plied their trade along pilgrimage routes, often posing as pilgrims. Other pilgrims emulated Chaucer's wife of Bath in going on a pilgrimage merely to see the sights, to get away from home, or to find a spouse. Most pilgrims did not consciously take part in a pilgrimage as a holiday, especially peasants who could ill-afford the expense or the time and would have had trouble leaving the manor on such an errand. However, from examining what few pilgrim narratives are extant, it seems that even the most devoted pilgrims took notice of the sights along their routes (Howard, Zacher).

In the 11th, 12th and 13th centuries the ecclesiastical and secular authorities seem to have encouraged pilgrimage as a noble endeavor for all elements of society save one—the monastic community. Although the religious hierarchy was aware of the spiritual benefits that accrued from taking part in a pilgrimage, they feared the temptations of the road and the threat to monastic discipline posed by pilgrimage (Constable). Monks and nuns could take part in pilgrimages but only after receiving the permission of their superiors. Even though this permission was not always forthcoming, a suspicion arises that monks and nuns set off anyway. From the tone of the Archbishop of Canterbury's (Robert Winchelsey) letter in 1310 it seems that he was addressing a reoccuring problem in forbidding the monastic clergy from setting off on a pilgrimage without first obtaining their superior's permission (*Registrum Winchelsey* 1:43-14).

Where did pilgrims go? Throughout the Middle Ages Jerusalem was the goal of devout Pilgrims, but one attainable by few. The nobility might be able to leave home for more than a year for a pilgrimage to the Holy Land, but few peasants or merchants could do so. The shrine of St. James at Santiago de Compostella was a popular one during the Middle Ages, one that Englishmen of all classes visited although at great sacrifice for the poor (*Paston Letters* 1: 465, Oursel). Rome too was popular. Nearer to home, Englishmen had an international shrine with the tomb of St. Thomas Becket at Canterbury. Even though pilgrims thronged the major pilgrimage sites, and Canterbury and the shrine of Our Lady at Walsingham remained popular throughout the Middle Ages, most pilgrims did not visit these major shrines. Instead, they visited the shrines of saints close to home.

The proximity of saints' tombs was an important consideration for many pilgrims. When driven by medical necessity, it made sense for the ailing to seek first the aid of local saints. If a local saint failed to give relief, a sufferer then turned to a saint farther afield. For example a man from Ropham, Lincolnshire, first sought the aid of St. Edmund and received some measure of relief at Bury St. Edmunds, but St. Edmund appeared in a dream and told him to go on to St. William's tomb at Norwich to complete his cure (Thomas of Monmouth 236-39). Some saints drew pilgrims from a quite small area. Forty-two percent of the 13th century St. Thomas Cantilupe's miracles were recorded from a distance of 20 miles of less from his tomb at Hereford and only 13% from a distance greater than 100 miles.[2] St. Thomas Becket's miracles displayed the opposite relationship with only 15% of the miracles from distances less than 20 miles and 54% from distances greater than 100 miles (William of Canterbury, Benedict of Peterborough). A more common ratio can be seen in the cults of Simon de Montfort and Henry VI with the bulk of their miracles falling between 20 and 100 miles (64% and 65% respectively) from their tombs.[3] Although not all miracle recipients journeyed to the saint's tomb, enough did so that these percentages give an indication of where pilgrims came from. Local pilgrims could hardly be classified as tourists, but saints also attracted pilgrims who had to travel two or more days in order to reach their tombs. Two examples serve to illustrate this point: Eremburga, an old woman from London, traveled to Becket's tomb at Canterbury in 1171 and was cured of her dumbness there, while a man from Werrington, Staffordshire, was cured of his gout on a pilgrimage in Simon de Montfort's tomb at Evesham, 65 miles from Werrington (William of Canterbury 53, Benedict of Peterborough 92, *Montfort* 75).

Pilgrimage was ostensibly an individual spiritual encounter, but pilgrims wanted others to know of their travels, just as is the case with many tourists today. Pilgrims often dressed the part; the usual sign of a pilgrim was the staff and the script. A person cured of a limp at a saint's tomb had a tangible sign of his pilgrimage when he returned home. Others returned with souvenirs of their journey such as a conch shell from Compostella or a palm from Jericho. Although it is impossible to know when pilgrims first began to acquire badges or other souvenirs, they were commonplace by the high Middle Ages. For example, pilgrims to St. Thomas Becket's tomb acquired small vials of water that were proclaimed to contain a drop of the martyr's blood. Becket's water, as it was called, itself had curative powers. Benedict of Peterborough reported that William of London regained the sight of one eye when a drop of Becket's water was applied and obtained full sight after completing a pilgrimage to Canterbury (83). Badges were available at the tombs of other saints as well; there are at least 90 varieties of badges depicting Henry VI as a saint (Spencer 238). A well-traveled pilgrim might even display several saints' badges on his hat proclaiming the extent of his journeys. The custodians of saints' tombs encouraged the use of badges instead of practices such as chipping away a piece of the tomb itself (Thomas of Monmouth).

This latter practice leads to the consideration of pilgrim actions in general. On the whole, pilgrims were well-behaved, although some took the opportunity of a pilgrimage for roistering or even story telling as did Chaucer's pilgrims. The clerical custodians of the shrines were aware of the impure motives of some pilgrims. Benedict of Peterborough, the recorder of St. Thomas Becket's miracles, was suspicious of the validity of a cure of blindness of a woman from Oxfordshire even though he credited St. Thomas with the cure (139-40). The ailments of other pilgrims were more genuine but the cries of the insane hardly led to a dignified atmosphere at pilgrim shrines. Even the devout could be troublesome. Margery Kempe's continual weeping at the passion of Christ partially explains her difficulty in keeping traveling companions on her journeys to Canterbury, the Holy Land, and Compostella.

The custodians of saints' shrines were not totally innocent when it came to pilgrim misbehavior. It was to their benefit to encourage large numbers of pilgrims to visit their shrines because a flood of pilgrims and miracles helped to provide evidence of the sanctity for a yet as uncanonized saint. Care was taken to record all miracles that occurred as a result of the saint's intervention, even those of questionable validity. The Church hierarchy was aware of such practices, and by the late 13th century part of the canonization process included a full investigation of the prospective saint's reputed miracles (Kemp, 104-05). These investigations were time-consuming because witnesses had to be examined.When the papal commissioners visited Hereford in 1305 to examine Thomas of Cantilupe's miracles, they had time to investigate only 17 of his more than 400 miracles (*Acta Sanctorum* 1: 609-39). Clerics had another motive for encouraging large numbers of pilgrims to visit their shrines: the offerings left by pilgrims. Part of the St. Andrew's aisle in Gloucester cathedral was financed by the offerings made at the tomb of King Edward II, a reputed saint, albeit an unlikely one.[4] St. Thomas of Cantilupe's shrine at Hereford also proved profitable to the cathedral chapter, yielding 178 10s. 7d in 1290-91 (Yates 79, Morgan). The shrines of St. Thomas Becket at Canterbury and Archbishop Richard Scrope (a reputed 15th century saint) at York also were profitable for their cathedrals.[5] Unfortunately for most cathedral chapters, the fame of their saint declined over time and so did the donations. By 1 386-87 the once popular Cantilupe shrine provided only 1 6s. 8d (Yates 79).

Enhancing the prestige of their cathedral or monastery also motivated clerical supporters of saints cults. This search for prestige (and revenue) led to outright theft at times as representatives from one monastery stole the relics of another (Geary, Hermann-Mascard 364-402). The Church roundly condemned relic theft in the high and late Middle Ages, and there appears to be little evidence of it in England. On the other hand, in 1498 the Westminster cathedral chapter, the custodians of St. George's Chapel at Windsor, and Chertsey Abbey in Berkshire all claimed to be the legitimate final resting place for the remains of Henry VI. All three had good reasons for claiming the body. Henry was first interred in the Lady Chapel of Chertsey Abbey following his murder in 1471. In 1484 Richard III had the body disinterred and reburied in St. George's Chapel. Westminster was already the resting places of other English kings, particularly St. Edward the Confessor. Even though the dispute was resolved in favor of Westminster, the reinterment never took place (Wilkins 3: 635-36, Stanley 506-21). If Henry VII had carried through the projected attempt to secure Henry VI's canonization, the possession of the new saint's remains would have become a valuable addition to the relics at Westminster Abbey.

The 13th century was the heyday of pilgrimages with a wide variety of new and old shrines, official approval of pilgrimages, and an improving economy to support them. In the 14th and 15th centuries official and popular attitudes toward pilgrimage underwent changes, changes that ultimately called the validity of the institution into question.

Already in the 13th century, and more often in the 14th and 15th centuries, there were other movements that led the poor to take to the road. Late in the 13th century some people began to leave their homes to follow leaders who proclaimed that the millennium was nigh. In the 14th century the massive social dislocation and sheer terror caused by the spread of the plague from 1348 onward induced people to join flagellant processions. Initially these groups included members of the middle class and even the nobility, but gradually these people dropped out and criminals or radical leaders took control of the flagellants. On the continent clerical and secular authorities were coming to regard flagellants and the various other millenial groups as a danger by the end of the 14th century and took measures to suppress them. Any movement that involved the peasantry in large numbers became suspect. Pilgrimages were not condemned, but the authorities became more wary of them. Although there is little evidence of large-scale millennial movements in England, a fear of this sort of social disorder existed. The chronicles are uniformly hostile to what they saw as milleniarism in the speeches of the priest John Ball to the peasants during the Peasants' Revolt of 1381.[6]

In addition to setting some of the millennial groups in motion, the Black Death decimated the population of Western Europe. Landlords in England no longer had enough free or unfree peasants to work their land. The labor shortage existed well into the 15th century, leading some landlords to be chary of allowing peasants to leave the village community for any reason. No English monarch went so far as to prohibit pilgrimage. Nonetheless, the crown was aware of the dangers of unrestrained pilgrimage. In 1388 the Statute of Canterbury ordered that a laborer setting off on a pilgrimage should have a letter patent stating where he was going, why, and when he would return. Moreover, the laborer could not tarry in any one place along the way for more than one day unless he was ill.[7] The Statute of Cambridge was an effort to curtail the mobility of laborers, but in the 15th century attention was turned to the disturbance of public order caused by poor pilgrims. Edward IV came close to Winchelsey's command to the monastic community in 1473 when he ordered that "no person go in pilgrimage not able to perform it without begging, unless he have letters testimonial under the great seal ordained for the same, testifying the cause of his going and the place whence he came and whither he shall go" (*Calendar of Close Rolls, 1465-1476 299*). Edward's order, which reiterated earlier prohibitions, would have severely circumscribed pilgrimages by the poor, but there is no way of knowing how vigilantly it was enforced.

By the late 15th century secular authorities were trying to curtail pilgrimage, and when the Reformation occurred in the 16th century the institution came under further attack. When saints' tombs were destroyed, there no longer existed an excuse for traveling to other parts of the country. The Elizabethan poor laws made it clear that local authorities were to return idlers with no purpose in the parish to their point of origin (or at least get them out of the parish). This is not to say that England suddenly became a cheerless society in the 16th century, but that one acceptable reason for leaving the village community had been removed.

The Protestant reformers of the 16th century strongly opposed the cult of the saints and its appurtenances, but even in the 15th century there were signs that the spiritual value of saints and pilgrimage was being questioned by some Englishmen. One reason was that the Lollards, followers of the teaching of John Wyclif, denied the religious validity of the saints in addition to pointing out the expense of pilgrimages and the often unholy side effects associated with them. The cult of St. Thomas Becket in particular came in for criticism with some Lollards asserting that Becket was a traitor not a saint (Thompson, Davis). Lollardy did not have a wide following, but it helped to raise questions about the value of pilgrimage. Attitudes toward pilgrimage among the reforming elite hardened in the 16th century, as seen in Erasmus's satire in "A Pilgrimage for Religion's Sake" (285-312).

A second reason for the 16th century reformer's attack on pilgrimage was that the institution had changed by the 15th century. The spiritual aspects of pilgrimage had been in decline for some time, and by the 15th century this was evident. The use of penitential pilgrimages as part of the judicial machinery of the Church and the state deminished their holy aura. There had always been saints of less than perfect reputation. The increase in the number of saints' cults by the late Middle Ages made it more likely that people would be exposed to a "saint" who exhibited few saintly virtues such as the cult of Richard Fitzalan, earl of Arundel in the last years of Richard II's reign. After Richard had the earl executed for treason in 1397, a cult formed around his tomb and people claimed that the head had been rejoined to the trunk.[8] The cult was patently political in nature, but by extension it called into question the motivation for other cults. Even the business-like fashion in which some clerics regarded pilgrimage harmed its reputation.

Spirituality and public regard for it comprised the third reason for the decline of the pilgrimage. By the 15th century pilgrimage, along with other ritual aspects of religion, was being transformed into civic ritual in some areas. Groups of people often joined together on a pilgrimage throughout the Middle Ages. Their aim was to enjoy the fellowship of the group and to obtain protection as they took part in the pilgrimage. Chaucer's pilgrims were from a more disparate background than most groups, but their love of good fellowship was no exaggeration. Groups such as the London Mercers Company in the 15th century also took part in pilgrimages, but they had the additional motivation of publicly showing their religious devotion as a specific group (*Acts of Court* 139). As Mervyn James has demonstrated in regard to Corpus Christie processions (another aspect of mass religious ritual), urban society was becoming hostile to public ritual of this sort in the 15th century, emphasizing instead private ritual (21-26, also Thomas 51-77). Most Englishmen still believed in the efficacy of pilgrimage in the 15th century, but as the opponents of pilgrimage as an institution combined with those who feared it as a potential cause of disorder, it became doomed to steady decline.

Even though reformers, and ultimately the state, attacked pilgrimage, they only drove it underground. As J.J. Scarisbrick has observed, the English Reformation was imposed from the top down; people continued to believe in the ritual of the medieval church (54-56). One consequence of being driven underground was that Roman Catholic religious practice became more personal and private, a trend that was already underway. Elsewhere, too, collective religious practices were giving way to individual action (Christian 207). Only with the return of toleration in the 19th century came a return of mass pilgrimages in England. Today, Canterbury pilgrimages have been revived albeit as primarily tourist opportunities. In Roman Catholic countries pilgrimage survived the Reformation. The site of St. Patrick's Purgatory in Laugh Derg in County Donegal, Ireland, has overcome the vicissitudes of changes in official attitude and continues to flourish today (Turner and Turner 104-39). There are differences in 20th century and late medieval pilgrimages. Marian pilgrimages predominate in the 20th century, but, as Stephen Wilson has shown, the saints still come in for their share of attention. Many of the old attitudes also remain. The diversity of pilgrim motives remains: from the spiritual to the self-serving. A spirit of hucksterism also can be found that stretches from Harry Bailly to advertisements that promise a tour of the Holy Land "where Jesus walked."

Because of its diminution in the 16th century, pilgrimage was in some ways a false beginning for tourism. But even though direct comparisons are not reliable, the English examples pictured here suggest some insights. Pilgrimage provided a socially acceptable means for mobility in a closed society, although normally as a secondary motive. Today, some tourists claim that visiting Disneyland is a learning experience and that seeing the sights is secondary. There was a strong financial side to pilgrimage from the costs to the pilgrim for the trip and souvenirs to the profits for the owners of the saints' relics. At times pilgrims behaved in less than admirable fashion and so too did the custodians of the shrines. Both medieval pilgrimage and modern tourism helped break down social barriers through exposing people to new people and places. There are, of course, major differences; the most fundamental is the religious motivation that is at the core of pilgrimage. Medieval pilgrimage was a religious activity with a concern for the spiritual improvement of society at its core. Pilgrimage has undergone changes, and today it is difficult at times to distinguish between pilgrims and tourists. Indeed, major religious sites, such as Chartres Cathedral, are themselves the goal of many tourists.

Pilgrimage first set people on the road in large numbers, and it is unnecessary to belabor the point by suggesting further examples of pilgrim behavior that can be found in modified form in 20th century tourism. Through examining pilgrimage as an aspect of popular culture in the past, we are able to see 20th century tourism in sharpened focus.

Notes

[1]A convenient starting point for examination of medieval pilgrimage is Sumption. See, also: Ladner, Vauchez, and Theilmann, "Communities." For the general question of travel see Jusserand.

[2]*Acts Sanctorum,* 1: 609-61. Ms. Vat. lat. 401 f 123-45. The Cantilupe miracles are discussed in Bannister and Finucane.

[3]*Miracles of Montfort.* Henrici VI Angliae regis. Henry's miracles are discussed in Theilmann, "Miracles."

[4]*Historia et cartularium monasterii Sancti Petri Gloucestriae,* 1: 46.

[5]Woodruff; *Testamentia Eboracensia,* 232; *Fabric Rolls of York,* 214, 32, 37.

[6]Walsingham, *Historia Anglicana,* 2: 32-33. Continuation of *Chronicon Henrici Knighton,* 2: 139-40.

[7]Statute 12 Richard II, caps. 3, 7, in *Statutes of the Realm,* 2: 56-59.

[8]Walsingham, *Annales Ricardi Secundi,* 3: 218. For 14th century sainthood see Bray and Kieckhefer.

Surprised by Love

The Wakefield Shepherds' Pageant has been one of the most discussed of medieval dramas and deservedly so. Edmund Taft's fresh and insightful essay provides a provocative view of the play as popular drama, produced by the middle-class and largely for the middle class. The popular appeal of this drama rests in the technique of dramatic surprise, used so effectively by the Wakefield Master to focus on such contemporary social and moral issues as oppression of shepherds, farmers and hired hands, unfeeling masters, unwanted children and marriages of contract only. The shepherds' play, with its powerful spiritual message of love and charity, reflects not only the Church which directed the drama but also the contemporary world of those medieval burghers who produced it.

Edmund M. Taft is a Ph.D. candidate in English at the Pennsylvania State University; his main area of interest is the drama.

Surprised By Love:
The Dramatic Structure and Popular Appeal
of the *Wakefield Second Shepherds' Pageant*

Edmund M. Taft

3 Pastor. Fare wordys may ther be, bot luf is there non
This yere.
(The *Second Shepherds' Pageant*, 11. 569-70)

Late medieval and early Renaissance drama, especially the mystery plays, reflect a culture that is essentially both religious and popular. Written by town clerics yet acted by local tradesmen, associated with the Feast of Corpus Christi yet an occasion for commercial enterprise, the cycle plays or pageants attracted a large and varied audience, "bothe more and lesse, / Gentillys and yemanry of good lyff lad" (11. 7-8),[1] according to the N Town *Banns*. Indeed, the composition of the typical audience was even more diverse than the *Banns* suggest, as Arnold Williams explains:

Remember that the audiences towards which the great cycle plays were directed were popular, the burgesses of provincial towns, their servants, the gentry, free folk, and perhaps serfs of the surrounding countryside, a sprinkling of the clergy and the nobility, on occasion even including a royal visitor.[2]

No playwright could ask for a more heterogeneous audience or, what is more important, for a better occasion to effect meaningful reform through what Sir Philip Sidney would later term the artist's responsibility "to teach and delight."[3]

108

We can be sure that the greatest of the medieval playwrights, the Wakefield Master, was well aware of this opportunity when he began to write his most famous play, the *Second Shepherds' Pageant*. Yet the Wakefield Master faced certain difficulties in writing this play as well, difficulties which he confides to the audience near the end of the *Second Shepherds' Pageant*. Daw's authorial comment—"Forsothe, allredy it semys to be told / Full oft" (11. 749-50)—admits the danger of presenting the nativity, a story that has been told and retold so often that its plot may seem perfunctory and its theme obvious or even commonplace. Poised at the outset of the play between opportunity and difficulty, then, the Wakefield Master needed to find some way to present the birth of Christ from a new, fresh perspective that would guarantee the attention of the audience and simultaneously focus on the need for reform, always a central concern of this playwright.

The Wakefield Master solved this dramatic problem neatly and brilliantly by using the technique of surprise. Because the *Second Shepherds' Pageant* is so familiar to us, we sometimes fail to appreciate how it must have affected the members of a medieval audience. They would expect the play to open in the past, during the period of the Old Law, but the pageant begins essentially in the present, under the New Law, with three contemporary shepherds who face the same problems as many in the audience. The spectators would anticipate moving quickly from the complaints of the shepherds to the nativity itself, but the Wakefield Master postpones Christ's birth until the last one hundred lines of the play. What is more, between the shepherds' complaints and the nativity scene the dramatist places the misadventures of Mak the sheep-stealer, surely the greatest surprise of all.

Though modern audiences have been pleasantly surprised by these innovations, the same cannot always be said for modern critics of the pageant. Influenced by the 20th-century concern for unity of structure and theme, A.C. Baugh's often quoted complaint—"The length of the Mak episode is hopelessly out of proportion to the proper matter of the play"[4]—mirrors the confusion and misunderstanding on the part of many critics. To add to the difficulty, the standard critical approaches, typology[5] and tropology,[6] provide only peripheral insights and fail to reveal fully the Wakefield Master's artistic intention. The central theme of the *Second Shepherds' Pageant*—the theme which each part of the play develops and emphasizes—is the need for a social order founded on mutual love and respect, in short, the need to rediscover and re-implement Christ's gift to mankind: the New Law. Because the playwright's subject is the necessity of recovering the New Law, he fills the beginning of the play with "anachronisms," references to the present time of the audience. In this way such problems as the oppression of peasant farmers and hired hands, the terror of unfeeling masters and proud, disdainful servants, and the misery of unwanted children and marriages held together only by contract all combine to present the members of the audience with an image of their own world in which the New Law seems lost or forgotten, despite Christ's sacrifice of Himself for all mankind. In addition, the Wakefield Master's subtle connection between the present and the past would not be lost on an audience expecting a nativity play: if men forget, misunderstand, or trivialize the meaning of the Incarnation, then life seems more hopeless after Christ's birth than before.

The Wakefield Master's emphasis on the present brings the complaints of the three shepherds into focus, for each of them poses essentially the same question: Where are the justice and mercy promised by the New Law to be found? At the start of the play, Christ seems present only in their oaths, not in their lives. When Daw asks why the world "is wars then it was," he is not complaining about "inversions" of the Old Law;[7] rather, as a contemporary shepherd, he questions the New Law, for the condition of mankind after the Incarnation appears worse than it was before Christ's birth. As the pageant begins, Coll worries about the same problem:

> Lord, what these weders are cold! Am I am still happyd.
> I am nerehande dold, so long have I nappyd.
> My legys thay fold, my fingers ar chappyd.
> It is not as I wold, for I am all lappyd
> In sorow.
> In stormes and tempest,
> Now in the eest, now in the west,
> Wo is him has never rest
> Midday nor morow!
>
> Bot we sely husbandys that walkys on the moore,
> In faith, we are nerehandys outt of the doore.
> No wonder, as it standys, if we be poore,
> For the tilthe of oure landys lyis falow as the floore,
> As ye ken.
> We are so hamyd,
> Fortaxed and ramyd,
> We ar mayde handtamyd
> With thise gentlery-men. (11. 1-18)

After Coll grows numb from the cold, he grows numb with sorrow, for the particular storm he is experiencing becomes a metaphor for his own life: filled with tempests, buffeted on all sides, without a time to rest. The source of the first shepherd's dismay ("It is not as I wold") is really his feeling of restriction and frustration because of the injustices in the world, a point of view which the deprived and the disadvantaged in the audience recognize immediately as essentially their own. In addition, the well-to-do in the audience perceive at once that they are responsible for the plight of the poor and the underprivileged—either directly, through their own lack of charity, or indirectly, through the excesses of their subordinates. The opening of the play, then, illustrates that justice and mercy are missing from the playwright's artfully constructed mirror of the 15th-century world. Everyone, especially the rich and the powerful, needs to rediscover Christ's legacy to mankind: the New Law.

Both Gib and Daw share Coll's frustration and his sense of restricton, of being bound so tight that action seems either impossible or totally unavailing. Gib complains that once a man is married, "Woe is him that is bun", / For he must abide (11. 80-81), and Daw notes with amazement how recent floods have paralyzed the people and filled them with doubt and wonder (11. 127-35). William Manly and, more recently, Linda E. Marshall have argued that the shepherds' observations about nature and their complaints about social inequities create a climate of foreboding and impending doom; such signs, according to them, hail the advent of Antichrist, whose agent is that devil incarnate, Mak.[8] Yet to feel that the world is going downhill fast, as all three shepherds do, is a perpetual characteristic of human nature; every generation tends to think that life has become unbearable and that, in general, things cannot get much worse than they are now. The Wakefield Master exploits this psychological reaction so that the audience perceives the three shepherds as fundamental representatives of mankind. As D.W. Robertson, Jr., writes, "To return to the mystery plays, we may conclude that their relevance arises from their bearing on the present seen as a manifestation of events perennially recurring not in literal space and time but within the human heart."[9] Thus, the problems of the shepherds are recurring, not anomalous, and from a psychological point of view the audience would believe that the timeless plight of the shepherds reflects the present with fidelity.

The appearance of Mak is not only another surprise to the audience but also a calculated attempt by the Wakefield Master to explore one kind of response to the shepherds' perception that their lives lack the justice and mercy promised by the New Law. For the most part, Mak sees the world as the three shepherds themselves see it. William Empson emphasizes that Mak and Gill are "fundamental symbols of humanity,"[10] and the evidence in the play bears this out, especially in regard to Mak, who at one time or another feels threatened by the weather, complains about injustice, laments his poverty, bemoans the state of matrimony and despairs at the prospect of providing for all his children. Josie P. Campbell points out that "Mak is like a mirror reflecting the shepherds' concerns, but they refuse to see their own reflections."[11] This is never more apparent than in Mak's first speech:

Now, Lord, for thy names seven, that made both moyn and starnes
Well mo then I can neven; *thy will, Lorde, of me tharnys.*
I am all uneven; that moves oft my harnes.
Now wold God I were in heven, for the[re] wepe no barnes
So still. (11. 190-94, emphasis added)

Mak's world, like that of the shepherds, appears intolerable, and existence is basically a mystery which puzzles and perplexes him. If Daw laments the state of nature in which "all things writhys," Mak finds the same mutability and lack of fundamental order within himself: "I am all uneven." However, what limits and restricts the three shepherds becomes, paradoxically, a source of "freedom" for Mak. Whereas the shepherds shrink from a world that fails to live up to their expectations, Mak tries to manipulate the world by adopting whatever pose fits or seems to fit the situation:

What! ich be a yoman, I tell you, of the king,
The self and some, sond from a greatt lording,
And sich.
Fi[e] on you! Goith hence
Out of my presence!
I must have reverence.
Why, who be ich? (11. 201-207, emphasis added)

Mak directs his final question to the audience as well as the shepherds. At stake are two opposing conceptions of the self. Although the shepherds can define Mak only in one way (as a thief), Mak finds that the possibilities inherent in the self are nearly endless. Before he is finally exposed, Mak will change shapes with comic rapidity; in the course of the sheep-stealing farce he feigns sickness, pretends to be first a yeoman and then a magician, plays the loving father of a newborn son, and even mimics his own hanging, as Gill notes when Mak arrives home for the second time (11. 408-12).

Seldom has one speech functioned with as much economy as Mak's burlesque of the king's yeoman. In addition to its philosophical implicatons, the speech demands to be acted in such a way that we learn something about Mak and something of the Wakefield Master's artistic intention. As Mak struts before the shepherds, posturing and waving his hands in an exaggerated, "official" manner, the spectators realize that here is a man who, at bottom, yearns for a secure place in society, a position of respect and admiration which will reinforce his personal sense of worth ("I must have reverence"). If, as many commentators speculate, the actor who plays Mak also plays the Angel when the three shepherds wake for the second time, the playwright wryly fulfills his character's wish, for Mak becomes, as Maynard Mack, Jr., rightly points out, "more and more the messenger 'from a greatt lordyng,' (1. 202), 'a yoman, I tell you, of the kyng' (1. 201), in ways unimaginable when he first claimed such authority."[12] Moreover, by indirections the Wakefield Master finds directions out, working through Mak's hilarious impersonation of authority to afford most of the audience a chance to laugh at their "betters," while inviting these same "betters" to perceive their absurdity and to laugh at themselves.

The reactions of the audience reflect the ambivalence built into the character of Mak. On the one hand, the spectators who tend sheep for a living and who are accountable for them probably react to Mak much as the first shepherd, who succinctly tells Mak where he can "sett in a torde." On the other hand, Mak's energy and zest contrast favorably to the weary shepherds who lie "stone-still" as he goes about his vocation. While the sleeping shepherds lie huddled together in a momentary attempt to escape from a world of misery and woe, Mak takes the opposite tack by attempting to steal from the world what it cannot give: "Now were time for a man that lakkys what he wold / To stalk prevely than unto a fold" (11. 269-70). On a literal level, what Mak does is wrong, and there is no doubt that the audience judges him harshly for stealing a sheep. But from a metaphysical and an iconographical point of view, Mak tries to steal the mercy and grace which seem absent from his own life. A medieval audience would know perfectly well that Mak takes more than just a sheep: he steals the Lamb of God Who takes away the sins of the world and Who grants us mercy and peace. After the theft, Mak tells his wife, "Thus it fell to my lott, Gill: I had sich grace" (1. 314). Lawrence J. Ross has demonstrated that the author is careful to keep both the literal lamb and its symbolic importance in the forefront as the sheep-stealing farce unfolds,[13] and a medieval audience aware that it is watching a burlesque of the nativity could not fail to recognize the humor and the pathos inherent in Mak's wrongheaded prank. Equally important, Mak's theft shocks the three shepherds into action, and their quest after the lost sheep is also a metaphoric search for grace and mercy.

Those who view Mak as the Devil or as an agent of Antichrist have on their side the ominous opening of the pageant and the repeated references in the play to Mak as a devil. One might add that Mak practises "false doctrine" insofar as his willingness to take on whatever image the situation calls for embodies his fear that the universe is without order and without an ethical center—two concepts that neither the Wakefield Master nor his audience would accept. Yet precisely this kind of universe seems to threaten the three shepherds as the play begins. Mak differs from the shepherds only inasmuch as he tries and fails to deal with the world on its own terms.

This is a very human kind of error, one which many in the audience would recognize in themselves. Rather than have the audience see the contrast between the shepherds and Mak in terms of good versus evil, the Wakefield Master aims at making the members of the audience understand why they all act like Mak sometimes. Mak's behavior is perfectly rational if self-interest is the only absolute value. His actions are irrational and self-defeating if, despite appearances, the New Law really does exist.

Moreover, there are at least four objections to identifying Mak with Antichrist or with the Devil. If the audience really thought that Mak represented either one, the spectators would wish him hanged once the shepherds expose him; yet the Wakefield Master denies this kind of punishment for Mak. Next, if Mak were really evil, his spells and incantations would have some power. Clearly, however, the three shepherds fall asleep because they are tired, not because of Mak's black magic. Third, the three shepherds accept Mak as fundamentally like themselves—as Gib says, "Mak, freyndys will we be, for we ar all oone" (1. 566). Lastly, Mak repents and willingly submits to punishment (11. 622-23)—two acts of which Antichrist, the Devil, or any of their party are incapable. All in all, then, the Wakefield Master presents Mak as devilish, not as a devil.

Discovering the right way to respond to Mak and his family leads the shepherds and the audience to the thematic center of the subplot, the recovery of the lost sheep. D.W. Robertson, Jr., provides the best explanation of what happens during this scene, although he sees the time of the action as essentially before Corpus Christi:

When the shepherds, under the inspiration of the "youth" among them who shows from the outset glimmerings of wisdom, and whose charitable impulse leads to the discovery of the stolen sheep, are led to perform an act of mercy, substituting a toss in a blanket for the legal death penalty for stealing after Mak has shown repentance (lines 622-623), they have, in effect, implemented the New Law and are thus in a position to discover Christ.[14]

Robertson is undoubtedly correct in seeing Daw's impulse of love as the pivot of the play: "Mak, with youre leyfe, let me gif youre barne / Bot six pence" (ll. 578-79); furthermore, in terms of the play's structure and plot, Daw's act of charity prepares the audience for the nativity scene to come, as does Mak's toss in a blanket, which signifies the audience's desire to see

justice tempered with mercy, signals the end of the farce, and announces
that the play is hastening to its close: the manger scene and the birth of
Christ.[15] However, from a thematic point of view the three contemporary
shepherds have not implemented the New Law but re-implemented it; just
as the sheep, the Lamb of God, has been lost and then found, so the New
Law, Christ's gift to mankind, has been lost and then recovered. Thus, the
shepherds' rediscovered capacity to love and to show their love by action
answers the question that they themselves posed at the opening of the play:
Where are the justice and mercy promised by the New Law to be found? The
three shepherds demonstrate to themselves, to Mak and Gill, and to the
audience that the New Law cannot be discovered in the world, but it can be
found in the human heart. What is more, by recapturing what seemed lost or
forgotten—the meaning of the nativity—the three shepherds emphasize the
need for and the possibility of change, despite the intransigence of the world
and of the worldly. Forgoing the death penalty is a revolutionary act, albeit
a small one, which emulates the greatest of all revolutionary acts: that God
would send His only begotten Son to suffer and to die for all men, to win
them a better life in this world and the promise of an eternal life in the next.

Viewing the subplot of the *Second Shepherds' Pageant* in this manner
explains the "contemporary relevance" of the play as well as the process
through which the Wakefield Master puts the audience. Like the three
shepherds, the audience dispenses with the official penalty for sheep-
stealing and conquers its anger at Mak and its frustration at a world in
which love seems absent. When they do so, the members of the audience
discover what the three shepherds discover: the New Law exists in their
own minds and hearts. Moreover, the complexity of the Wakefield Master's
theme—where and in what way the New Law operates—determines the
construction of his play and explains why those who see the subplot only as
a preliminary to Christ's birth feel that the complaints of the shepherds and
the sheep-stealing farce are "hopelessly out of proportion" to the main
plot—the birth of Christ. However, if the theme of the pageant is really the
New Law and how it applies to the spectators watching the play, then the
emphasis which the Wakefield Master places on the subplot becomes
evidence of is his comic genius.

Because structure reinforces theme in the *Second Shepherds' Pageant*,
the main plot focuses immediately on Christ's birth by providing the
familiar signs of the nativity: the Herald Angel singing "Gloria in
Excelsis," and the star to lead the way to Bethlehem. In other words, once
the shepherds and the audience have been "surprised by love," they are
ready to understand that the Incarnation, the supreme gift, demonstrates
both the origin and the essence of the New Law:

Angelus. Rise, hyrd-men heynd, for now is he borne
        That shall take fro the feynd that Adam had lorne;
        That warloo to sheynd, this night is he borne.
        God is made youre freynd now at this morne,
        He behestys.
        At Bedlem go se
        In a crib full poorely,
        Betwix two bestys. (ll. 638-46, emphasis added)

God reveals through his messenger that love is the principle of order and harmony in the universe, the gentle bond which unites "high" and "low," even the Creator with the created; and the members of the audience discover that Gib's gift of friendship to a sheep-stealer—"Mak, freyndys will we be, for we ar all oone" (l. 566)—echoes Christ's gift to them: "God is made your freynd now at this morne."

After the Angel departs, the shepherds delay the most important journey of their lives long enough to join together and imitate the celestial harmony of the Herald's song:

2 Pastor. Say, what was his song? Hard ye not how he crakyd it,
        Thre brefes to a long?
3 Pastor.   Yee, Mary, he hakt it.
      Was no crochett wrong, nor nothing that lakt it.

(ll. 656-58)

Thus, nature imitates supernature and the community of man, represented by the three shepherds, consciously attempts to reflect the divine order in a song of praise whose very rhythm ("Thre brefes to a long") signifies not only the mystery of the Trinity but also the eternal perspective from which the audience is to view Christ's nativity. The prophets and prophesies recalled by the shepherds on their journey, the manger scene recreated in the theatrical present, and Mary's parting command to the shepherds, "Tell furth as ye go" (l. 744), unite memory, perception and hope, that is, past, present and future into one moment of historical time when the ideal became real, a moment of perfection which endures, so long as men remember it vividly and properly, as *the* model of familial, social and universal harmony through mutual love.[16]

When the three shepherds join the Holy Family in the manger, both "high" and "low" are united by gift-giving, by love in action. Although the symbolic import of the shepherd's gifts is intentionally general, Daw's tennis ball, a present from one youth to another, illustrates the proper relationship between those of high and low degree. Distressed at the Infant's poverty and His old clothes, Daw gives a gift which acknowledges Christ's true position in society, for tennis was a game of the nobility. In return, Christ's unspoken gift of Himself—so at odds with the actions in the subplot of gentrymen, retainers, and "men that are gretter" (l. 36)—sets the standard for all, particularly for those whom Christ has left in positions of temporal or spiritual authority.

Restrospectively the audience realizes that the Wakefield Master's diversity of technique has led to unity of theme. The double plot of the *Second Shepherds' Pageant*, the play's sophisticated time scheme, and the engaging character of Mak are all designed to capture and maintain the interest and attention of the audience so that the message of this pageant— the necessity for a fair and just social order based on the New Law—will not be lost. Daw's wry comment about how often the story of Christ's birth has been told not only reveals to the audience the author's problems in writing a nativity pageant but also leads the spectators out of the main plot, from the demonstration of harmony and order provided by the scene in Bethlehem to the world at large as it was reflected in the subplot. At the conclusion of the pageant the three shepherds walk off into this world as well, leaving behind a sacred tableau which reminds the spectators of their duty to be caretakers of the New Law and to make God's work their own.

Notes

[1] All quotations from the mystery plays are from *Medieval Drama*, ed. David Bevington (Boston: Houghton Mifflin, 1975).

[2] "Typology and the Cycle Plays: Some Criteria," *Speculum*, 43 (1968), 677-84.

[3] *The Defense of Poesy*, in *The Renaissance in England*, ed. Hyder E. Rollins and Herschel Baker (Lexington, Mass.: D.C. Heath, 1954), p. 608.

[4] *A Literary History of England* (New York: Appleton-Century-Crofts, 1948), p. 281.

[5] Largely because of Rosemary Woolf's fine article, "The Effect of Typology on the English Mediaeval Plays of Abraham and Isaac," *Speculum*, 22 (1957), 805-25, "typology" or figural exegesis has become an important way of analysing medieval drama. Although no one doubts that, for example, Isaac, whose sacrifice anticipates the crucifixion, prefigures or is a "type" of Christ, the uncritical use of typology too often makes no more than a technical puzzle out of what is really imaginative drama. See Arnold Williams' essay (note 2 above) for some helpful distinctions about the use and misuse of typology.

[6] D.W. Robertson, Jr., "The Question of 'Typology' and the Wakefield *Mactacio Abel*," *American Benedictine Review*, 25 (1974), 157-73, criticizes the use of typology because "it is a severely limited subject, theoretical rather than practical" (p. 158), and the author goes on to suggest that typology implies "tropology"—employing contemporary verisimilitude to insure that Biblical stories apply to the everyday life of the audience. Robertson's explication of *The Killing of Abel*, utilizing his understanding of tropological effects, is both learned and convincing, as is his tropological analysis of the *Second Shepherds' Pageant*. Nevertheless, the massing of "anachronisms" in the first two-thirds of the Wakefield Master's second nativity play seems to me to go beyond tropology and to firmly establish the time of the action as the present. This is the basic premise from which my argument begins.

[7] Robertson argues that "The complaints of the shepherds at the opening of *Secunda pastorum* are essentially complaints about the reign of the Old Law, with its attendant inversions, in contemporary society" (p. 163). But when these "inversions" begin to pile up, they become the rule, not the exception, and the natural result is to wonder about the New Law, whether or not somehow men have lost or forgotten it.

[8] William M. Manly, "Shepherds and Prophets: Religious Unity in the Towneley *Secunda Pastorum*, *PMLA*, 78 (1963), 151-55; Linda E. Marshall, " 'Sacral Parody' in the *Secunda Pastorum*," *Speculum*, 47 (1972), 720-36.

[9] Robertson, p. 164.

[10] *English Pastoral Poetry* (New York: Norton, 1938), p. 29.

[11] "The Polarization of Authority: A Study of the Towneley Cycle," Diss. Pennsylvania State University 1972, p. 122.

[12] "The *Second Shepherds' Play*: A Reconsideration," *PMLA*, 93 (1978), p. 83.

[13] In this important and influencial article, "Symbol and Structure in the *Secunda Pastorum*," *Comparative Drama*, 1 (1968), 122-149, Lawrence J. Ross not only points out the relationship between the stolen sheep and the Lamb of God (pp.136-37) but also asserts that both the comic subplot and the main plot are united by the theme of "the recovery, at the birth of a child, of what was lost" (p.138). Properly relating this insight to the beginning of the pageant clarifies the complaints of the three shepherds in the first part of the play and provides a perspective which reveals the thematic unity of the entire work.

For more recent studies of structural and thematic unity in the *Second Shepherds' Pageant* not alluded to elsewhere in my essay see David Lyle Jeffrey, "Pastoral Care in the Wakefield Shepherd Plays," *American Benedictine Review*, 22 (1971), 208-21; Lynn Remly, "Deus Caritas: The Christian Message of the *Secunda Pastorum*," *Neuphilogische Mitteilungen*, 72 (1971), 742-48; and John Gardner, *The Construction of the Wakefield Cycle* (Southern Illinois Univ. Press, 1974), pp.85-95.

[14] Robertson, p.165.

[15] Maynard Mack, Jr., writes of Mak's punishment, "Claude Chidamian, 'Mak and the Tossing in the Blanket,' *Speculum*, 22 (1947), 186-90, suggests that the blanket tossing was

symbolic as well, being a traditional way of hastening childbirth, but this seems hardly relevant since it is Mak, not Gyll, who is so punished" (p.85, note 8). But if, as Maynard Mack, Jr., himself argues, "Mak is the play's energizer" (p.80), then clearly the blanket toss not only symbolizes the function of both Mak and the sheep-stealing episode but also points us toward the nativity scene to come.

[16]Josie P. Campbell has pointed out to me the resemblance between the Wakefield Master's use of time in the *Second Shepherds' Pageant* and T.S. Eliot's in "Burnt Norton":

> Time present and time past
> Are both perhaps present in time future
> And time future contained in time past. (11. 1-3)

Milton's conception of time in "On the Morning of Christ's Nativity" also invites comparison.

"Quike Bookis"

In the Middle Ages, when schools and literacy were rare, and when priests were often ignorant of the central tenets of their faith, children could learn more of the Bible from Corpus Christi drama than from many other sources. Perhaps for this reason, a Wycliffite preacher who strongly disapproved of the plays condemned them as "quike bookis," or living books.

As Professor Hanks points out, children learned more than Bible stories from the "quike bookis." They learned a philosophical and theological concept of time and a view of history which was "at once universal, providential, and apocalyptic." They also learned—perhaps to a modern reader's surprise—an attitude toward contemporary spiritual and secular upper classes which amounted to condemnation.

Thus, according to Hanks, the cycle dramas were not only richly entertaining and profoundly moving, but they were in their way revolutionary in their view of the contemporary society.

D. Thomas Hanks, Jr. is an Associate Professor in the Department of English, Baylor University.

"Quike Bookis"—The Corpus Christi Drama and English Children in the Middle Ages[1]

D. Thomas Hanks, Jr.

That each generation of human beings devotes a great deal of time to passing its values on to its children is a commonplace observation. The observation is only commonplace, however, because of the importance recent generations have attached to the activity of inculcating values in youth. Widespread "free" education, the education industry, the past decade's worries about the loss of values and the consequent need for "value education" in the school all attest to our concern for transmitting values to our children.

This concern was perhaps less often voiced in the English Middle Ages but it was still a preoccupation of adult society. The major transmission of values during this period doubtless took place in the home, and to a degree in religious services. It must be remembered, though, that the bulk of the church service was in Latin, and that sermons in English, especially on the parish level, were infrequent (see the oopening chapter to H.S. Bennett's *Life on the English Manor: 1150-1400*. [Cambridge, Eng.: Cambridge University Press, 1937], especially pages 32-33, for a "real-life" exposition of this fact). Schools too were much fewer, and illiteracy was, of course, widespread.

How then were the values spread which in our culture come to youth via television, newspapers, schools, churches, etc.? A full answer to this question would require a longer discussion than is appropriate here, but part of that answer is the matter of this essay. As the title suggests, and as I shall argue here, the Corpus Christi drama of the English Middle Ages was one of the major means by which the adult generation transmitted some of its values to the younger generation.

English children were attending religious plays at least as early as the 12th century, according to William Kettell. Ketell writes (*ca.* 1150) of a play of Christ's resurrection presented in the Beverley churchyard. A great crowd attended—so great a crowd, in fact, that many children could not see over the heads and shoulders of the adults. The children, frustrated, went into the church and began to climb about. One boy climbed too high, lost his hold, and, to the noisy horror of the onlookers, fell to his death on the stone floor. Luckily Bishop John of Beverley came hastening at the outcry and was able miraculously to restore the boy to life.[2]

No such melodrama is recorded for the later Corpus Christi drama of medieval (and Renaissance) England. One cannot doubt, though, that children attended the cycle plays of Corpus Christi as eagerly as they had attended the liturgical drama of an earlier day. Scholars agree that all medieval English literature was equally accessible to children and adults;[3] the most accessible literature would have been the cycle plays—which played in nearly every major English town every year from 1335 to about 1600.[4]

*   *   *

Certainly children would have attended—and paid attention to—the cycle plays. Wholly aside from the obvious point that children like spectacle—especially spectacle hallowed by adult interest, like Christmas parades—the cycles attracted the young by portraying children on stage, by presenting villains of entertaining but scary frightfulness, and even by incorporating children's games into the plays.

Children appeared on-stage in all the extant cycles.[5] In many cases they the had decidedly minor parts—the infant Christ, for example, was presumably represented by a doll, as certainly the male children must have been in each cycle's slaughter of the Innocents—but the four "boys" of *Chester's* "Shepherd's Play" present lengthy speeches (*Chester*, pp. 151-154), as does the boy Isaac in three of the cycles where he is a boy (*Chester, Ludus Coventriae* and *Towneley*). *Ludus Coventriae* presented the best roles for children; both the infant Mary in "Mary in the Temple" (pp. 71-82) and the youthful Christ of "Christ and the Doctors" (pp. 178-187) are the protagonists of their plays. Mary appears "as a childe of iij yere age" (*Ludus Coventriae*, p. 71, 1. 9 and stage direction) and Christ is a character young enough to be teased with being called "lytyl babe" and directed to go home, sit on his mother's lap, nurse for his meal, and wear a bib (*Ludus Coventriae*, p. 179, ll.41-43). Young though they are, each soon dominates her or his play and the adults who appear in it (this would certainly have gratified watching children).A youthful Christ also dominates *York's* "Christ and the Doctors" (pp. 174-181). Each cycle, in short, presented one or two major roles for children as well as several minor ones. These stage-children—most or all of whom would have been portrayed by local youths—

would certainly have riveted the attention of child spectators.

Perhaps even more attractive were the cycles' villains, each both funny and frightful Herod in *Chester's* "Three Kings" is a good example: he brandishes, in turn, a staff, a sword, a bill, his sword again (which he throws down with a clatter, then breaks), his staff once more, and a second sword—all in the space of ten minutes or less, as he rages, throws his staff into the air, and repeatedly promises to chop off the head of the new king of whom the magi tells him (*Chester*, pp. 163-174). Herod's actions are certainly funny, and his sanguinary threats as frighteningly attractive as a later's age, "I smell the blood of an Englishman! Be he alive or be he dead, I'll grind his bones to make my bread!"

Herod is less funny and more frightening as he later calls up his two knights, Sir Grymball and Sir Lancherdeepe, and orders them to murder all new-born males: "Goe slaye that shrewe; ... Dryve down the dyrtie-arses .... All knave-children ... you must sley this nighte" (*Chester*, p. 190, ll. 139-152).

Recall that Herod is only one of a distinguished group of gratifyingly evil villains: Cain, King Balaack, Pharaoh, Herod the Great, Caiaphas, Pilate and various *tortores* add their wrongdoings and rages to the cycles' portrayal of the City of Man, while Satan and his demons appear at intervals to testify to or fulfill the destiny of the unGodly (in *Ludus Coventriae*, for example, "Diabolus" carries King Herod and his murderous knights off to hell immediately following the slaughter of the Innocents—p. 176, ll. 232ff). These villains and their comeuppances would certainly have been as enjoyable to medieval children as my generation found the black-hatted enemies of Tom Mix and their inevitable defeat.

Youthful spectators would have found the game element of the cycles as interesting as the plays' portrayals of children or villains. Much of that game element V.A. Kolve has already discussed in "The Passion and Resurrection in Play and Game" in his *Play Called Corpus Christi* (Stanford: Stanford Univ. Press, 1966, pp. 175-205). The most notable of the games he finds portrayed in the cycles is probably "Hot Cockles," a game which medieval English children played by having one of their number kneel, cover his or her eyes, lay his or her head in another child's lap, and, as the other children lightly struck him or her, try to guess who struck the blow.[6] In the Passion plays of the Corpus Christi drama Christ is always "it," and "Hot Cockles" becomes the buffeting of the biblical accounts of Christ's arraignment before Caiaphas (in Matthew 26:67-68, Mark 14:65, Luke 22:63-64, but not appearing in John). In the biblical accounts, Christ's captors blindfold Him (in Mark and Luke) and buffet Him, demanding (in all three gospels which contain the buffeting) that He "prophesy" who struck Him. This event, already containing several of the ingredients of "Hot Cockles," quickly became a dark version of that game in the playwrights' hands. Thus in *Towneley* the "primus tortor" refers to the buffeting as "a new play of yoyll [yule]" which the tormentors will teach Christ (p. 239, l. 344); they blindfold Him, then strike Him in turns, rivaling one another in the shrewdness of the blows and demanding as they bring their game to a close,

> 'Sit up and prophesy!'
> 'But make us no lie.'
> 'Who smote thee last?'
> 'Was it I?'[7]

The game element—especially in the "players' " rivalry—is clear in *Towneley*. It is still clearer in *Ludus Coventriae*, where a game rhyme accompanies the buffeter's blow:

> 'Wheel and pill, wheel and pill,
> Come to the hall whoso will,
> Who was *that*?' (he strikes).[8]

There are other games in the cycles, some darker of humor than "Hot Cockles," others nearer the cheerful everyday games of children. Kolve comments upon the game which the tormentors make of the Crucifixion;[9] I shall not repeat him, but instead turn to the more lighthearted games. They appear prior to the Passion, and take place more or less in passing. Wrestling is one such game; the *Chester* shepherds wrestle with their "Garcius," or "boy," on stage (pp. 135-138). The boy calls the wrestling a "game" (p. 136, l. 246) and enjoys it hugely. He throws all three of his elders and goes his way rejoicing as they lie groaning. The *Towneley* shepherds of the "First Shepherds' Play" do not wrestle, but they too engage in game: Gib, counting his chickens well before they're hatched, imagines himself driving non-existent sheep over pasture claimed by John Horne, who takes umbrage and insists the "sheep" be driven elsewhere. The two nearly come to blows before a third shepherd intervenes in the game of "let's pretend" which is becoming serious (*Towneley*, pp. 103-104, ll. 101-142). The *Towneley* "Second Shepherds' Play" mentions yet another game, in a curious context: Daw, the third shepherd, gives to the Christ child the gift of a ball, saying, "have and play the[c] with all, / And go to the tenys" (*Towneley*, p. 139, ll. 735-736).[9]

Whether tennis, wrestling or "Hot Cockles," the game element of the cycles joined with their portrayal of children and their horrific villains to ensnare the attention of medieval English children.

*   *   *

What, then, would these children have seen in the plays aside from other children, villains and games? Most noticeable, as I suggested earlier, would have been the spectacle: horse-drawn pageant-wagons, (where they were used); costumes and special effects like the smoke and flames from Hellmouth, or Christ's ascension into the clouds, or the "flying" of *York's* angels. Only slightly less noticeable would have been the sheer entertainment offered by such scenes as Mak's being tossed in a blanket in the *Towneley* "Second Shepherds' Play" (p. 136) or the panicked flight of "Juvenis" as he brandishes a sword in one hand and holds up his trousers with the other in the *Ludus Coventriae* "Woman Taken in Adultery" (p. 204). Certainly there was much of spectacle and entertainment in the plays.

There was also much serious content. While children found considerable delight in the cycle drama, they also found a great deal of instruction in the values of their culture. Specifically, they learned a philosophical and theological concept of history implicit in cycle structure; they learned the devotional stories central to their Christian tradition; and, surprisingly, they learned an attitude of outright condemnation of the upper classes, both secular and religious.

The structure of the cycles was Christ-centered, as indeed was the medieval English concept of time. Children learned this view of time simply by watching the cycles unfold: each began with the Creation, moved quickly through major Old Testament events, arrived at Christ's conception, birth, youth, passion and resurrection—events which make up the bulk of each cycle—then ended with Doomsday, or the Last Judgment. This sequence mirrors a view of time and history which began with Plato's *Timaeus* (transmitted by Chalcidius), developed in the works of Augustine, Boethius and Aquinas, and flowered into the patristic concept of *figura*—the single concept which, more than any other, shapes the cycle plays.

Chalcidius' translation of Plato's *Timaeus* (fourth century A.D.) presented to the Fathers the idea of sacred time as opposed to profane time. The *Timaeus* avers that "deus," existing unmoving in eternity, created a moving image of that eternity. This image is time (eternity, meanwhile, remains separate from time, intact and singular). We may apply terms like "was" and "will be" only to time, the *Timaeus* continues, but not to eternity; eternity remains perpetual and immutable, and of it we can only say, "It is." In short, God—Who exists in eternity—exists outside time in His own sacred time which is best termed an "eternal present."[10] Augustine, Boethius and Aquinas adopted this dual view of God's time and earthly time; Augustine summarizes the concept as he writes of God's perception of His creation in *The City of God*:

He does not pass from this to that by transition of thought, but beholds all things with absolute unchangeableness; so that of those things which emerge in time, the future, indeed, are not yet, and the present are now, and the past no longer are, but all of these are by Him comprehended in His stable and eternal presence (Bk. XI, Ch. 21).[11]

This idea that God perceives all events in time at once in His eternal *now*, led the Fathers very early to the concept of *figura*.[12] *Figura* embodies the concept of God's simultaneous perception of all events: it is essentially the belief that events distant from one another in chronological time are nonetheless closely related in "God's time" (or, more accurately, God's timelessness). Thus—as Erich Auerbach explains in "Figura"[13]—a significant person or event (the "figure"), real in itself, prefigures another significant person or event. Put more simply, this usually meant that "the persons and events of the Old Testament were prefigurations of the New Testament and its history of salvation."[14] Thus, Cain's murder of Abel is a *figura* of the Crucifixion of Christ, as is the (near-) sacrifice of Isaac, the only child, by his father Abraham. Likewise, Moses' delivery of the Israelites is a *figura* of Christ's delivery of mankind from its sins, and the story of Noah and the flood is a *figura* of the Last Judgment—where God will save the good and damn the wicked.

The concept of *figura* was accepted throughout medieval England as through all Europe.[15] The most obvious evidence of its acceptance in England is the Corpus Christi drama itself: the cycle plays embody *figura* in virtually every episode. The examples just cited demonstrate the cycles' use of *figura*: Cain's slaughter of Abel appears in all four extant cycles, as do the sacrifice of Isaac, the play of Noah, the Crucifixion, the Last Judgment and many other figures and fulfillments.

The playwrights were clearly aware that they were employing the concept: *Ludus Coventriae's* Jonah announces in the "Prophets" play that Christ will rise from death on the third day, as was

> fyguryd in me þe which longe beforn
> lay iij days beryd with in þe qwall.

(Ludus Coventriae, p. 60, ll. 69-70)

In the same play Solomon refers to his famous temple as a "fygure" of the maid who is to bear the Messiah (p. 59, ll. 40-42), and Daniel makes a similar reference to "fygure" (p. 59, ll. 60-62). In *Chester's* "Last Supper" Christ uses the term; He tells His disciples

> ... the tyme is come
> that sygnes and shadowes be all donne.
> Therfore, make haste, that we maye soone
> all figures clean rejecte.

(Chester, p. 271, ll. 69-72)

I have not found the term *figura* elsewhere in the plays, but these explicit references, plus the numerous uses of the customary figures and their fulfillments, make it clear that the concept permeated and unified the cycles.

The point of this necessarily lengthy discursus is this: from the plays they saw yearly, children would have learned painlessly what it has taken me several painful paragraphs to summarize: a view of history which is at once universal, providential and apocalyptic, a history whose theme is "the general development of God's purposes for human life."[16]

Such a view of history is profoundly meaningful to the maturing child; it leads the child to see his or her universe as orderly, ordered and ruled by a God who sees all. The existential *anomie* of the modern cannot exist in individuals with this world view. They must see their world as filled with interrelated events moving to a known end, an end which for each individual is the logical outcome of the choices he or she has made during earthly life. Thus in the Judgment plays of the cycles, "Regina Damnata" laments choosing lechery instead of chastity in the *Chester* "Judgment" (p. 447, ll. 269-76), the *Ludus Coventriae* "Anime dampnandum" bewail their "mysdede" in "Doomsday" (p. 375, l. 67); and, more positively, the *Towneley* Christ informs the "Boni" that when others had needs, they gave help—and thus they shall rest with Him in Heaven ("The Judgment," pp. 382-83, ll. 450-73). St. Paul's "all things work together for good" comes close to summarizing this ideology; it is an ideology which informs each cycle. Even the Fall of Man works eventual good: in time to come, a seraph tells Adam and Eve in the *Ludus Coventriae* "Fall of Man," a child shall be born of a maid and "saue all that ye haue forlorn / Your welth for to restore."

The child's developing ego needs an ideology, as Erik Erikson has pointed out in detail.[17] In the cycle plays, medieval English children found the chief ideology of their age, an ideology which made sense of their universe and also made their universe a hopeful one.

Inseparable from the ideology communicated by cycle-play structure are the devotional stories which flesh out that structure. Children learned from the plays the matter as well as the form of their tradition; they learned the story of Creation, of man's fall, of the Patriarchs, of Christ and His life, death and resurrection, and of His final judgment of mankind. In an age when Sunday schools and literacy were equally rare, and when priests were often either ignorant of the central elements of their faith or reluctant to communicate what they did know,[18] the child would learn more of his Bible from the cycle plays than from any other source—perhaps more than from all other sources. To quote a Wycliffite preacher who strongly disapproved of the plays, they were "quike bookis"—living books[19]—for children, most of whom had no other access to Book or books.

Children learned more than Bible stories from the "quike bookis" of the cycle plays. They also learned—to a modern reader's surprise—an attitude toward the contemporary religious and secular upper classes which amounted to outright condemnation. Consider the following reconstruction of the *Towneley* "Buffeting" (pp.228-242):

> two knights chivvy the captive Christ to a pageant in the play area. Its curtain opens to disclose two resplendent figures seated on ornate chairs. Both wear gold and silver mitres, amices and ornately embroidered dalmatics over scarlet albs (the headgear and clothing of medieval English bishops). Each grasps a crosier. The two are Cayphas and Anna, prelates and lords in degree (*Towneley*, p. 233, l. 154). They hear the two knights' "charges" against Christ.
>
> The more brightly clad of the two soon flies into a rage at Jesus, who stands silent. Cursing and threatening, Cayphas is barely prevented from striking, then stabbing, the quiet defendant. Anna[s] finally quiets Cayphas by agreeing to allow the two knights to beat Jesus. The two cheerfully prepare to "clowte well his kap" (*Towneley,* p. 238, l. 335), but the first knight asks a favor:

> > 'But or we go to this thyng,
> > sayn vs, lord, with thy ryng'
> >
> > (*Townley*, p. 239, ll. 339-340)

In short, he asks Bishop Cayphas for his blessing—for the sign of the cross made with the hand that bears the episcopal ring. Cayphas genially responds:

> > 'Now he shall haue my blyssyng
> > That knokys hym the best'
> >
> > (*Towneley*, p. 239, ll. 341-342)

Thus spiritually fortified, the two knights set to it.

What have watching children seen? They have seen their Lord driven like an animal, then beaten by two English knights—members of the lesser aristocracy. They have seen Him harangued and sentenced to a beating by a bishop—one of the "lords spiritual" who tour their town and its environs upon occasion. The Jewish high priest and member of the Sanhedrin has not appeared on this stage. Instead, a contemporary bishop has offered his blessing to the tormentor of his Lord. This may surprise a modern reader, but bishops are villains in all the cycles: in *Ludus Coventriae* a sympathetic Pilate tells Christ that "Busshoppys and prestys" love Him not (p. 291, l. 587); in *York* Cayphas the "Busshoppe" (so termed on p. 248, l. 183 and p. 251, l. 327) says of Jesus, "This same day muste he be slayne" (p. 253, l388); and in *Chester* it is "bushoppe" Cayphas who orders the blind Longeus to spear Christ on the cross (p. 320, ll. 372-378).

Secular lords appear to equal disadvantage. Knights (lesser aristocrats) capture, torment and crucify Christ in the cycles—and slaughter the Innocents as well. The higher aristocracy, as is only fitting, are the greater villains: Herod the Great, Herod Antipas and Pilate.

Herod the Great, we learn in *Ludus Coventriae*, is attended by knights and dukes and is a crowned king (p. 152, ll. 13-16; pp. 154-155, ll. 82-83). He is also a despotic oppressor who rages intemperately, orders the slaying of the innocents, and threatens to hang and draw or otherwise slay "traytors" who threaten his kingship (*Ludus Coventriae*, p. 272, ll. 11-29; cf. *Chester's* Herod, pp. 163-174, 185-204; *Towneley's* Herod, pp, 140-181; and *York's* Herod, pp. 16646-173). Herod Antipas is cut from much the same cloth: in *Chester, Ludus Coventriae* and *York* he tries Christ in court and taunts Him before he returns Him to Pilate (see, e.g., *York*, pp. 275-80. Herod Antipas does not appear in *Towneley*).

Pilate, like the knights and the Herods, is both aristocrat and villain. Like Herod the Great he is a "kyng with crowne" and a "rewler of great renowne"(*Towneley*, p. 204, ll. 11-13), who frequently addresses his peers in the Norman French of the upper class (as in *Chester*, p. 339, ll. 1-8). He is also the very type of ruler who, through weakness (*York*) or malevolence (*Towneley*) condemns the innocent. Though he is a king (or "prince"—the plays use both terms), he appears in the cycle plays primarily as a judge (except in *Chester*, which allows him only brief appearances modelled strictly on his role in the gospel accounts of the Passion, pp. 290-324).

The York cycle speaks of Pilate's giving "judgment" on Christ while sitting "in parlement" (*York*, p. 284, 1.. 34; p. 393, ll. 49-50). The other plays are more explicit yet; *Ludus Coventriae* allows Pilate to preside over a court of law, and *Towneley's* Pilate welcomes false indictors, qluestmongers, jurors, and other false men of law *(Towneley*, p. 205, 11. 22-7). Pilate in short is both an aristocratic ruler and an unjust judge.[20]

Both religious and secular aristocrats, then, appear as the villains in the Corpus Christi drama. These aristocrats abuse and crush the common people, including their Lord Himself. The lesson to the watching children must have been very clear: the upper classes are our enemies!

That the upper classes were indeed the enemies of the commoners is an assertion to which many scholars have testified.[21] The commoners indeed saw them as enemies: in the Peasants' Revolt of 1381 the rebelling peasants joyfully welcomed John Ball's advice to slay "the great lords of the kingdom"[22] and later presented to King Richard II a list of some sixteen religious and secular lords whom they wished beheaded.[23] Nor did they stop there; John Stow, the antiquarian/historian, reports in *Chronicles of England* (London: Newberie, 1580) that the aroused peasants took it upon themselves to behead several primates and secular lords high in the king's council (p. 482). It seems the medieval English commoner considered the religious and secular aristocracy exactly the scoundrels portrayed in the cycle plays. That the cycles reflected this view so clearly makes them fascinating social documents as well as literature engrossing both to adults and children.

*   *   *

It is clear that medieval English children would have attended the

Corpus Christi plays and watched them with great interest, enjoying the stage-children, villains and familiar games as they learned their society's concept of history, its chief religious stories and a revolutionary view of the upper classes. Fraught with all these riches, the cycle plays lasted either from dawn to dusk or through parts of several days; in view of those riches, it is not surprising that the audience, both children and adults, remained watching from Creation to Doomsday. This was great drama—and a major vehicle for transmitting social and religious values from the older generation to the younger.

Notes

[1]Research for this essay was supported by a released-time fellowship from Baylor University.

[2]"Miracula Alia Sancti Johannis Episcopi," *The Historians of the Church of York and Its Archbishops*, ed. James Raine (3 vols. Rolls Series, 1879), 71;1, 328-30.

[3]See, e.g., Meradith Tilbury McMunn and William Robert McMunn, "Children's Literature in the Middle Ages," *Children's Literature* 1 (1972), 24, or Bennett A. Brockman, "Children and Literature in Late Medieval England," *Children's Literature* 4 (1975), 58-59. One must of course remember that manuscript literature was unavailable to the great majority of English children owing to its high cost and their illiteracy.

[4]The earliest date for the cycle plays was until recently considered 1376: A.C. Cawley, ed., *Everyman and Medieval Miracle Plays* (London: Dutton, 1956), x. Siegfried Wenzel has now presented evidence of their performance in 1335: "An Early Reference to a Corpus Christi Play," *Modern Philology*, 74 (1977), 390-394. For later dates and places of presentation, see E.K. Chambers, "Representations of Medieval Plays," *The Mediaeval Stage* II (London: Oxford Univ. Press, 1903), 329-406.

[5]*The Chester Mystery Cycle*, ed. R.M. Lumiansky and David Mills, EETS,SS, 3 (London, New York, and Toronto: Oxford Univ. Press, 1974); *Ludus Coventriae or the Plaie called Corpus Christi*, ed. K.S. Block, EETS, ES, 120 (1922; rpt. London, New York, and Toronto: Oxford Univ. Press, 1960); *The Towneley Plays*, ed. George England and Alfred W. Pollard, EETS, ES, 71 (1897; rpt. London, New York and Toronto: Oxford Univ. Press, 1966); *The York Plays*, ed. Richard Beadle (London: Arnold, 1982). I ignore the remaining fragment of the Coventry cycle; in my essay I refer to the four complete cycles parenthetically by short title, page and line numbers hereafter.

[6]Joseph Strutt, *The Sports and Pastimes of the People of England ____ from the Earliest Period to the Present Time*, ed. William Hone (London: Chatto & Windus, 1898), p. 501. In Kolve's chapter see pp. 185-86.

[7]The entire episode appears in Towneley, pp. 239-241, ll. 343-414. Here I translate it into modern English.

[8]My translation of *Ludus Coventriae*, p. 277, ll. 170-72.

[9]*The Play Called Corpus Christi*, pp. 188-193.

[10]*Timaeus A Calcidio Translatus Commentarioque Instructus*, ed. J.H. Waszink (London and Leiden: E.J. Brill, 1962), p. 30, ll. 2-13.

[11]Cf. Boethius' *Consolation of Philosophy* Book V, Prose vi, and Aquinas' *Summa Theologica*, Part I, Question x, Articles 1 and 2.

[12]I am indebted to J.D. Hurrell's "The Figural Approach to Medieval Drama," *College English*, 26 (1965), 598-604, for much of my discussion of figura.

[13]*Scenes from the Drama of European Literature* trans. Ralph Manheim (New York: Meridian, 1959), pp. 11-76.

[14]*Ibid.*, p. 30.

[15]See Erich Auerbach, "Typological Symbolism in Medieval Literature," *Gesammelte Aufsatze zur Romanischen Philologie* (Bern: Francke, 1967), p. 111.

[16]R.G. Collingwood, *The Idea of History* (Oxford: Clarendon Press, 1946), pp. 49-50; quotation p. 49.

[17]*Childhood and Society*, 2nd ed. (New York: Norton, 1963), p. 263; *Identity: Youth and Crisis* (New York: Norton, 1968), pp. 133-134 and, especially, pp. 188-191.

[18]H.S. Bennett, *Life on the English Manor* (1937; rpt. Cambridge, Eng.: Cambridge Univ. Press, 1974), pp. 32-33, 325-329.

[19]"A Sermon Against Miracle-Plays," *Reliquiae Antiquae*, II, ed. Thomas Wright and James O. Halliwell (London: Pickering, 1843), 50, 46.

[20]For an excellent discussion of Pilate as unjust judge, and of the social comment this implies, see Arnold Williams' *Characterization of Pilate in the Towneley Plays* (East Lansing: Michigan State College Press, 1950).

[21]See L.F. Salzmann, *Medieval Byways* (London: Constable, 1913), pp. 125-158; H.S. Bennett, *Life passim*; May McKisack, *The Fourteenth Century: 1307-1399*, vol. 5 of the *Oxford History of England* (Oxford: Clarendon Press, 1959), pp. 422-423; E.F. Jacob, *The Fifteenth Century: 1399-1485*, Vol. 6 of the *Oxford History of England* (Oxford: Clarendon 1961), pp. 496-499; Robert Weimann, "Die furchtbare Komik des Herodes," *Archiv*, 204 (1967), 113-123; Theodore R. De Welles, "The Social and Political Context of the Towneley Cycle," Diss. Univ. of Toronto, 1982; *DAI*, 42:10 (1982), 4456A.

[22]Thomas Walsingham, *Historia Anglicana*, 2 (Rolls Series, 1863), 32; cited in *English Historical Documents*, 4, ed. A. R. Myers (London: Eyre and Spottiswoode, 1969), 141.

[23]*Anonimalle Chronicle, 1333 to 1381*, ed. V. H. Galbraith (Manchester: Manchester Univ. Press, 1927), p. 139.

English Cycle Drama

Over 600 years separate us from the earliest production of medieval cycle drama, and it is impossible to recreate its full meaning or the emotional responses to it. It is possible, however, to inquire into the contribution as a work of art over a long period of time, a work that made stunning use of social norms, both legitimizing and criticizing them. The cycle drama represents the idea of pilgrimage within a closed system of salvation history; its center has to do with renewal, a beginning again. Although the story told in the cycle plays is of cosmic proportion, the history is a human one. If for no other reason, we have a desire to understand and interpret the text of these plays. Although the medieval world represented in the cycle drama appears different from our own, in some important ways, it remains our world.

Josie P. Campbell is a professor of English at the University of Rhode Island; she has published on medieval and renaissance drama and on contemporary American and Canadian fiction.

English Cycle Drama: "Thou art a pilgreme..."

There are four great English cycle dramas extant: the York, Chester, Wakefield (Towneley), and Coventry (*Ludas Coventriae* or N-Towne) cycles. For over two hundred years, from 1335-1600, the cycle dramas were performed every year in virtually every major English town.[1] It was popular drama, written by the local clergy, staged and acted by local guilds and townspeople, and performed for a local but widely heterogeneous audience. The action encompassed by the cycles is large and spacious; it includes all time—from Creation to Judgment Day—and all space—Heaven, Earth, and Hell. Such inclusiveness, spatial and temporal, overflows and embraces the public life that sustains and is sustained by it. These vast and enormous dramas were prepared over many months by an entire town and performed by hundreds of actors and walk-ons. Often the actors were from the very town they played in; thus they were both set apart and not set apart from the townspeople. Similarly the audience participated in the drama yet remained outside it, watching and observing the action. The world itself became a theater, with the action taking place out of doors—in the streets or open spaces of a town.

Much attention has been given to analysis of the principles which govern the selection of the episodes in the Middle English cycle dramas.[2] In recent years scholars have increasingly turned to civic and church documents to discover the cycles' use of elaborate stage craft and spectacular visual effects.[3] In addition, attempts have been made to "read" the cycle dramas by using the techniques of the art historian with reference to the painting, sculpture, and tapestry of the era.[4]

128

It is clear that no one scholarly method has provided—nor is it likely to—a definitive key to our understanding of the drama or of its popular appeal, although all have increased our knowledge of the cycles. Professor Bruce Rosenberg's question in his essay, "Was There a Popular Culture in the Middle Ages," is relevant here: how much have we learned about medieval culture as a whole by looking at certain artifacts such as the drama of that culture? Probably not as much as we would like or hope to. Yet Professor Altman's look at church sculpture, as well as all of the essays in this book, contribute collectively to our discoveries of medieval culture in the only way possible, as Rosenberg suggests, by the analysis of significant segments of that culture.

Altman's advice to take into account, where possible, the specific entrepreneurial voices of the text is important to the study of popular culture in all ages.[5] In the Middle Ages such voices often belong to the Church and to the powerful rising merchant class, as is the case with church sculpture and to some extent the cycle drama. Although it would be a mistake to assume the entrepreneurs as univocal, nonetheless the Church and the merchant class had a vested—and a voiced—interest in the cycle dramas as vehicles of instruction. Moreover the power in their voices reveals itself in the capacity for irony, parody, satire, and other modes of self-criticism. At the same time, one must remember the importance of the craftsmen's guilds in the financing, organization, and production of the cycles. They were both an integral yet underprivileged part of the feudal order and were most likely closer to the rural population than to any of the upper classes.[6] Moreover, they most certainly would be opposed to the individual economic enterprise of the merchant. Perhaps the significance of these voices can be seen in how well they accommodate as well as demonstrate some of the enormous stresses of the 14th and 15th centuries: the exploitation of many by both the Church and the upper classes, the tormenting hunger and poverty of the masses, and the threat of pestilence, violence, and horrendous deaths for all. The realities of the Black Death and the Peasants Revolt should dispel any romanticized or nostalgic notion of a joyous and cohesive medieval community. The "mad priest of Kent," John Ball, for some twenty years (1360-81) found an audience for his sermons, crying out: "Good people, things will never go well in England so long as goods be not in common and so long as there be villains and gentlemen." The radical spirit of this priest is condensed into the popular medieval rhyme: "When Adam delved and Eve span, who was then the gentleman?" It was the Peasants Revolt that inspired Wyclif's *Of Servants and Lords* in which he urges a community system of mutual obligations. The cycle dramas depict not only those forces fracturing the society but also the desire for unity among humankind and with God.

The extended two-hundred-year run enjoyed by the medieval cycle drama stems from its use of conventions and formulas that remained popular for a long period of time. This drama is not one of suspense but of irony; the audience knows the plot from the beginning when God proclaims the [hi]story of humankind. Any lapses of audience memory during the cycle are restored through the use of numerous prologues and set speeches (though this is not necessarily their primary function) which open many of the episodes in all of the cycles. The story having already taken place in

Christian history is irreversible; Judgment Day *will* come. Although the plotline is irreversible, there are dramatic reversals within the individual units: Eva becomes Ave; Lucifer is overthrown; humankind's debt to God repaid; death overcome. The dramatic units provide a series of contrasts and oppositions, of crises and solutions. The characters themselves have a series of gestures and voices that recur: the villains rage intemperately; the good display charity. Moreover, a repertoire of topoi or recurrent situations reiterate certain patterns of dramatic action so that the audience recovers point by point what it already knows, what it desires to know again.

The reiterative structure of the cycle dramas reveals two major and powerful formulas: the idea of pilgrimage and the story of salvation. Although the two patterns are intertwined, the journey or pilgrimage provides an architectural or exterior framework for its interior story of salvation. The idea of pilgrimage lends the cycle drama its episodic and processional shape: the story of salvation insures the completion of the journey. The popularity of these formulas can be seen not only by their use in the cycle dramas but in morality plays such as *Everyman* and *The Castle of Perseverance;* they are also found in sermon literature and in the visual arts as well as in the institution of the pilgrimage itself.[7] Pilgrimage in the Middle Ages was a commonplace metaphor for the journey of life itself, from birth to salvation. Ideally the journey was one-way to the Heavenly Jerusalem; although all might not reach this destination, all were pilgrims on the road to it. Terror lay in the possibility of falling by the wayside or in taking a wrong turn.

John Cawelti notes in "Myth, Symbol, and Formula," that formulaic structures in popular literature of all ages "combine a minimal variety of existing cultural and artistic interests and concerns (at the same time that) they maximize a great many interests."[8] Although both the pilgrimage and salvation formulas contain a number of socio/political ideologies, the authors and audience share "certain fundamental attitudes." Analysis of the function of such formulas, as Cawelti suggests, is a step towards understanding some of the "attitudes" or values of a culture on the one hand and of the concerns and desires of a particular era on the other.

When God creates the world in the cycle dramas, He sets in motion not only Lucifer but a teeming field of folk akin to Langland's in *Piers Plowman.* Lucifer's attempt to disrupt God's time and place and make it his own repeats itself countless times in the actions of the devil and of numerous villains. Although pride may be the deadliest of sins, in these plays envy seems to be the mainspring of a murderous violence that alienates as it works to gain and consolidate power. As Lucifer tries to imitate God with bravura—albeit "bad"—acting, so too do a host of others with less skill try to embody God's authority. Indeed once Adam and Eve turn away from God in a vain attempt to gain equal power with Him, the entire cycle from Creation to Doomsday can be seen as a journey fraught with the anxiety and extraordinary tension that come from conflicting desires. On the one hand there is the desire to be reunited with God and on the other an absurd but violent counter-desire to appropriate His power and to abuse it. The journey constantly threatens to collapse under the weight of these desires, just as the plays themselves consistently move towards dissolution. That the journey does not grind to a halt, but keeps going, comes from those significant moments ("marked" time as Clifford Davidson calls them[9]) when God bends down to humankind to re-create a covenant with them.

Journeying or pilgrimage—I use the words interchangeably in this essay—has synecdochic and incremental functions in the cycle drama. Almost all of the plays in the cycle have to do with journeys, and each journey comes a step closer to man's ultimate journey to judgment. Indeed, the whole journey of man's life on earth is presented during the course of the cycle. The Wakefield passion plays, like those in the other cycle dramas, provide a horrific paradigm of the use of journeys in the cycles. The action of "The Conspiracy" flows into the beginning of "The Buffeting": the torturers' journey, as they drive Christ from Pilate's hall to the hall of Cayphas (Caiaphas), is circular; at the end of the play, the torturers, followed by Cayphas and Annas, return Christ to Pilate. "The Buffeting" in turn disappears into "The Scourging," or rather, moves into a repetition of itself. The journey from one hall to another, from one play to another, strengthens the continuity within the plays also. Movement to and from the various pageants, Calvary Hill, and the area of reception and places of torture within the halls of Cayphas and Pilate offer ample opportunities for the torturers and rulers to reveal themselves:

> Sir, we wold fayn witt / all were ar oure bonys;
> we haue had a fytt / right yil for the nonys,
>   So tarid.[10]
> (p. 249, 49-50)

The torturers' whining complaints about the weariness of their bodies reveal a blindness to the meaning of their journey as they deliver Christ into the hands of rulers fearful of losing their power.

Journeys are times off from the torture scenes. Kolve comments that gaming—such as the game of Hot Cockles—breaks the predictable flow of the familiar events of the passion, and so allows for the audience to experience the events for the first time (V.A. Kolve, *The Play Called Corpus Christi* [London, 1966], pp. 185, 207). In a similar way the journeys break the known pattern of inquisition and torture to add a new dimension: the audience attends to the action of the processions and recessions, listens to the banter of the torturers and the nervousness of the prelates, and only at the stop of the movement must it again respond to the horror of the action. Moreover, their response is intensified by the very fact that, because of the staging, they have been part of the journeying itself. For example, in the recent production of the Wakefield cycle at the University of Toronto (May 25-26, 1985), place and scaffold staging was used; in order to see the action, the audience had to follow the torturers and Christ on their journey between Pilate and Cayphas. The distance beween the world of play or theater and the world of the audience was very much foreshortened.

The journeying itself can become a game in Kolve's use of the term. At the beginning of "The Buffeting," for instance, the torturers take fun in forcing Christ to trot. The play ends as it begins, with the first torturer addressing Christ as a donkey, driving Him forth:

> Come furth, old crate,
> Be lyfe!
> we shall lede the a trott.
> (p. 242, 427-429)

Froward, one of those meddlesome, vicious, poor servant-boys in the cycle
dramas, whose actions mirror those of his masters, had already included
himself in the Hot Cockles game and now decides he has nothing better to
do than join the others in their torment of Christ: "Then nedys me do nott /
Bot com after and dryfe." If, as in the Toronto production, the torturers drive
Christ through the audience from one place to another, and if the audience
closes ranks to follow on the journey, the participation comes close to
overwhelming the audience's detachment of distance. The journeying game
becomes nearly unbearable in "The Scourging" by the time Simon, the too-
busy merchant, meets Christ and the torturers on their way to Calvary Hill.
    The dramatist reiterates the action of journeying with significant word
play. Much reference is made to Christ's walking, His trespassing, His
misleading, and His earthly journey among the people. Christ Himself
refers to His divine journey:

> ffor after this shall thou se / when that [I] do com downe
> In brightnes on he / in clowdys from abone.
> ("The Buffeting," p. 236, 253-54)

The tension between Christ's journey among humankind and His coming
resurrection defines the larger significance and the incremental aspect of
journeying.
    The passion plays represent only one or two days of Christ's time on
earth, but the unjust and inhuman treatment He receives emphasizes the
importance of His short earthly journey and increases the drama of the
scenes of His death and rebirth. In the monumental journey of the cycle
dramas towards the final judgment of humankind, the torturers' acts
amplify the acts of all others who are sinful: those "Busshoppys and
prestys" who love Him not; the secular lords, the knights, the lesser
aristocrats, who capture, torment, and crucify Christ in all the cycles. As
Thomas Hanks reminds us in his essay, "Quike Bookis," they slaughter the
innocents. From the higher aristocracy come the chief villains: Herod the
Great, Herod Antipas, and Pilate. Of these Pilate is perhaps most
interesting; a "kyng with crowne," he appears in all the cycle plays (save
Chester) as a judge.[11] In the York cycle, Pilate gives judgment on Christ
while sitting "in parlement" (p. 308); *Ludus Coventriae* makes Pilate's court
one of law, complete with legal bar (pp. 293-94). Lucas even calls Pilate a
"hyz justyce" and his court a "gre A-syse." It is in the Wakefield cycle,
however, that Pilate's role as an unjust judge is most clearly contemporary;
he first announces himself to be "leder of lawes," then adds that though he
feigns to ordain the right, in reality he welcomes false indictors, quest
mongers, jurors, "all thise fals out rydars" ("The Conspiracy," p. 205, 26).
As both aristocrat and judge, Pilate is "full of soteltry, / ffalshed, gyle, and
trechery" (p. 243, 10-11).[12] He is proud that he is a "bad actor"—"Therfor am
I namyd by clergy / As *mali actoris*." The upper classes are clearly

represented as the enemies of the poor, just as the legal and ecclesiastical institutions they control are perceived as corrupt.

The commoners certainly saw the upper classes as enemies: during the Peasants Revolt of 1381, the peasants took seriously John Ball's advice to kill "the great lords of the kingdom"—peasant spokesmen swore to kill "all lawyers and servants of the King they could find"—and presented to Richard II a list of over a dozen religious and secular lords whom they wanted beheaded.[13] Indeed, the peasants beheaded a number of ecclesiastical and secular lords of the king's council.

But it is not only the aristocracy that falls short in the cycle drama; the rising merchant class looks only slightly better in their actions. Perhaps one of the most appalling journeys aside from (and beside!) Christ's is that of Simon, the merchant-businessman who tries to refuse the task of carrying Christ's cross to Calvary. Simon appears in all of the cycle dramas, although only in Chester does he overtly state he is a reluctant witness of Christ's crucifixion; he takes up Christ's cross "by distres," as he curses the jews for their part in the heinous crime. In the other three cycles, Simon is depicted as a man in a hurry, one who is on an extended "greatt Iornay" (Wakefield, "The Scourging," p. 256); and as a man whose "wayes are lang wand wyde," a man who has promised a surety which must be kept, "Or it will [im]paire my [e]state" (York, p. 345). In the Coventry cycle, Simon has "gret errandys for to do" (p. 295) and begs release from carrying the cross. With the possible exception of the Chester cycle, all the dramas represent Simon as one of those people too busy to help Christ; only when the torturers threaten physical punishment does Simon find the time to carry Christ's cross. The irony of Simon's attempt at evasion—"I shall com full soyn agane,/To help this man" (Wakefield, "The Scourging," p. 256, 384-385)—is obvious, as he pleads to be allowed to continue on his way. There is nothing compassionate about the motives of the torturers in seeking help; Christ is unable to carry the cross much further, and the journey to Calvary is about to halt as a result. Simon's act, not out of charity but self-preservation, paradoxically saves Christ's strength so that He may die to save mankind.

In contrast to villainy being generally an upper-class vocation, goodness for the most part belongs to the lower classes. The husbandman of the vineyards, the plowman of the fields, the fishermen, and the shepherds are called as witnesses and servants of the Lord. This is not to say that to be poor is to be pure; even those Christ chooses as his apostles are less than perfect. Abraham, Isaac, Abel, though, all obey God's commandments. The simple maiden Mary becomes the handmaiden and mother of Christ. God bends down to a simple knave, Noah, who is "old, / seke, sory, and cold, / As muk upon mold" (Wakefield, "Noah," p. 25, 60-63), and Noah responds with steadfastness to the power that is God.

Looked at this way, the cycle dramas suggest a degree of social self-consciousness on the part of the craftsmen/yeomen that seems well-defined, especially in their view of the upper classes. Moving hierarchically downward, from king through bishop to knight, powerful secular and religious aristocrats appear as villains who torment and slay the poor and oppressed, including Christ. Christ Himself is an example of the common man who is also noble; His betrayal is a betrayal of the common people to the powerful of the world. To betray the New Law of Christ is to turn one's back on "the brotherhede" of all men; indeed Christ's chief crime is social in that He comes to overturn the old laws that are divisive. Yet for all the satire and parody directed toward the upper classes, the curve of action in the plays remains conservative. For the most part, one must literally wait until Doomsday for justice. What Altman argues so eloquently in his essay, "The Medieval Marquee," about church portal sculpture is equally relevant to the cycle drama: both shore up the common people's belief in salvation and serve to divert criticism which the lower classes might be tempted to level at the upper and more powerful classes. At the same time, the very fact that the plays juggle a variety of social tensions perhaps explains their wide appeal and enormous popularity over an extended period of time. These tensions are accommodated within a framework that insists all humankind makes the self-same journey from birth to judgment—to salvation, if one does not lose the way.

If the cycle dramas are a mimetic correlative of the social tensions of the age—of the growing gaps between individual action and social circumstances in the 14th and 15th centuries—these same dramas also mediate the gaps by representing a desired unity between God and humankind. This mediation finds expression in the salvation formula which continually pushes the drama forward at the same time that it threatens to collapse. The salvation formula contains the story of creation, loss, and re-creation, a pattern that serves both the individual units and the whole of the cycles. All of the cycles have a tripartite structure of repetitive forms or acts—redundancies—each initiated by a creation mystery: God's first creation of Adam; His second the Virgin birth of Christ; and His third, the Deliverance of Souls. Following each of these creations are acts of faithlessness by humankind, one to the other, and to God. Each of the creations provides not only a promise or a fulfillment of unity between God and His creatures, but each also introduces a falling away from God that carries within it the seeds of its own dissolution.

The "Noah" play provides one of the best examples of how the pilgrimage and salvation formulas function dramatically within the cycle dramas, both revealing tensions and at the same time mediating them. In the "Noah" play, the world is about to dissolve in the flood; the cycle drama itself seems to move rapidly towards its own closure. The flood results directly from the sinfulness of humankind as manifested by their disregard for each other and for God. When God speaks to Noah, He forges a creative partnership: He not only gives Noah the blueprints for the ark, He suggests how to rebuild the relationships between man and God, man and community, man and family, and man and nature that are essential to perpetuate the life of the earth. Noah, "trew as stele," makes a commitment not only to build an ark but to build a personal relationship with his God and the world. Thus the journey—and the cycle drama—can begin again.

Noah, with his family, is thrown out onto the flood in order to create the world anew. Undergirding his commitment to this new beginning is love, God's love for man, which if returned, vitalizes the earth. Noah instinctively recognizes the power of this love when he says:

Noah's Ark Salisbury Chapter House
Noah enters the Ark, and receives the dove. Scene 17, Salisbury Chapter House
(Personal slide collection).

I thank the, lord, so dere / that wold vowch sayf
This low to appere / to a symple knayf;
Blis vs, lord, here / for charity I hit crafe,
The better may we stere / the ship that we shall hafe,
Certayn.
(Wakefield, "Noah," p. 28, 172-176.

It is this power of love that Noah will eventually take with him on his journey in that fragile ark so that they "shall wax and multiply, / and fill the erth agane." Although Noah might be the last person one would expect to be entrusted with such a task—he is old, sick, at times a drunkard, quick-tempered, and an ill-provider—yet he of all people is selected to bring to the new world the best out of the old.

Journeys in the cycle dramas often have to do with such beginnings, beginnings which provide both an action and a consciousness. To begin anew in the cycle dramas is always an attempt to make a difference, but a difference which is the result of combining the new with the already familiar. When the Old Testament God chooses to begin the world again, he does it with Noah and a reiterated covenant. A part of the old world journeys out to create the new.

After "The Deliverance of Souls," the journeys at the end of the cycle dramas seem to be journeys thrown into reverse, but they too are begin-nings, as humandkind seeks to resume its initial connection with God. Yet even here, in the final third of the cycles, the pilgrims falter and their journeys tend to break down. Perhaps the most dramatic evidence of this tendency is in the "*Peregrini*" of "The Pilgrims," a play found in all of the cycles. "The Pilgrims" is one of the most ironic plays in the cycle drama; in the Wakefield play, Lucas and Cleophas meet a fellow pilgrim who happens to be Christ and proceed to tell Him the events of His own crucifixion. Even though they lament the crucifixion, they miss its true meaning, until Christ informs them that it is only part of the story. As the prophets have foretold, "thrugh his pauste [power]," He will "Ryse up in flesh and fell." But the Pilgrims distrust prophecy just as they distrusted the message of the three Maries who found Christ's tomb empty. Indeed, their distrust was so strong that they themselves viewed the tomb, and in seeing it empty found even greater cause for mourning.

To Christ this must appear to be the dark wood of error all over again, even though there is no malice in Lucas and Cleophas. Christ's rejoinder to their ignorance has a note of asperity in it:

ye foyles, ye ar not stabyll!
    where is youre witt, I say?
wilsom of hart ye ar vnabyll
    And outt of the right way,
ffor to trow it is no fabyll
    that at is fallen this same day.
(Wakefield, "Pilgrims," p. 331, 202-207)

His fulfillment of prophecy has been undertaken for men who apparently fail to believe in it.

The only real insight that Lucas and Cleophas have of the meaning of the crucifixion and the resurrection reveals itself in their spontaneous gesture urging Christ to stay with them for "charite" and "for godys sake." Lucas reminds Him that they are brothers: "Thou art a pilgreme, as we ar." Christ surely must have smiled at this final remonstrance, as he agrees to remain. The communion feast that occurs among the three allows Lucas and Cleophas to recognize their own deficiencies and ignorance: "we were full blynde, euer alas." Christ's appearance as a pilgrim beguiled them into believing He was simply another man:

> Wee are to blame, yee, veramente,
>   That we toke no better tente....
> (p. 335, 334-335)

Christ's breaking bread with them in "charite" reveals His Godhead, as He instantly vanishes from the stage; His sudden disappearance must have been theatrically spectacular and effective. The pilgrim's final recognition of Christ brings about a reversal from disbelief to belief, and their journey is given a direction it did not have before. They go to spread the news of Christ's resurrection.

Noah, the pilgrims, and others like them are constantly on the move in the cycle dramas, and in each case they have singular goals: Noah to save the world, the magi and the shepherds to worship the child, Mary and Joseph to save that child, the pilgrims to tell the good news. They journey, however haltingly at times, into the world to voice and to act upon the word of God. In contrast, Satan, Cain, and all "cursyd tyrantys," voice and act upon their own concerns. They are filled with self-explanation and bombast. The tyrants, Herod, Annas, Cayphas, and Pilate, frequently use direct audience address and introduce themselves as villains, their self-consciousness a deliberate dramatic device on the part of the playwrights to project a variety of self-references onto the contemporary medieval secular and ecclesiastical upper classes. Satan and Cain more often hurl direct challenges to the audience demanding and quickening some sort of moral response. For example, Cain's malevolent boy says to the audience at the beginning of the play:

> Som of you ar his men.
> Bot let youre lippis couer youre ten,
> harlottis, euerichon!
> (Wakefield, "Killing of Abel," p. 10, 20-22)

Cain himself takes in the audience with a conspiratorial wink but a hardly veiled threat after he kills his brother:

> And if any of you thynk I did amys
> I shal it amend wars then it is,
>   that all men may it se:
> well wars then it is
>   right so shall it be.
> (p. 18, 331-335)

Magi
The Ride of the Magi. Stained Glass, 173E4, N. Choir Aisle, Canterbury Cathedral
(Reprinted with permission of Woodmansterne Publications Ltd.)

Even at the end of the play, in Cain's despair, he includes the audience:

> Now fayre well, felows all
>   ffor I must nedis weynd,
> And to the dwill be thrall,
>   warld withourtten end.
> (p. 22, 462-465)

Like the good characters in the cycles, all of the villains are on the journey to Judgment Day, although they remain oblivious of it until too late; they attempt to hold fast to their space and time. With the powerful lords, this attempt is dramatically reinforced by the fact that few journey forth from their palaces or courts: Herod directs the magi to return to him to report on the birth of Christ and later commands his knights to go forth and slay the innocents. Annas, Cayphas, and Pilate all have Christ brought before their tribunals; again the knights must do the dirty work: they drive Christ back and forth among the rulers and finally to Calvary. There is a great bustling and busy-ness—and much stage business—with all of these characters, but they end as they begin. Pilate sums it up in his reiterated and vain "we think to abyde." Similarly, Satan holds tightly to his kingdom behind his "bandys of bras." Their journeys are not quite circular, for their movement is of one piece and in one place.

There are few moments of [ar]rest in the great movement of the cycle drama. The highly significant moments of mediation in the drama are just that—brief moments. They have an intensity resulting from time "marked" off from the journeying at the same time they propel it forward to salvation. The dramatic power of these mediating moments is perhaps most strongly felt in the cluster of plays containing the Incarnation and the Nativity, the very heart of the salvation story itself. Even in the play of "The Incarnation" the quiet confrontation between Mary and Gabriel comes into dramatic collision with the frenetic—and funny—flight of the bewildered Joseph to the wilderness. Joseph's agitation is related to the fierce farce of the Wakefield shepherds which preceded the actual nativity and adoration of the Christ child.

In both the Incarnation and the Nativity plays, the untouchable security of Mary calls for a moment of reflection. Her serene gaze at the Child and at the shepherds not only arrests movement in the scene but also arrests the audience's gaze as well. As Edmund Taft writes in his essay "Surprised by Love," Mary's parting command to the shepherds, "Tell furth as ye go," unites "memory, perception and hope, that is, past, present, and future into one moment of historical time when the ideal became real, a moment of perfection which endures, so long as men remember it vividly and properly, as *the* model of familial, social and universal harmony through mutual love."

That such moments of mediation bring the journey back on track is evidenced by "The Offering of the Magi." In the Wakefield plays, little dialogue occurs that does not contain references to a journey: the Magi travel through "way[e]s wylde," they are "led" by a star; they "weynd" their ways and "neuer ryst by day nor nyght." It is not frantic movement, but purposeful, as they seek the Christ child. Jaspar expresses the idea behind

Adoration
Adoration of Magi and Shepherds. Stained Glass, 173E6, N. Choir Aisle, Canterbury
(Reprinted with permission of Woodmansterne Publications Ltd).

this particular journey and the whole idea of pilgrimage in the Middle Ages:

> A, lordyngys dere! the sothe to say,
> we haue made a good Iornay;
> we loue this lord, that shall last ay
>   with outten ende:
> he is oure beyld, both nyght and day,
>   where so we weynd.
> (p. 158, 577-582)

Melchior adds that they "haue traueld lang, / And restyd haue [they] lytyll," as they prepare to sleep. But they are allowed no rest and must leave at once, taking their various ways, as the "fals fo" they flee. The repeated emphasis on movement, particularly after the Magi see the Christ child, not only creates an urgency in the drama but underscores the medieval conception "of the wayfarer in a strange world, who is also a pilgrim toward order...."[11] Surely the Magi are pilgrims *par excellence.*

Only one brief moment of quiet and stillness exists in "The Offering of the Magi"; as in the Shepherds' Plays, it is the adoration of the Christ child. The rest is filled with the rage of Herod and the movement of kings, desirous of finding the child. The Magi find little rest; their short stay with Herod is filled with anxiety, and their one sleep is disrupted by the vision of an angel warning them to be on their way. Jaspar speaks for all three, when he says in parting, "ilk on weynd by dyuers way," but perhaps in a larger sense he speaks for all humankind.

The modern poet T.S. Eliot writes of the Incarnation that "The Word in the desert / Is most attacked by voices of temptation" ("Burnt Norton" in *Four Quartets* [N.Y.:L Harcourt Brace and World, 1943]). The voices become more shrill and insistent immediately after the shepherds leave the stage, and the pattern of movement becomes increasingly urgent and anxious. In the center of the salvation story is the stillness of the virgin mother in "The Salutation of Elizabeth," a play that might better be called a hymn of praise. "The chyld makys Ioy, as any byrd,/That I embody bere," says Mary, who is called blessed for what "shall betyde" in the promise of unity "ffrom kynde to kynde." Mary and Elizabeth are placed in an easily recognizable situation, where the two mothers begin their visit with news of the family and where it closes with Mary's tender "mym awnt dere," while Elizabeth reminds her to "Crete well all oure kyn of bloode." The intimacy of the scenes at the beginning and end of the play, enclosing one of the central Christian mysteries, serves to remind the audience that the infinite is to be found within the finite—within the very familial and social fabric. If the center of life and tiem can be seen in the Incarnation, then, dramatically speaking, this is the center of the cycle itself. Thus the play fits appropriately in the cycle as the one truly quiet moment for the mother "who gathers to herself the processional masque of the kings and shepherds."[15] It remains the only completely peaceful moment in the cycle dramas, a brief interlude between the Old Testament world, which awaits Christ so anxiously, and the New, which as His passion approaches, rejects Him so violently.

Over 600 years separate us from the earliest production of the medieval cycle drama, and it is impossible to recreate its full meaning or the emotional responses to it. It is possible, however, to inquire into its contribution as a work of art over a long period of time, a work that made stunning use of a number of social norms, both legitimizing and criticizing them. The cycle drama represents the idea of pilgrimage within a closed system of salvation history; its center has to do with renewal, a beginning again. At the same time, under the affirmation inherent in salvation, we find a strong spirit of contradiction or of negativity. If there are continuities expressed in this drama, there are also expressed equally strong discontinuities. The plays themselves exhibit a brokenness, a tendency to fall apart or to collapse under their own weight. The few spontaneous gestures of charity from a shepherd, king, or pilgrim are not enough to keep the journey going; nor is the hope for faith in salvation. Divine mediation is both desired and required.

The plays reveal a disconcerting amount of attention to what we might call "getting ahead" or at least "staying in place." The desire for power, place, and property is represented across all class lines from king to shepherd to meanest boy; only a few characters lack acquisitiveness in some form. This desire for appropriation is both conflictual and divisive; its tendency is towards individualism, not brotherhood. At the same time, the plays also represent reconciliation, renewal, and—in the face of the thrust towards individualism—the radicalism of true communion and community. This equally strong desire for re/union reveals the strength of the inner spiritual and artistic life of the Middle Ages. The two formulas I have analysed—the idea of pilgrimage and the story of salvation—reflect both the stresses pushing the Middle Ages into the Renaissance and the longing for a medieval community that may have existed only in the structures of the imagination—in desire itself.

Notes

[1]Siegfried Wenzel cites evidence of cycle drama performance in 1335: "An Early Reference to a Corpus Christi Play," *Modern Philology,* 74 (May 1977), 390-394. A.C. Cawley puts the date at 1376 in his edition, *Everyman and Medieval Miracle Plays* (London: Dutton, 1956), p. x. For later dates, see E.K. Chambers, *The Medieval Stage* (London: Oxford Univ. Press, 1903), pp. 329-406.

[2]Rosemary Woolf, "The Development of the Cycle Form," Ch. IV, *The English Mystery Plays* (Berkeley: Univ. of California Press, 1972), 54-76.

[3]*Records of Early English Drama* (REED) is a research and editorial project whose aim is to find, transcribe, and publish external evidence of dramatic, ceremonial, and minstrel activity in Great Britain before 1642.

[4]Medieval Institute Publications (Kalamazoo, Mich.: Western Michigan Univ.) continues to publish an excellent monograph series on cycle drama and medieval art (as well as medieval music).

[5]See especially Herbert J. Gans' excellent text, *Popular Culture and High Culture: An Analysis and Evaluation of Taste* (N.Y.: Basic Books, Inc., 1974) for what Gans calls "mediating voices" (*passim*).

[6]Robert Weimann, *Shakesperare and the Popular Tradition in the Theater,* ed. Robert Schwartz (Baltimore: The Johns Hopkins Univ. Press, 1978), pp. 60-61.

[7]See Donald R. Howard's brief book, *Writers and Pilgrims: Medieval Pilgrimage Narratives and Their Posterity,* (Berkeley: Univ. of California Press, 1980), for a succinct and excellent discussion of the idea of pilgrimage. My comments about the idea of pilgrimage are derived from Howard's work.

[8]*Journal of Popular Culture,* 8 (Summer 1974), p. 4. For more extensive treatment of literary formulas, see Cawelti's *Adventure, Mystery, and Romance: Formula Stories as Art and Popular Culture* (Chicago: Univ. of Chicago Press, 1976).

[9]"Space and Time in Medieval Drama: Meditations on Orientation in the Early Theater," in *Word, Picture, and Spectacle,* ed. by Clifford Davidson, Early Drama, Art and Music, Monograph Series, 5 (Kalamazoo, Mich.: Medieval Institute Publications, 1984), 51-58.

[10]All references to the cycle drama plays are from the following editions: *The Chester Plays,* ed. Hermann Deimling and J. Mathews, EETS, E.S. 62, 115 (London: Oxford Univ. Press, 1892, 1916); *Ludas Coventriae,* ed. K.S. Block, EETS, E.S. 120 (London: Oxford Univ. Press, 1922); *The Towneley Plays,* ed. George England, EETS, E.S., 71 (London: Oxford Univ. Press, 1897); *The York Plays,* ed. Lucy Toulmin Smith (Oxford: Clarendon Press, 1885). Page and line numbers are given in the text.

[11]See D. Thomas Hanks, Jr.'s " 'Quike Bookis'—The Corpus Christi Drama and English Children in the Middle Ages," printed below. Professor Hanks' essay overlaps with my own, although our arguments take us in somewhat different directions.

[12]Arnold Williams has an excellent discussion of Pilate in his *Characterization of Pilate in the Towneley Plays* (East Lansing, Mich.: Michigan State College Press, 1950).

[13]Barbara W. Tuchman, *A Distant Mirror: The Calamitous 14th Century* (N.Y.: Ballantine, 1978), pp. 372-378. See also Hanks' comments on the Peasants Revolt.

[14]My essay, "The Idea of Order in the Wakefield Noah," *Chaucer Review* 19 (1975), 76-78, is a fuller discussion of the interconnections between the ideas of salvation and pilgrimage in the drama.

[15]Gerhart B. Ladner, *"Homo Viator:* Medieval Ideas on Alienation and Order," *Speculum* 41 (April 1967), 256.

[16]Northrop Frye, *Anatomy of Criticism: Four Essay* Princeton: Princeton Univ. Press, 1957), p. 292.

Innocence and Suffering in the Middle Ages

Michael Stugrin's essay is both theoretical and practical: he suggests that texts, when viewed as "structures of perception," give us the "voices of the reality which they were part of and helped shape." He then proceeds to apply this theory to a number of spiritual texts popular during the Middle Ages to give us an idea of popular taste at that time. Such texts were structured in a highly affective way to affirm testimonies of faith and to commemorate God's promises to men. But perhaps most importantly, these spiritual texts, along with such texts as Sir Gawain and the Green Knight *and countless prose treatises and sermons, provided medieval audiences with a way of "knowing" within the context of human experience in a time of great cultural stress.*

Michael Stugrin, assistant professor of English at the University of Pittsburgh, is editor of New Directions in Medieval Literary Studies, *currently in press, The Pennsylvania State University Press.*

Innocence and Suffering in the Middle Ages: An Essay about Popular Taste and Popular Literature

Michael Stugrin

Why in this wretchedness do you linger on more wretchedly? Why do you take pleasure in this wordly glory, you who are going to die, leaving everything behind? Death, who spares no one, will take away your joys.[1]

While the terms in the title of this essay are not quite freely interchangeable, and thus in various euphonic combinations capable of meaning a great deal or nothing at all, the terms are covalent, and they must unavoidably be used in discussing life, culture, and the literature of the late Middle Ages. One cannot look long for texts which can be proved to have been in the hands of, or to have been read to, the layfolk without coming upon a mass of vernacular sermons, devotional guides, saints' lives, and exempla—all of which in some way chart the course of an *Itinerarium mentis ad Deum.* And one cannot read long in these spiritual texts without acquiring an acute sense of the writers' and their audiences' awareness of human suffering, of the ebbing—or, often, violent destruction—of human innocence. Then, too, one cannot escape at least tacit recognition that the popular taste of the late Middle Ages was conspicuously emotional,

144

sensitive to the pathetic and, in general, preoccupied with the heavy costs of moving through the world enroute, hopefully, to salvation. Such a sensibility scarcely masks a vulnerability and, as some people argue, an anxious uncertainty, about both temporal existence and eternal weal. Piers asks of St. Truth, "Teche me to so tresore, but telle me this ilke,/ How I may saue my soule," and echoes the concern of countless pilgrims.

My concern in studying the largely unstudied, and not even completely collected and catalogued, spiritual texts of Ricardian England has been not merely to determine their historical place in the development of late medieval spirituality or of vernacular prose, but to determine the function—rhetorically, generically, psychologically, and epistemologically—of their deliberate, varied exploitation of emotional tactics. Whether it is a sermon about the Passion, or a scene from the Hegge Passion in which Jesus is stripped of every human dignity, or a passage from Nicholas Love's enormously popular *Myrrour of the Blessed Lyf of Jesu Christ*—the tenor of these texts is intensely affective, calculated to work an effect upon an audience that is not merely one of familiar emotional experience, nor merely didactic. As my broader remarks about how such texts should be read, and as the more detailed brief discussion of a fifteenth-century devotional text will suggest, such texts do not intend *merely* to rephrase in lay terms basic tenets of faith, nor *merely* allow a reader or listener to escape through religious euphoria the rigors of daily existence. Their mimetic effectiveness and cultural significance lie within the participating readers' structure of reality—that structure of language, religious tenet, daily existence, and emotion.[2]

It is a tempting enterprise to ferret out causal equations in order to account for a culture's incredibly emotional sensibility. Clearly, cultural conditions are integrally involved, but data about religious and political change cannot alone suffice. Huizinga's dramatic portrayal of the 'waning of the Middle Ages' and Leff's skillfully wrought discussion of the 'dissolution of the medieval outlook' are the two most convincing, yet seriously reductionist, treatments of the reality of existence in the late Middle Ages.[3] And even the amorphous concepts of "popular religion" and "popular spirituality" misleadingly call attention to disparities between the spiritual lives and concerns of the learned and ignorant, in the same way that study of "popular" and "high" culture command different, and thus probably unwise, assumptions and critical methodologies.

It has been traditional to conceive of late medieval spirituality and its texts as homogenous effusions of fervid religious emotion. Even a relatively intelligent reading of Richard Rolle's *Incendium Amoris,* of the Harley Passion lyrics, and of sermons suggests doctrinal orthodoxy, and rather obvious literary characteristics. And about whatever *appears* as atypical in these texts, such as the English Mystics' extreme religious eroticism, scholars have explained by resort to biographical evidence or to arguments of stylistic idiosyncrasy, rather than working toward a full sense of the texts' psychological tactics. I would argue that late medieval popular spiritual texts are differentiated both by generic identities and by the rich, varied nature of religious experience, neither of which we understand very well. These texts, regardless of how they are classed and labeled, contribute to a culture's construction of its sense of reality, of its total living experience. Terry Eagleton's insistence that the critic examine the collective perceptions a society uses in constructing its sense of reality is especially pertinent: "Literary works are not mysteriously [or divinely] inspired, or explicable simply in terms of their authors' psychology. They are forms of perception, particular ways of seeing the world; and as such they have a relation to that dominant way of seeing the world which is the 'social mentality'...of an age."[4] And thus texts, when viewed as structures of perception, yield up voices of the reality which they were part of and helped shape. The great value of studying any literary text, but especially texts which we know were close to the emotions and thoughts of a people, is that the texts themselves, a Passion play or devotional guide, become metaphors of communal and individual existence. The issue, of course, is the means by which a community finds its truth, its ultimate values, and its symbolic language. Systems of spirituality and their literary texts constantly, creatively, luxuriate in the tension between insight and illusion and among possibilities of confirming what they have taken as truth.

Christ, of course, belongs to our human community; he is one of us. This startingly, simple realization cannot help but shape our response to a typical fifteenth-century preacher: "Beholde than that good lorde cheuerynge & quakynge all this naked bounde to a pyler / about hym standynge wicked men without any reason sore sorgynge pat blessyd body without ony pyte" (see below). Such charges, many which are even more insistent, typify much of the devotional rhetoric of the late Middle Ages. Such a tactic, in all our lives, utilizing a fusion of literal and imaginative conceptualization to move an individual to a heightened level of spiritual experience, is hardly a unique phenomenon. But such texts are culturally more significant; they are at once calculated testimonies of faith affirmed, commemorations of God's promises to mankind redeemed by his son, and intensely emotional, subjective constructions of knowledge existing within the context of daily human experience.

We have few testimonies, other than letters of a few people as self-conscious of their lives as the Pastons, of daily perceptions of reality. What we do have, however, are such texts as the *Canterbury Tales, Sir Gawain and the Green Knight,* and innumerable lyrics, prose treatises, and sermons which, though utilizing different codes of languages and different generic forms, reflect similar perceptions of the emotional costs of human experience. Gawain's cold, miserable journey to meet the Green Knight— "Wylde wayez in the worlde Wowen [Gawain] now rydez" (2479) and his profound lesson in humility and fallibility are proximate to the Harley lyric, "Lollay, lollay":

Child, thou nert a pilgrim but an uncuthe guest:/ Thy dawes beth itold, thy jurneys beth icest./ Whoder thou shalt wend, north eother est,/ Deth thee shall betide with bittre bale in brest.[5]

Both passages, together with, for example, the great body of *contemptus mundi* literature, bespeak an urgency to secure a tenable model of experience in the midst of cultural stress. The essence of what is called "affective spirituality" is a dual response to human experience and a broadening and deepening understanding of the centrality of human emotion as a component of man's ability to exist in the world. More formally, it is an occurrence best considered as a series of shifts in sensibility and taste, remarkable for its emphasis upon the intrinsic value of the individual's earthly and spiritual being. In art as early as the ninth century, and with dramatic prominence in the twelfth and thirteenth centuries the figures of the Christ Child and Mary, of the crucified Christ and his suffering mother, are presented in increasingly human, identifiable terms.[6] And at the same time, the intricacies of self-perception shift to the validity and importance of the individual. As R.W. Southern writes, men could now think of themselves "less as stationary objects of attack by spiritual foes, and more as pilgrims and seekers"[7] In theology and psychology, Abelard's and Hugh of St. Victor's argument for the primacy of intention in the moral act—*Quantum vis, tantum mereris* (merit is measured by the will)—underlies intense interest in the penitential experience. Indeed, the Fourth Lateran Council's decree of 1215, *Utriusque sexus,* mandating the sacrament of penance as a normal aspect of Christian life, accelerated the shift from rigidity to the subjective and emotional, from penance as a system of penalities to, in Alain de Lille's image, a spiritual medicine and ethical analysis.[8] This pisgah moment in the history of man's perception of man signals the rise of evangelical Christianity and of literary texts informed by and intended to extend participation in the humanity—and thus in the death—of Christ. This love for Christ's humanity (*carnalis amor Christi)* becomes the dominant theme of the late Middle Ages. It is a vastly consequential epistemological metaphor in which abstract and real, vision and experience meet. As Bonaventura writes:

The true Christian...who desires to resemble the crucified Saviour completely, ought to strive above all to carry the Cross of Christ Jesus either in his soul or in his flesh in order to feel himself, like St. Paul, truly nailed to the cross with Christ.... Now he alone is worthy to experience the ardour of such a feeling who, calling to mind with thankfulness the passion of the Lord, contemplates the labour, the sufferings and the love of Christ crucified....[9]

This is formal as well as popular theology, the articulation of a markedly new sensibility that informs sermon and hagiography, lyrics and works of private contemplation and devotion.

It is, at least in retrospect, entirely expected that during the fourteenth and fifteenth centuries there was renewed, intensified interest in the writings on spirituality of Anselm, Bernard, and Bonaventura.[10] The psyhoclogy and sensibility of the individual addressed the rise in the culture's emotional tenor. The intensification and pessimism, the concern with death and the macabre, with a queer escapism into cults, with the extensive playing of the Christ-drama, with subjectivity transformed into the hysterical—are all changes in the model of experience people shaped to enable them to deal with a world deeply troubled, not only by religious tensions, but more immediately by an economic decline that began with the great famine of 1315-17 and by the intermittent, sometimes serious, disruption and loss caused by the Hundred Years' War which began in 1337. The Black Death, most serious of all these traumas, attacked England during 1348-50, claiming at least twenty percent of the population. It recurred in 1361-62, this time claiming many more children than adults, and causing a devastating murrain among the livestock. Economic depression, of course, occurred amidst all this and led, for the survivors, both to new opportunities in the cities and to continual insecurity and terror. Affective spirituality and psychology, originally helping in the discovery of private self, now made possible the self's continued existence, its continued ability to know its place in the world, its belief in its place in the drama of salvation. One lived and worked to feel faith.

How, then, does a modern person accurately and fully read the spiritual texts that emerged from this period of anxiety and intensely emotional spirituality? I have implied that conventional procedures of textual analysis, if not placed in the context of at least some version of a medieval model produce readings that only flatly confirm religious orthodoxy. And certainly literalistic applications of economic and social models would be interesting, but would exclude so much of the vibrant complexity of perception and experience that defines life in any time.

The problem of reading medieval affective texts is nothing less than attempting to understand how the register of human emotions functions in an individual's—and in culture's—continuing activity of *knowing*. It is a knowing which takes many shapes and which is always made part of a comprehensive model of experience which has not exclusively or even primarily to do with the organization and tenets of a religious system or with literary analysis of a system's texts, but with something profoundly interior in an individual. I suggest that religious texts of the late medieval period in which the innocence and suffering of Christ are calculated to work an effect upon an audience function as externalized perception and knowledge of a world in which temporal and timeless *must* merge if one is to survive. Such mimetic structures fuse public knowledge and promise of Christian doctrine with the intimate *feeling* of the pain and the hope, of knowledge that experience inevitably, though unpredictably, brings. In this structure figures of mediation and of identification are crucial; and rhetorical power and emotional manipulation are requisites of any epistemology that stands a chance of withstanding the challenges of both faith and bewildering experience.

The following passage from a fairly representative medieval affective text illustrates:

Thou mayst here imagyne in thy herte as yf thou sawe thy lorde take of his enemyes with many repreues & despsytes / brought before a Iuge / falsely there accused of many wycked men / & he answered ryght nought but mekely suffred theyr wordes. They wolde nedes haue hym deed / but fyrst to suffre paynes. Beholde than that good lorde cheuerynge & quakynge all his body naked bounde to a pyler / about hym standynge wicked men without only reason sore sorgynge that blessyd body without ony pyte. Se how they cesse not from theyr angry strokes tyll they se hym stande in his blood vp to his ancles / from the toppe of his heed to the sole of his foot hole skynne they lefte none / his flesshe they rased to the bones / & for werynes of themselfe they lefte hym almoost dede. Loke than asyde vpon his blessyd moder / se what sorrow whe made for her dere sone / & haue compassyon of her payne that laye there aswowne. Torne agayne to thy lorde & se howe they vnbynde hym / how hastly they draw hymforth to do hym more dysease. A garlonde of thornes they put vpon his heed tyll the blood ran down in to his eyen / nose / mouth & eeres. Than they kneled downe with scornes, & arose vp with repreue & spette in his face. See than how that blessyd lady beteth her breste / draweth her clothes / & wryngeth her hondes / & I trowe thou wylt wepe for that pyteful syght. Loke yet agayn to thy lorde & se how they hurle hym forth to an hyghe hylle there to nayle hym hande & foot vpon the rode tree.[11]

The passage is representative of the affective vernacular works circulating throughout England and the continent in the late Middle Ages, perhaps the most famous of which is the pseudo-Bonaventuran *Meditationes Vitae Christi*. The vividness of imagery depicting the horrors of Jesus' suffering parallels the increasing intensity of the late medieval iconographic tradition of the Passion. The psychology here, even when one does not work through the intricacies of affective psychology, assumes that the imagistic power of language and the infinite power of the Passion to move even the hardest hearts would work at least some softening effect upon a reader. But I am struck by the spatial organization and the movement of this narrative. It begins, predictably, with the figure of suffering Jesus imaged in gruesome detail in the central focus. Jesus's suffering and humiliation as he hears the verbal abuse of the torturers, and then as he endures the viscious scourging, until he "stande in his blood vp to his ancles," could, depending upon the reader's degree of concentration and receptivity, move him to a remembering of Jesus's human suffering and thus to a remembering of its significance to man. Augustine well described this faculty: "Thus in this mortal life, wandering from God, if we wish to return to our native country where we can be blessed we should use this world . . . so that the 'invisible things' of God 'being understood by the things that are made' . . . may be seen, that is, so that by means of corporal and temporal things we may comprehend the eternal and spiritual."[12]

But the visual focus and the energy of the writer's efforts shift, in an extra-biblical intrusion, to rivet the reader-viewer's attention on Mary. The presence of Mary in most medieval spiritual literature is well-known, as is the cult-like devotion to the Mother of God as an intermediary between man and God.[13] But in such singularly powerful scenes as this, and in the Passion plays, too, there is full rhetorical and narrative exploitation of the rather unique human suffering of child and mother. It seems that a tension is created between faith and grief, a tension between knowing what the salvational act means for mankind and the incredible expenditure of human pain and grief required of the participants *and* of their fellow humans. To "loke than asyde vpon his blessyd moder" and then to "torne agayne to thy lorde," and to "see than how that blessyde lady beteth her breste / draweth her clothes / & wryngeth her hondes" is to enter into an emotional, painful landscape and into an act of profound knowing.

In the intended experience of this text any sense of historical or sacramental time is of only limited relevance. Rather, the experience involves the meeting of an individual receptive to profoundly moving emotion (made possible by the gradual absorption in the narrative) and a mechanism, an object of identification, quite distinct from either God-man or an ordinary man. Mary as exalted human, as ultimate embodiment of sex and purity, of humility and perfection, has long played an integral psycho-historical role in the evolution of Christian faith. Her presence in this scene not only adds intimate poignancy, but makes possible the transcendence into the realm of religious experience which is so elusive, which has so often been expressed in sexual metaphor.

The ultimate significance of popular texts which pursue various strategies aimed at bringing the participating reader into the remembering, both private and communal, is that profound transcendence becomes a psychologically literal reliving of the event. The experience of suffering and the loss of innocence in daily life correlate only imprecisely with the tenor of a culture's spirituality; but more certain, yet even less provable, is that extremely felt human experience is a route into our most profound capacities of knowing. The knowledge of reading or seeing a reenactment of the Passion can become platitudinous, but various texts and particular times coincide to make possible for some humans an experience that is neither articulatable knowledge nor, mere transitory feeling. Augustine's observation about the dynamic, transcendent nature of the human mind and of simplicity, religious experience applies here:

I will soar therefore beyond this faculty of my nature, still rising by degrees unto him who hath made both me and that nature. And I come into these fields and spacious places of my memory, where the treasures of innumerable forms brought into it from these things that have been perceived by the senses to be hoarded up. There is laid up whatsoever besides we think, either by way of enlarging or diminishing, or any other ways varying of those things which the sense hath come at: yea, and if there by anything recommended to it and there laid up, which forgetfullness hath not swallowed up and buried. To this treasury whenever I have recourse, I will demand to have anything brought forth whatsoever I will.[14]

That prose texts such as the one cited earlier and the incredible treatments of the Passion in drama existed, flourished, and appear to have answered a popular taste during a period of English history which has, fittingly, been called an "age of adversity" gives us an opportunity to study ways in which literary texts both reflect and help shape perception and knowledge. How does this knowledge contribute to an individual's life? To a life in a period of particular stress? Answers concerned with ontological security, with a sense of community coherence, with tapping innate structures which predispose humans to a "sense" of God are surely at least a little true. But perhaps it is in considering the experience of a spiritual text as an act of knowing, rather than as a finished event and "piece" of knowledge, that we come closest to understanding. Medieval man, afterall, had all the answers. What he had to do, of course, was to bring together, as we all must, knowing and living. His considerable human resources of intellect and emotion enabled him to transcend the faculty of his nature and so to use those "treasures of innumerable forms."

Notes

[1] This Latin Poem is found in several fifteenth-century manuscripts (Cambridge University Library MS Ii, 4.9, fol. 69) and is representative of the vast body of deeply pessimistic literature which has never been fully assimilated into our understanding of the late Middle Ages. The poem has been translated by Donald R. Howard and appears in "Renaissance World-Alienation," in *The Darker Vision of the Renaissance,* ed. Robert S. Kinsman (Berkeley: University of California Press, 1974), p.54.

[2] Even though scholars have long acknowledged the significance of medieval devotional

literature, much of it, admittedly, minor, in understanding the culture and spirituality of the period, there are few studies that go beyond the merely descriptive. I am, as the following discussion demonstrates, indebted to the work of John Hirsh, "The Experience of God: A New Classification of Certain Late Medieval Affective Texts," *Chaucer Review*, 11 (1976), 11-21.

[3]John Huizinga, *The Waning of the Middle Ages* (Garden City, New Jersey: Doubleday and Company, 1954); Gordon Leff, *The Dissolution of the Medieval Outlook: An Essay on Intellectual and Spiritual Change in the Fourteenth Century* (New York: Harper and Row, 1976). For a valuable corrective to reductionist views of the late Middle Ages see Heiko A. Oberman, "Fourteenth-Century Religious Thought: A Premature Profile," *Speculum*, 53 (1978), 80-93.

[4]Terry Eagleton, *Marxism and Literary Criticism* (Berkeley: University of California Press, 1976), p.6.

[5]R.T. Davies, ed., *Medieval English Lyrics* (Evanston: Northwestern University Press, 1964), p.107.

[6]See Dorothy C. Shorr, *The Christ Child in Devoitional Images in Italy During the XIV Century* (New York: George Wittenborn, Inc., 1959) and Millard Meiss, *Painting in Florence and Siena after the Black Death* (New York: Harper and Row, 1964).

[7]R.W. Southern, *The Making of the Middle Ages* (New Haven: Yale University Press, 1961), p.222.

[8]Most historical surveys of medieval philosophy discuss these events and seminal texts, but the most helpful studies for purposes of understanding the intricacies of Christian spirituality seem to be François Vandenbroucke, *A History of Christian Spirituality: The Spirituality of the Middle Ages* (London: Burns and Oates, 1968); and Pierre Pourrat, *Christian Spirituality in the Middle Ages*, trans. S.P. Jacques (London: Burns, Oates, and Washbourne, Ltd., 1924).

[9]*Lignum Vitae*, Cant. 1.12, quoted in Pourrat, *Christian Spirituality*, p.183.

[10]For full documentation of this renaissance of interest see Giles Constable, "The Popularity of Twelfth Century Spiritual Writers in the Late Middle Ages," edd. A Molho and J.A. Tedeschi, *Renaissance Studies in Honor of Hans Baron* (Dekalb: Northern Illinois University Press, 1971), pp.3-28.

[11]In Carl Horstman, ed., *Yorkshire Writers: Richard Rolle of Hampole and his Followers*, II (London: Swan Sonnenschein and Co., 1896), p.103.

[12]*De doctrina christiana*, I.4.4, trans. D.W. Robertson, Jr. (Indianapolis: Bobbs-Merrill Company, 1958), p.10.

[13]This tradition is described in Marina Warner, *Alone of All Her Sex: The Myth and the Cult of the Virgin Mary* (New York: Alfred A. Knopf, Inc., 1976).

[14]*Confessiones*, X.viii, trans. William Watts (Cambridge: Harvard University Press, 1961), p.93.

Was There A Popular Culture In the Middle Ages?

With Bruce A. Rosenberg's article, "Was There a Popular Culture in the Middle Ages," we come full circle, returning to some of the comments made by Charles Altman. Rosenberg's cautionary remark that segmenting the experienced world into "popular," "folk," and "elite," is arbitrary and artificial does not discount the practical value and necessity of constructing analytic categories in popular culture studies. What is essential, however, is that those of us studying "popular" artifacts must also examine the ways in which they interact with other cultural aspects or segments.

Bruce A. Rosenberg is professor of English at Brown University and has published widely on medieval literature, folklore, and popular culture; he has been an Andrew W. Mellon Professor of English at the University of Pittsburgh, 1979-80.

Was There a Popular Culture in the Middle Ages?

Bruce A. Rosenberg

In an editorial in the (Mormon) *Millenial Star* of 1 March, 1856, Franklin D. Richards, president of the Perpetual Emigration Fund, proclaimed that

When Ancient Israel fled from bondage into the wilderness, they had not even the privilege of taking provisions for their journey, but had to trust to the good hand of God for their daily bread. If the Saints in these lands have not seen such times, the future will reveal them.... Ancient Israel traveled to the promised land on foot, with their wives and little ones. The lord calls upon modern Israel to do the same.[1]

In the spring of that year the first handcart companies set out from Iowa City to make the 1,400 mile crossing of the Great American Desert on foot, pushing and pulling their provisions and belongings (sometimes each other) in handcarts. The carts themselves were uniform in design, generally, though varied in size and construction. They resembled those carts used by porters and street cleaners in several American cities. Little or no iron was used; axles were made of single poles of hickory; they were about 6 or 7 feet long, 2 feet or more high, and carried 400-500 pounds of supplies. These were pushed and pulled from Iowa to Zion (Salt Lake City) enabling the immigration to continue at a very modest cost: drought and grasshopper infestation had ravaged Mormon crops, making cheaper immigrant transportation necessary.[2] The first two expeditions—in 1856 and 1857—were quite successful, despite the heat, privation, and fatigue inevitable in such a journey made by such means over more than a thousand miles of inhospitable land. But late companies fell victim to early winter snows; Willie's company buried seventy-five of its original four hundred members, and Martin's contingent of five-hundred and seventy-six lost about one-hundred fifty of its number to winter.

The most famous "folk" song to commemorate these odysseys is entitled, simply, "The Handcart Song," one of whose verses declares:

> As on the road the carts are pulled
> 'Twould very much surprise the world
> To see the old and feeble dame
> Thus lend a hand to pull the same.
> And maidens fair will dance and sing,
> Young men more happy than a king,
> And children will laugh and play
> Their strength increasing day by day.

The chorus is equally blithe about the journey:

> For some must push and some must pull
> As we go marching up the hill;
> So merrily on our way we go
> Until we reach the valley-o.[3]

The buoyancy of the spirit of the song was certainly felt by those who welcomed the travelers on their arrival in Zion, as a *Millenial Star* reporter remembered: "my heart is gladdened as I write this, for methinks I see their merry countenance and boyant [sic] step, and the strains of the handcart song at eventide or in a dream."[4] No doubt the pioneers' hearts were uplifted as they approached Zion, and the last mile or so was traversed with a lively step and a jubilant heart; but the sentiments expressed in the song do not match what in fact their diaries and letters indicate they suffered.

And so it comes as no surprise to learn that "The Handcart Song" is Church sponsored, that it did not originate among the "folk"—the people who actually pushed and pulled those handcarts across the plains. If not actually commissioned by the Church, it was certainly fostered by the Elders. (The author is said, variously, to be a Williams Hobbs or Elder J.T.D. McAllister.) We may be offended or inspired by it, but our credulity is taxed when we hear that the handcart companies went "merrily" on their way, that the "old and feeble dame" will lend a hand eagerly, that "maidens fair" will "dance and sing," and that young men will be happier than "a king." That does not seem to be the response of "the folk" to such a trek. But it is precisely the image, tone, and message that the Mormon Church wished to project. And eventually—how soon is not known—"The Handcart Song" entered the oral tradition of the Mormons, and has now become so popular that Thomas Cheney's edition of *Mormon Songs From the Rocky Mountains* remarks that "scarcely a record of Mormon songs has appeared without it."[5]

"The Handcart Song" appears to be a cultural artifact analogous to the popular church statuary identified by Professor Altman as "popular culture." An item, in the Morman case a song, has entered oral tradition and appears to be a folk product, but has in fact been "mediated" by an entrepeneur, the Church, and "sold" to a public. The same situation is true of certain church statuary of the late Middle Ages—as well as, one might add, the church-sponsored and produced *mystery* plays, which commonly popularized Scriptural narratives. According to our definitions of "popular culture" both a medieval statue of Lazarus and a church-sponsored song of the handcart migration will have to be considered examples of popular artifacts. Do such typological additions enlarge our perception of either medieval or nineteenth-century culture?

Even if we grant "The Handcart Song" to be "popular" rather than "folk," questions remain. Henry Glassie has recently described the conditions in which an item can be classed or excluded as folk: "a tale or a wagon built by a person who does not have that tale or wagon as a part of his own tradition cannot be folk."[6] If we are to follow these guidelines, we would then want to know in intimate detail the relationship of the carvers of medieval tympanum to the traditions and the culture in which they lived; we would want to know if they were part of the folk group ("a homogeneous, sacred, self-perpetuating, largely self-sufficient group isolated by any of many means..."[7]) which provided at least part of the audience—in this case the parishoners.

We study popular culture, isolating and classifying certain cultural items for a useful purpose. The bottom line—or one of the bottom lines—of popular culture study as well as the study of folklore, is an interpretation of culture. Few would contend that Neil Simon, for instance, was aesthetically comparable with Shakespeare, particularly since not only the critical vocabulary but the criteria for judging both were designed to describe and evaluate such poets as "the Bard." Simon would be playing in the wrong game with the wrong rules if such a competition were staged. Not only would it be a no-win game; the disparity of the contestants works against such a match ever being arranged.

No one who studies popular culture seriously will get caught in this elitist trap: the attempt to ascertain quality according to genre or type, by which *a priori* assumptions *The Deerslayer* is incontestably better than any dime novel. But how many people ever read, say, *Moby Dick,* during Melville's lifetime, compared with the audience for Prentice Ingraham, Ned Buntline, or Frederick Whittaker? Which books more closely reflect American taste during the late nineteenth century and which are more influential with the American public? Which says more about American civilization? Professors of English will go on insisting that the sonnet is inherently superior to the limerick (for instance), and since the academic sub-culture defines aesthetic quality in culturally determined terms, its members will never be deflected from that view—like the Idaho farmer who plows his field a certain way because that's the way it seems "right" to him.

So too, matters of taste and excellence, a fact which is usually overlooked, are culturally determined. Chaucer, despite his lack of high seriousness, is high-brow; Len Deighton is low. This, despite our understanding that standards of taste are more ephemeral than, say, the dime novel or the hard-boiled detective story. Even the idea of an operative, viable cultural structure—folk, mass, and elite—is artificial, implying that we could actually make clear class statements about the tastes of these groups as groups. Modifying an informal remark of John Cawelti's, I will call this the "Brow Theory" of cultural analysis.

We all recognize that the distinctions among "elite," "popular," and "folk" culture are arbitrary and "analytic" rather than native. That is, such distinctions usually do not exist in the culture at large, but are the categories of academicians and those of that ilk. Much of Shakespeare was popular in this day, but all of it is elite now. *Robinson Crusoe* seems to have slipped somewhat from one category to another in the decades following its first appearance, and people still refer to the Kingston Trio or Joan Baez as "folk" artists.

Still, it is often useful for us to attempt to make cultural distinctions among creators, performers, and texts. The way Judy Collins sings "The Banks of Ohio," or Baez "Barbara Allen," is not the way those songs are performed in people's homes in southern Virginia and Tennessee. Style—intonation, phrasing, melody, accompaniment, text, etc.—are important data in a cultural interpretation. Neither Collins nor Baez, though excellent, will provide that data. Neither may tell us very much about the community preferences of (say) Whitesburg, Ky., but they might about that grand abstraction, the American public. So it can be important to make distinctions based on cultural "levels."

As Professor Altman suggests, a more useful means of distinction may be made in terms of the mediator in popular culture (an idea also suggested by John Cawelti several years ago in a National Humanities Institute seminar at Chicago); in popular productions, an entrepeneur sponsors specific works from the artist and packages them for the audience. In folk art the artist performs what he perceives his audience wants to experience, and this communication is direct.

Academic interest in popular culture seems to have arisen largely out of a desire to understand a "new" class of artifacts, which in turn offers a new way of understanding the culture that produced them. Thus, popular culture is closely identified with mechanical repetition (mass production), whether of MacDonald's "quarter pounders" or the songs of "Creedence Clearwater Revival." Both of these products, and thousands of items like them (mechanically reproduced artifacts) have an impact upon us and our culture, and the study of their form, composition, and use can lead to cultural analyses and evaluations. It seems to me that those who define "popular culture" in this way have segmented external phenomena in a useful way. The categories which most students of popular culture now use—one can almost speak of "classic" pop culture studies—are useful because they enable us to aproach our society in ways that can lead to useful observations about ourselves. It has always been useful to distinguish—however oversimplified the methodology—between the products of a culture's academically trained artisans and those which have been perpetuated through tradition and custom.

I don't wish to argue, here, at any great length on behalf of the conceptions of many anthropologists toward culture, and the danger of arbitrarily segmenting our experienced world into "elite," "popular," and "folk." Victor Turner has recently noted the tendency toward a holistic approach toward culture: "some anthropologists, and scholars in adjacent fields...are beginning to turn their attention to both folk and high culture of complex societies and civilizations...."[8] He thinks that we now have a great opportunity for those scholars who are interested in "the popular and high performative genres which continually scrutinize, criticize, subvert, uphold, and attempt to modify the behavior of the personnel, their values, activities and relationship...." For the future study of culture, Turner envisions "a creative collaboration among literary critics, anthropologists, sociologists, historians, art historians, philosophers, historians of religion, and other kinds of scholars...in shared fields of interest" (p.73).

The point is well taken; but nevertheless, we are able to begin to learn a lot about ourselves when we examine the ways in which these segments interact and play off against each other within a complex culture such as ours. We should be aware that segmenting is arbitrary and artificial ("analytical"), and probably does not bear a very close similarity to the way our world is segmented—if it is at all. Nevertheless, it will probably be necessary for us to continue to construct analytic categories in order to deal coherently with the materials of the culture we study.

Which brings us back to the Middle Ages. One is convinced by Professor Altman's argument: after the eleventh century a number of churches dedicated religious art of the *Westwerk* to pious advertising, and that sculpture—so different from the plastic art of the interiors and the eastern end—may be properly called "popular." And once having made that classification we are left with the question about how much we have thus learned. A little about the Church Militant, certainly, and its relations with the lay world. But almost nothing additional, I think, about the nature of medieval culture: religious carving of the *Westwerk* is not a significant enough body of medieval materials to see it interacting with other aspects of medieval culture as a whole. If our categories are going to be arbitrary, they should serve some analytic purpose. Our present taxonomies enable us to deal adequately with such problem items as "The Handcart Song." And they are elastic enough to stretch back into the twelfth century and to include Professor Altman's statuary; we can now say that there was popular art in the Middle Ages. We must next decide of what importance that is, what and how much that tells us about life and culture in that time and place. These will be the tests of the value of our definitions and taxonomies. Art historians have identified hortatory plastic art in the European Middle Ages, and have discussed its use, aesthetic worth, and function. Of how much value is it for us to realize that this is popular art? The answer to that question also evaluates the criteria which make that question possible.

Notes

[1]Leroy R. and Ann W. Hafen, *Handcarts to Zion* (Glendale, CA: Arthur H. Clark Co., 1960), pp.35-36.

[2]Hafen, *Handcarts,* pp.28 ff.

[3]Thomas E. Cheney, *Mormon Songs From the Rocky Mountains,* Publications of the American Folklore Society: Memoir Series, No. 53 (Austin: University of Texas Press, 1968), p.66.

[4]Hafen, *Handcarts,* pp.64-65.,

[5]Cheney, *Songs,* p.64.

[6]Henry Glassie, *Pattern in the Material Folk Culture of the Eastern United States* (Philadelphia: University of Pennsylvania Press, 1968), p.5.

[7]Glassie, *Patterns,* p.3.

[8]Victor Turner, "Process, System, and Symbol: A New Anthropological Synthesis," *Daedalus,* 106 (Summer, 1977), 72.